A THOUSAND DAYS *of* WONDER

A THOUSAND
DAYS *of* WONDER

A Scientist's Chronicle of
His Daughter's Developing Mind

Charles Fernyhough

AVERY

a member of Penguin Group (USA) Inc.

New York

Published by the Penguin Group

Penguin Group (USA) Inc., 375 Hudson Street, New York, New York 10014, USA • Penguin Group (Canada), 90 Eglinton Avenue East, Suite 700, Toronto, Ontario M4P 2Y3, Canada (a division of Pearson Canada Inc.) • Penguin Books Ltd, 80 Strand, London WC2R 0RL, England • Penguin Ireland, 25 St Stephen's Green, Dublin 2, Ireland (a division of Penguin Books Ltd) • Penguin Group (Australia), 250 Camberwell Road, Camberwell, Victoria 3124, Australia (a division of Pearson Australia Group Pty Ltd) • Penguin Books India Pvt Ltd, 11 Community Centre, Panchsheel Park, New Delhi–110 017, India • Penguin Group (NZ), 67 Apollo Drive, Rosedale, North Shore 0632, New Zealand (a division of Pearson New Zealand Ltd) • Penguin Books (South Africa) (Pty) Ltd, 24 Sturdee Avenue, Rosebank, Johannesburg 2196, South Africa

Penguin Books Ltd, Registered Offices:
80 Strand, London WC2R 0RL, England

Originally published in the United Kingdom by Granta Books 2008
First published in the United States by Avery 2009

Most Avery books are available at special quantity discounts for bulk purchase for sales promotions, premiums, fund-raising, and educational needs. Special books or book excerpts also can be created to fit specific needs. For details, write Penguin Group (USA) Inc. Special Markets, 375 Hudson Street, New York, NY 10014.

Library of Congress Cataloging-in-Publication Data

Fernyhough, Charles, date.
A thousand days of wonder : a scientist's chronicle of his daughter's developing mind / Charles Fernyhough.
p.   cm.
Includes bibliographical references and index.
ISBN 978-1-58333-347-1
1. Fernyhough, Athena.   2. Toddlers—Biography.   3. Toddlers—Development.   4. Child development.   I. Title.
HQ774.5.F47   2009   2008050395
305.232092—dc22
[B]

Printed in the United States of America
1   3   5   7   9   10   8   6   4   2

BOOK DESIGN BY AMANDA DEWEY

For Squiggle and for Cherry

Contents

A THOUSAND DAYS *of* WONDER

One

IT'S LIKE THIS

Remembering a Beginning

I didn't know where to start, so I asked her.

"Athena?"

She was feeding me coffee dregs from a teaspoon. It was a cold, bright midmorning in June, and the shoppers had abandoned central Sydney to the part-time dads and a few hurrying office girls. We were sitting in a café on the first floor of the Queen Victoria Building, feeling the winter draft from the nearby escalator. She was nearly three.

"Do you remember being a little baby?"

"No."

"Do you remember *anything* about being a baby?"

"No."

She continued scraping the teaspoon around the rim of the empty cup.

"More? More?" she offered. "Shall I feed you?"

I leaned forward obediently. She dug deep with the spoon and scraped another bit of metallic-tasting coffee scum into my mouth.

"When you were a little tiny baby, what was it like?"

"I don't know. I don't know yet."

Yet. Was it all about to come back to her?

"Can you remember some of the things we used to do?"

"Oh, you *always* say that," she sighed.

I sat back, a little surprised by my daughter's tone. As I studied her determined, slightly cross-eyed scouring of my coffee cup, I wondered whether I had really asked this question before. I had probably come up with some that were equally impossible, and possibly equally absurd.

"That's because I'm interested."

"Why?"

"Because it's interesting. Because *you're* interesting."

She clattered the teaspoon into the saucer. "Now you be the clapper and I'll be the pig!"

"Can you remember?"

"Clap! You have to clap!"

I clapped. Office workers hurried past with plastic-lidded cappuccinos, bemused by the applause from the Old Vienna Coffee House.

"Athena, when you were a little tiny baby, what sort of games did we play?"

"Well," she replied, with somber certainty. "I think we used to play chaseys."

"What about before you could run around, when you were still a little tiny baby? Can you remember what it's like to be a little tiny baby?"

She pulled the straw out of her orange juice and trumpeted at me through it, spattering me with its sticky warmth. I felt a faint, familiar despair.

"Can you remember who looked after you when you were a little baby?"

"Mummy."

"Who else?"

She looked up at me with the straw still bitten between her teeth.

Wisps of blond hair curled into the corners of her eyes. Her blue irises were big and clear. My questions seemed to bounce off her. They were just the latest stuff being shot at her, to be dodged or endured. But I needed her answer. Something extraordinary had happened to our yowling newborn of nearly three years ago, and she was the only true witness to it. I had observed her transformation from the outside, documented her emergence into this flitty center of experience with which I could, with a little prompting or bribery, have a tentative conversation. But she was the only one who had lived through it. I had my notebooks, my jottings and theories, but careful observation would only take me so far. I needed my subject to remember it for herself.

Then she smiled. I like to think she smiled.

"Daddy," she said.

Looking back, I realize that I was asking a lot of a child so small. If Athena had been like me, or just about anyone else who has ever been asked the question, she would have been able to recall very little detail about the first two or three years of her life. No matter how you choose to quiz people about it, no one seems to have demonstrably accurate memories of their very early childhood. On the face of it, young children aren't just a blank slate, a tabula rasa—they're a nonstick surface. The events of life do not cling to them. There has not, Sigmund Freud once observed, been enough astonishment over this fact.

Psychologists have recently begun to make progress in understanding why memories of our earliest lives do not stay with us into childhood and beyond. One thing we know about memory is that different kinds of information are organized in different ways. Information about facts goes into one system, known as "semantic" memory; information about events that happen to us (our "autobiographical" knowledge) goes into another. At nearly three, Athena was already skilled at handling certain kinds of facts about the world, such as her date of birth, or the fact that the first train stop after the Harbour Bridge was Wynyard. But her capacity to organize her knowledge of things that had happened to her was only just beginning to develop. She was not yet an autobiographer. Her own life story was not, for her, a proper topic of study.

Perhaps that was because handling information about your own life requires something more than the retention of impersonal, objective bits of knowledge. To say that you possess semantic knowledge of, say, the capital city of a particular country, it is enough simply to know the fact: you don't need to recall the specific instant when that information became known to you. But when it comes to the details of our own lives, that personal, subjective quality is the essence of what we remember. It was not that Athena found it impossible to process facts about her own past. She had prodigious memory for various kinds of autobiographical information, such as promises we had made her in weak moments, or the clothes she had been wearing when she visited a certain place. But she couldn't re-create the visit itself; she couldn't put herself at the center of the recollection. In fact, memory researchers are now suggesting that this special, subjective aspect of memory may not start to develop until halfway through the third year of life. If this is true, then it would explain why our earliest years are a blank for most of us. In infancy, we are absent from our memories. We can live, but we cannot yet relive.

W hat are you writing?" she asked.
   I looked up from the crowded pages of my notebook. I'd been unaware that, once again, my observations of the thing had distracted me from the thing itself.

"I'm writing down what you say. I've been writing down all these notes since you were a baby."

"Why?" she said, looking faintly shocked.

"Because that's what Daddy does. He tries to understand how little children think. That's his job."

She laughed at that. Daddies stared at blank pieces of paper all day and then went for long walks, talking to themselves. That surely couldn't bring you to an understanding of anything.

"You know what?" she said, obligingly. "When I were a little baby, it were very sunny."

I nodded, trying to coax the thought into the open. I suspected that this summery recollection had something to do with the previous year's family holiday, but it may only have been the afterglow of the home movies we had recently been watching. Athena's grip on the memory was unsure, and I could understand why. If she had only begun to center herself in her memories at two and a half, then five-sixths of her life was forgotten. How did it feel, to have so much of your past immediately lost to you? Was life still a blooming, buzzing confusion, a movie in which she had only just begun to star? What was it *like* for her?

I had a particular interest in that question. I had studied children's development in the abstract, from a safe academic distance, for all my years as a graduate student and then part-time university lecturer. I had seen how much profound change happens in the first three years of life, in just about every aspect of a human being's psychology. Within a few years of her birth, a newborn baby has to build a mind out of chaos, gain control of her own actions, acquire the ability to talk about her experiences, and get a sense of herself as the sentient being at the center of those experiences. Even though she is born with certain complex and finely specialized talents, they would seem to equip her only lightly for the tasks ahead. Developmental psychologists have some of the biggest questions of all to grapple with: how a human being acquires both a private and a public self, whether language is a learnable skill or something reserved for those who have been biologically chosen, how the colors of consciousness can take root in a brain that starts out as raw, proliferating matter. Look closely enough at a developing mind, I would tell my students, and you can learn everything you need to know about being human.

Now these questions were coming alive for me in the most immediate way. With Athena's arrival, the phenomenon that had so fascinated me from a distance had installed itself, delightfully, right in front of my eyes. Among all the other emotions of those heady days of new parenthood, I felt something like the surprise you feel when your new next-door neighbor turns out to be your boss, and you see your precious work–home balance disappearing along with your nude sunbathing. Athena made demands on my professional responsibilities as well as my parental ones. She brought my work home with her. For the last three years I had observed this miracle in close-up, watching the momentous transformations of toddlerhood happen to my own precious firstborn. In those brief thousand days, our yowling neonate had turned into a person: social, moral, intelligent, articulate. I might not have been fully aware of when it happened, but somewhere along the line I had watched a consciousness emerge.

With each new milestone in Athena's development, I mused about how the theories I had studied matched up with the realities I was witnessing. But I also found myself constantly wondering about the other, subjective side of the objective story. I wanted to understand what it was like to inhabit a mind that was a different thing every day, whose understanding of itself was changing so rapidly. I could find few insider testimonies to guide me through this period of life, either in the scientific writings I was familiar with, or in grown-up literature, where the experiences of the under-threes have hardly found a voice at all. For all the richness of their depictions of adult subjectivity, their willingness to eavesdrop on different forms of experience, novelists and poets have shown little interest in the unremembered atmospheres of toddlerhood. That neglect was startling, when all our scientific probings of the infant mind were showing that it was an interesting place to be.

Beyond the ordinary pleasures of fatherhood, my time at home with Athena promised to give me that insider's view into a small child's mind. With a little imaginative projection, I had the chance to put some subjective detail into the scientific background. Was there anything comparable to being a newborn baby, an infant on the threshold of language, a fiercely self-sufficient toddler? Would careful observation and questioning, enriched by the insights thrown up by new research, give me some clues as to how those experiences could be described? What do young children understand of their own consciousness, of their capacity to be there at the center of these colorful, chaotic experiences? How do you make sense of yourself, when that self has no continuity in time? These were some of the questions that had drawn me to the subject in the first place, and now fatherhood was giving me a chance to ask them all over again. The answers, if I got any, would not make me any better at parenting Athena, but they might make her a little less of a mystery.

The day after our visit to the Old Vienna Coffee House, I was going through some of the videos of Athena as a baby. I had been transferring our home movies to the computer, and we had been watching them in the mornings, when she crashed down the stairs in her pajamas, puffy-faced and euphoric from sleep. To the child who sat down with me to watch these video extracts, the baby on the screen did not even trigger the memory boost of self-recognition. I, too, could hardly recognize my daughter in the moon-faced two-month-old who now gazed out from my laptop. For the last three years she had been overwriting herself too effectively, shredding the evidence of her former self as she went along. We were going to need all of my notebooks and these hours of video footage if we were ever going to understand this strange infant, lost in time.

She came in and climbed up onto my knee. On the screen was herself at nine and a half weeks. In the video clip she was sitting on my knee in a floral sleepsuit, propped up by my hands, working her tongue while I tickled her nose and cheeks and scurried my fingers around her bald head. I had zoomed in so that her face filled the screen. Athena's nearly-three-year-old self looked at her nine-and-a-half-week-old self, and her nine-and-a-half-week-old self looked back. The picture zoomed in even closer, so close that the autofocus was tricked and the image blurred, then clarified again. The now-Athena was captivated. The then-Athena opened her eyes wide and pulled up the sides of her mouth in a grin. I slowed the playback and let the camera zoom in on each eye in turn, on her flaring nose, her beaked, translucent mouth, the soft curve of her cheek, the miniature ivory-work of one ear. We moved over her baby-self from the shortest distance the focus would allow, as though filming a giant Buddha from a helicopter. Finally the camera settled on her left eye and zoomed in as close as it could. There was a single perfect crease above her eyelid. Her eyelashes were long and fine. Her iris was a dark circle, almost filled by the blacker pupil. Then, for me at least, a strange moment of recognition. It was as though I had stopped looking through a window and had started looking into it, into the mirror of it, to see the details of the room reflected there. Within the shiny blackness of her pupil was another, human roundness, a reflected silhouette. I saw myself looking in on her, caught in the mirror of her cornea: the eye in her eye, her constant observer.

Two

PRECONCEPTIONS

Life Before Birth

If I wanted a starting point, I could do worse than begin on Day One: that Sunday morning in the hospital delivery room when the clock started ticking on her life. Ten twenty-five on a hot, overcast July morning. The *Archers* radio omnibus nearly half an hour old. Her fate set, according to some ancient notion of how the gods of the week would shape her personality. Bonny and blithe and good and gay. And a birthday, too: an annual appointment, to be celebrated by friends and family for the rest of her life. That first gulp of air was supposed to be the ignition spark that primed her soul. A slew of gifts and flowers and pink-hued cards would soon be making the same point: she started here.

If you trusted the received wisdom about psychological development, you would have concluded that this was where mind, as well as soul, began its work. When I studied the subject at university, the textbooks began with happy scenes in the maternity ward and ended with adolescence, the stage at which, according to giants of the discipline like Jean Piaget, the individual becomes a paid-up member of Homo sapiens. In terms of setting the parameters for development, those limits were misplaced at both ends of the scale. Today's psychologists continue their studies of mental and behavioral change long after their subjects have reached adulthood, and building a mind is acknowledged to be a lifetime's work. Attitudes have also changed toward the study of development at the near end of the life span. A brain doesn't spring miraculously into existence on the day its owner happens to take a first breath of air. Athena's birth may have started something for me, but it didn't really start anything for Athena that wasn't already going. Her nervous system was up and running, priming her musculature for action, long before it had any work to do out here in the light. With the new imaging techniques at their disposal, psychologists can study a fetus's behavior in almost as much detail as they can a newborn baby's. The drama of life in the womb is no longer played out behind a closed door: nowadays it can be scrutinized almost as closely as any other part of our lives. If development is a task we are busy with throughout our entire lifetime, its starting point ought to be conception, not birth.

It might sound like fanciful thinking to say that we can go back even further than that. As far as genetic makeup is concerned, your fate as an individual is set when your parents' DNA goes into the lottery spinner of human sexual reproduction. But it is not just the genes you inherit from your parents that affect how you turn out. Even before the reassortment of chromosomes that makes for a viable embryo, Mum and Dad will have started influencing their future progeny in all sorts of ways. Parents have expectations of their children, formed long before the children are even conceived. Our daughter's life had begun some time before her little heart started beating as a four-week-old embryo; it started as soon as we decided to stop using contraception, and thus began the painstaking process of instilling the lives of our future offspring with all the dreams and aspirations we'd failed to reach in our own. They were, quite literally, preconceptions. We start creating our children long before we give birth to them. Even before they are a twinkle in our eye, they are on their way.

One of the most important ways in which these expectations are manifested is in the way people think and talk about their unborn children. Parents have psychological baggage from their own upbringing that will influence how they approach being parents themselves. A mother might remember her own mother as being cool and aloof, or as providing contradictory and frightening signals about how she should behave. More happily, she might recall her own mother as being emotionally available, loving, and supportive. Studies have shown that if you recall having had a secure emotional relationship with your own mother, it is highly likely that your child will have a similar relationship with you. Although we are still some way from explaining precisely how these patterns of love and mistrust cycle across the generations, it seems to have something to do with how parents-to-be conceive of their fetuses-in-progress. In one study, psychologists simply invited mothers and fathers in the third trimester of pregnancy to describe how they thought their baby would turn out at six months of age. The researchers weren't so interested in whether the predictions were accurate as in whether they were made at all. Talking about your prenate as a real person, long before you have made its physical acquaintance, suggests that you have already started to take that person seriously. As predicted, parents who gave richer projections of their babies' personalities were more likely, when observed in interaction with them at six months, to treat their infants as independent beings, with minds of their own.

In our case, it might have come down to something as simple as giving our unborn baby a name. Perhaps the surest way of showing that we conceived of her as an entity separate from us was the fact that we gave that entity a label. Athena, as a term of reference for this little being, came relatively late. In the womb she was Tiger, a name that had stuck after my wife's twelve-week scan, when Lizzie and I saw her fetal shadow kicking in an arc of static and blackness, and we learned from one of our free government baby brochures that she was now the size of a tiger prawn. Tiger. In the womb she growled and prowled. She was going to come out with a leap and a bound, like Tigger in Disney's *Winnie the Pooh,* and bat life across the room like a ball of wool. You could see her struggling to get out, making squirming landscapes with elbows and knees, animating Lizzie's tautened abdomen with the same strong-limbed writhings that would keep us awake at night for weeks after her birth. She was flexing her muscles, and to our minds she was also showing off a personality. Our preconceptions may have been running wild, but we had some notion of who she would be, long before she could really prove it for herself.

Unsurprisingly, those preconceptions affected how we responded to her. We had an idea of her, and we acted on that idea. We spoke to her, read to her, reassured her, encouraged her in her cramped task of brain-building. We felt pangs of guilt that we could not do anything to relieve her hiccups. We wondered, sometimes, whether anyone was listening, whether there was anything in her budding nervous system that might have been receptive to the incantations we murmured over her: *healthy baby, happy baby, clever baby* . . . all the things we wanted her to be, all the fates we could bring about if we only prayed hard enough. If our lessons of love were going to make any difference, our floating child would need to be able to hear them. As to whether she would remember them for the future, we would have to wait to find out.

As it turned out, the vocal route was a good way of trying to get our messages across. Of all the varieties of information that make it through into the muscular prison of the uterus, the most potent is probably sound. For one thing, the womb is not as well insulated from noise as it is from other forms of energy, such as light. Studies using inserted microphones have shown that the sonic pressure inside the amniotic sac can reach ninety-five decibels, as loud as a passenger jet on the Gatwick flight path. The noisiness of the womb gives psychologists a convenient way of investigating how much learning can happen during the fetal period. Experiments of this kind have shown that fetuses learn the sound of their mother's voice, and can distinguish it from a stranger's moments after birth. They can recognize music heard repeatedly in the womb. You test fetal memory through a technique known as exposure learning. Infants who have been repeatedly exposed to a particular stimulus in the womb are presented with the same stimulus soon after birth. If they remember the stimulus, they show signs of interest: that is, they become alert, they stop moving, and their heart rate slows. In one experiment, newborn infants showed exposure learning to the theme song from the soap *Neighbours*, which their mothers had been watching during pregnancy. They showed the interest response when played the *Neighbours* tune two to four days after birth, but they showed no such response to unfamiliar tunes. A control group of infants, whose mothers had not been *Neighbours* fans, showed no interest in the tune. The only way of explaining this pattern of findings is to say that the *Neighbours* infants have remembered the tune they heard in the womb.

Although these lessons are not retained much beyond the early weeks of life, studies such as these show that the basics of remembering are in place even before birth. For that to be possible, Athena's fetal nervous system must have been sophisticated enough to process and retain new information. If, on that dark afternoon in the ultrasound scanner's room, I had been able to observe my daughter's brain under a powerful microscope, I would have seen new nerve cells being formed at rates of up to ten thousand a second. Of the hundred billion neurons that would go to make up her adult brain, most would already have been manufactured by the end of the second trimester. To begin with, these billions of neurons are not yet sufficiently developed to fulfill the most basic function of a nerve cell: to make connections, or synapses, with other cells. In fact, up to half of the cells produced in those first few weeks are destined for an early death. This process of "neural pruning" ensures that only those neurons that have formed appropriate connections go forward to form the body's most complex organ. Even with these extraordinary rates of neural proliferation in the first few months, brain development is really as much about the decimation of a multitude as it is about abundant life.

The birthplace of the embryo's neurons is a rolled-up layer of cells known as the neural tube. Peaking between around two and four months after conception, neuron formation is centered in an area called the ventricular zone, a layer of cells that forms the lining of this primitive structure. Neurons born here migrate to their final positions along networks of pathways laid down by structural cells called glia, which radiate outward from the center of the embryonic brain like lines of rigging. Most of the research on brain development has focused on the region known as the neocortex, the highly folded outer layer of the brain that represents the fruits of several million years of evolution. The first part to form is an area called the subplate, which forms a temporary scaffold for the initial layering of the neocortex. The neurons that follow trace the paths of their glial guide ropes to form new layers ever closer to the surface of the brain. The result is a columnar structure, with each column built up from six layers distinguished by different cell types or density. The mass migrations of the early months of brain development eventually form half a million of these columns, each around a millimeter in diameter and containing about sixty thousand neurons. These columns are the building blocks of the cortex's activities. In the visual cortex, for example, at the back of the brain, each column will eventually respond to a certain kind of visual input—perhaps a bar of light in a particular orientation. Measurements with electrodes have found the same kinds of specialization in the columns of the auditory cortex, located in the temporal lobes

above the ears, and the somatosensory cortex, the region at the top of
the brain that processes information about touch and movement.

Once in place, a neuron can get on with its real business of forming
connections to other neurons. It does this by sending out structures
called neurites, which can turn into axons (the long fibers that conduct electrical signals to other neurons) or dendrites (the shorter,
highly branching threads that gather electrical impulses into the
neuron). To reach the cells they need to connect to, the neurites follow a chemical trail, sometimes laid by the target cells themselves.
But the process is also sensitive to electrical activity produced by
the neurons themselves. Although much of neurodevelopment pro-
ceeds according to a plan stored in the genes, what happens up there
is equally a story of responding to local conditions. In the brain, the
context of development is as important as the genetic blueprint. The
brain doesn't unfold like a flower, according to some immutable master plan; it adapts to local conditions, like a city. Stimulation from
elsewhere in the nervous system is necessary to get neurons embedded in working relationships with other neurons—the alternative is
the holocaust of neural pruning. Like a metropolis full of people, the
neurons need to be given work to do to ensure their survival. Those
that can't find a role die off in the cull.

The prevailing electrical climate also has a say in how different
parts of the brain become specialized for different functions, such
as vision, hearing, and touch. According to one theory, the issue of
how any particular part of the cortex finds its role depends on the kind
of sensory input it receives. Your visual cortex becomes adapted for
its task because it receives input from the eyes; otherwise it would
become dedicated to something else. Although sensory input in the
womb is not nearly as rich as it is after birth, there is enough for the
fetus to hear, smell, taste, and touch to get this process of differentiation started. What's more, the brain's capacity to adapt to events
elsewhere in the nervous system means that it can remain in a state

of plasticity until well into childhood. One result is that damage to a particular part of the cortex can lead to other, intact areas taking on the same role. In congenitally blind children, for example, the visual cortex can be co-opted into processing information about touch. Although the neurons that migrate to a particular cortical area often have certain specializations that allow them to fulfill their role, this kind of plasticity makes the human cortex extraordinarily adaptable. Developmental change in one area is accompanied by changes in a whole range of connecting areas. When one neighborhood moves up in the world, the others adapt accordingly. For all the popularity of the term in modern culture, the idea that our circuits are "hardwired" is only partially accurate. We are softwired, sensitive to disruption and damage at all stages of development, but we are also uniquely equipped to adapt positively to the damage by drawing on other neural resources.

With all this migration and specialization, it is not long before the developing nervous system starts to show signs of life. About eight weeks after Athena's conception, a sensitive electrode would have been able to distinguish the first traces of electrical activity in her primitive brain. At around the same time, an ultrasound scan might have detected the first movements of her little body, such as her startle response to a loud noise. A new imaging technique based on detailed ultrasound scans allows us to witness the complexity of fetal movement in striking detail. By ten weeks, Athena would have been touching her own face with her fingers, which were already beginning to move independently of each other. By four months she would have had around fifteen different movement patterns, such as stepping or head-turning, to choose from. Much of this organized activity would have been established well before Lizzie felt her daughter's first kicks through the muscular wall of the womb. Shortly after this, she may have been opening her eyes and looking around at her underwater world. She was in the dark, like we were. If I interpreted her struggles as attempts to communicate, to show off her rapidly expanding repertoire, it was just more evidence of the preconceptions with which we were approaching parenthood. She may only have been testing out her muscles, but to me it looked purposeful. My new neighbor seemed restless. She had things she could do, and she wanted to show them off.

For the moment, we were divided by a gulf of interpretation as much as by an abdominal wall. We were locked in different rooms, each aware of the other but powerless to get our messages through. If Athena could hear anything of me against the background of her mother's circulation, it was only because her sense of hearing was fortuitously tuned to the acoustic characteristics of a human voice. Body tissues and amniotic fluid would have filtered out all but the lowest frequencies. Athena would have heard the world as a scuba diver would: muffled voices, thumping footsteps, the constant *lub-dup* of her mother's heart. Voices, whether mine or Lizzie's, would have sounded like someone calling from a boat. Although the lights were out in her subaquatic cave, her fully formed vestibular system, located in the inner ear, would have given her a sense of where she was in space. From about the fifth month of pregnancy, she would have known which way was up.

So was she conscious? Was there anything comparable to being that floating creature with the time-lapse city between her ears? What would once have been a question for theologians and philosophers has become a hot topic for developmental neuroscientists. We won't be interviewing any of these second-trimester fetuses any time soon, of course. Instead, what we can do is look at the electrical activity in their little brains, observe how fetuses respond to certain stimuli, and see whether their brain structure shows the right amount of connectivity to make consciousness possible. If we look at the EEG of the fetal brain, we see patterns of electrical activity in the cortex that aren't so different from those observed in a wide-awake adult brain. But those electrical traces can be misleading. Wakeful-looking EEG patterns can also be seen in coma victims, whom we would probably not want to describe as conscious. Relying solely on behavioral responses to stimuli would be just as misguided. Those very early startle reflexes were probably just that: reflexes that went nowhere near the circuitry of consciousness. They showed that some of the sensory pathways were there, but they didn't show that the subjectivity was there, any more than a reflex knee-jerk indicates a conscious intention to move one's leg. Medical specialists have a particular interest in these sensory reactions because of their concerns about whether fetuses are capable of feeling pain. After careful weighing of the evidence, they have tended to conclude that feeling pain requires something more than the mere ability to respond to noxious stimuli. As many philosophers have noted, pain requires that a sensation be felt *as* pain: you feel a toothache, vividly, in your tooth, a stomachache in your abdomen. There must be something comparable to having a pain; it must have some interiority. Acting as though you are in pain is not the same thing as feeling it. To suggest otherwise, in the case of the developing fetus, would probably be to attribute too much subjectivity.

As neuroscientists have learned more about the brain systems that underlie consciousness, they have refined their criteria for ascribing conscious awareness to the unborn. Studies of brain surgery patients have led to the surprising conclusion that the most highly evolved part of the brain, the neocortex, may not actually be enough to support consciousness on its own. Even while undergoing extensive surgery to cortical areas, many such patients remain conscious. Consciousness seems to depend on connections being made between the developing layers of the cortex and more primitive, subcortical areas such as the thalamus, an area in the forebrain known to be involved in relaying sensory information to the cortex. These connections take time to become established. The first neural projections from the thalamus reach the subplate of the neocortex from around eighteen weeks after conception. No one knows whether these newly formed pathways can immediately open the doors to the feeling of pain: it seems unlikely, as the processing of pain is known to depend on all sorts of learning experiences. But it is at least possible that fetuses have the necessary structures in place for consciousness around the middle of the second trimester.

You could argue that it isn't enough just to have the structures in place; it is also necessary to show that the structures are functioning properly. Those early EEG patterns may look very much like the wakeful states observed in adults, but they are transient, fleeting moments of coordinated activity. It would take something more consistent and continuous, such as activity organized in regular cycles, to prove that the system was working properly. One sure demonstration that an organism has the capacity to be conscious is to witness it losing that consciousness; that is, to watch it fall asleep. By the beginning of the third trimester, Athena's fetal brain would have been sufficiently developed to allow the beginning of REM sleep. Normal adults enjoy rapid eye movement sleep, or dream sleep, for one or two hours a night; fetuses are at it all the time. It has been suggested that REM sleep is a way for the developing brain to tune itself for the sensory bombardment that will follow birth. Considered like this, adult dreaming is a hangover from these fetal tuning impulses. When you and I dream, our brains are flooded with bioelectrical impulses from deep down in the brain stem, and our higher cortical centers interpret the resulting activity. They read the tea leaves, if you like: they see this ancient, random pattern sparkling up through the nervous system and they do their best to attach meaning to it. Evidence from other areas of psychology, such as visual perception, suggests that this compulsive pattern-seeking is a kind of neural reflex over which we have next to no control. Our cerebral cortices are the biggest cranks of the lot: they'll see a pattern in anything, and have us staking our lives on it. That's what the brain is there for, to impose order on chaos. And this crankery is persuasive. The vividness of our dreams testifies to that.

The fetal Athena knew about that vividness. She was stuck on a ledge on the wrong side of a reality gap, and there was no reaching her. The fireworks sparking up from her self-tuning brain stem had her embryonic mind enthralled. I didn't know what dangerous habits she was getting into. There is a theory that cot death is caused, not by pillows, duvets, or other instruments of suffocation, but by dreaming. The newborn baby enters REM sleep, but, because it has not yet had any experience of life in the outside world, all it can dream about is life in the womb. In the womb you don't breathe. The infant dreams of being a fetus again, and forgets to keep breathing. Until now, no one has ever imagined that dreaming could be fatal. Dreams can portend death, of course, but they cannot actually cause it. If this theory were shown to be correct, then newborns would need to keep their wits about them, for they would be one slip of memory away from death. Thankfully, our grip on life is quite a bit stronger than that, and we are reminded to keep breathing by all sorts of subcortical safety mechanisms. The body has its own memory systems, which keep the heart ticking and the metabolic fires burning. Our conscious, or even unconscious, thoughts would never be entrusted with such life-and-death stuff.

There was something that it was like, but it was not like this. At night, when Lizzie and I held each other, our Tiger was there between us, squirming against the skin of my belly, dreaming her way into existence. And yet her booming, red-toned reveries with their dull flashes of illumination weren't the magical escapes that our dreams can be. For us, a dream means a chance to turn away, however temporarily, from what we know of the world's wearying realities. Athena had no such knowledge yet to turn away from. There was a real world out there, ready to swamp her with its big noises and bright lights, and pretty soon she would have to face up to it. For several shadowy, suboceanic months her nervous system had been tuning itself for action, and now it was going to face its biggest test. Would life outside the womb just be a continuation of the fetal dream, no more troubled by reality than that gorgeous prebirth drift? Or was reality going to be a hard lesson? The outside world was awaiting her. Any day now, she was going to have to find out.

Three

⌒

BLOOMING, BUZZING

First Impressions of the Newborn

We think of light after darkness, noise after quiet, coldness after amniotic warmth. Birth is a bombardment of the senses, a shock to the system with no parallel in life. It is a trauma so devastating that, some psychologists have insisted, it can be remembered into adulthood. But it's not just the objects of perception that must be terrifying: it's the rude fact of becoming an object oneself, of taking one's place as a thing in a world of things. What was once all flickering dream life now has a body: heavy, unwieldy, needing a wash. Birth shocks us because of the sensory assault it lets loose, but also because those shrieking stimuli now have something solid to act upon. You cannot hide from your own corporeality, even when it weighs less than a few kilos.

For Athena, it was almost very different. We had planned to use a birthing pool for the later stages of labor, and now, a few hours in, the body-temperature water was having its effect. Lizzie was making strange, deep, erotic wailing noises, something like a mermaid must make. Midwives were gathering from other parts of the hospital, quietly excited by the prospect of an underwater birth. The idea of water birth is to ease the transition from womb to outside world, to ensure that the newborn baby spends her first few moments in an environment that is as similar as possible to the uterus. The idea is also to put the fear of God into every middle-class parent with a secret penchant for "natural" solutions. "Won't she drown?" we asked, somehow knowing that she would be a she. No chance. Apparently it's the change of temperature that triggers the infant's first breath. You can't deny oxygen for long, but you can put it off for a few moments. By reducing the shock of birth, the idea is that the water baby is less stunned by the experience and is thus able to stay more alert and receptive in that crucial first hour, when newborns are typically at their most wakeful. Otherwise it would be like turning up to a party already drunk. There are important people to meet. You have to be at your best.

In the end, it didn't work out that way. After three hours in the pool, the new mother was starting to flag. The midwives were checking the baby's heartbeat after every contraction, looking for signs of fetal distress. Athena's heart rate was, as expected, dropping during contractions, but it was also failing to recover as quickly as it should. What was needed now was gravity and a hard bed. Our daughter would be born on dry land, like the vast majority of Western infants. If there was to have been some spiritual benefit in being delivered from water into water, she would have to make do without it, like everyone else.

So: light after darkness, noise after quiet. Well, perhaps. Athena would have heard enough of our voices in the booming confines of the womb to have formed some memory of them, a memory for their rhythms, rather than their tonal qualities or content. In fact, the most developed of her newborn senses would have been touch. Fetuses aborted during the third month of pregnancy have been shown to respond to the touch of a human hair around the mouth. Babies born three months prematurely are sensitive enough to respond to a hair touch anywhere on the body. Surely such a developed tactile sense would make being squeezed down the birth canal an excruciating experience? Those who have studied it think not. Our hypersensitive fetuses might respond to the hair touch, but they don't necessarily experience it as anything like discomfort. Until the required connections between thalamus and cortex are established at about eighteen weeks of gestation, they probably cannot consciously experience it as anything. Even after those neurological advances, you might still want to be cautious about describing the baby's sensations of birth as genuine pain. Pain is as much a learned reaction as anything else, part of the body's response to a divergence from a familiar sequence of sensory stimuli. When the shock to the system is so total, there is nothing to compare it with—which is why a soldier can have a limb blown off on the battlefield and not feel it for hours afterward. Newborn babies are in a similar position: they have no idea what life is supposed to feel like, so they have no way of knowing whether this is a painful bit or not.

Which is not to say that our new baby would have been numb. She would have felt the pressures of the birth canal, certainly. The coldness of the air in the delivery room would have been a shock. When she was lifted up on to her mother's belly to make the acquaintance of the nipple, the sensation of that expanse of maternal skin against her own nakedness must have felt like drowning in something else. They tell us that the skin is the largest organ in the human body. Something that had been cushioned by warm water for months was suddenly exposed to air and human flesh. Although her bone-crushing squeeze down the birth canal would have taken some of the edges off the lesson, she had nevertheless started to learn what it was like to be a physical being in a world of physical beings. Our daughter had attained stuffness. She had fallen to earth with a bump.

But all that light: what was she to make of that? In the short video clip we took when she was five minutes old, her eyes are puffy and pinkish, but very definitely open. Her vision would have been blurred, but shortsightedness is no protection against dazzlement. An influential thought experiment in philosophy asks whether someone who had never experienced a feature of consciousness, such as redness, could ever know what it was. The same argument can be applied to any subjective quality of sensation. How can you understand what sort of thing light is if it has never actually shone on you? To us, it would be like suddenly acquiring a new sense, something we can hardly imagine without trying to compare it to our other, existing senses. But such comparisons don't work. Light is not like anything. You have either seen it, or you have not.

She would have seen her mother's face, other faces, the head of a bed, the functional details of a hospital room. After months of fetal immunity, the outside world had finally turned up. She was well into her first lesson in objective reality, although possibly too out of it to care. The physical trauma of birth, in particular the constriction of her oxygen supply as she passed down the birth canal, would have left her slightly hypoxic, like that spaced-out high you get after you've been running. There may have been a slight headache. In their memorable description of neonatal hypoxia, Daphne and Charles Maurer liken it to running long and hard along a busy, brilliantly lighted street: the hubbub stimulates while the hypoxia strings you out into space. It's like the end of an all-night bender. You've run out of taxi money, so you've taken to your heels. Your tour of the city's parties is almost at an end. You've made this great friend—you call her "Ma"—and she's as out of it as you are. You're going home to crash for about three days. You lost your coat somewhere, and you're freezing. But what a rave, what a light show. What a night.

For an hour or so, the newborn is as alert as she will be for weeks. Like her mother, she has probably gone beyond tiredness, and entered that wobbly world where sobering-up teenagers talk philosophy and watch the sun come up. It used to be thought that this was a crucial window of opportunity for bonding, an appointment arranged by natural selection to make sure the newborn and the new mother can get off on the right foot. It may in fact just be an accidental by-product of all that sensory stimulation, a more-or-less meaningless adrenaline rush. Anyway, the "bonding" hypothesis is now largely discredited, and parents are told to get on and enjoy that magical first hour without feeling that they need to be doing anything in particular. In some hospitals, they might have to fight off the scientists who also want to take advantage of this moment of lucidity. In a study such as the *Neighbours* experiment, psychologists have to be certain that any learning that is detected cannot possibly have happened since birth. For this reason, many modern psychology departments have outposts in maternity hospitals, so that infants can fulfill their experimental duties as soon as is decent. The youngest participant in one classic study of imitation in infants was only forty-two minutes old. Even this newborn baby showed signs of being able to imitate facial expressions, strongly suggesting that this capacity is innate, and not learned after birth.

For the moment, Athena's career as an experimental participant lay a little way in the future. Within a few hours I was watching her sleep soundly in her incubation cot, being heated gently by a bank of tiny electrical elements. Like most newborns, her temperature had plummeted after birth. If she awoke now she might have heard the comings and goings in the corridor outside, the arrival and departure of doctors and dinner trolleys, and the sound of her mother's breathing as she slept. Where previously the higher frequencies would have been filtered out by the fluid and body tissue that surrounded her, she would now have begun to hear them clearly. It would have been a shrill world in which to try and get some sleep. I watched her breathing, wondering how long she could keep up this new trick of hers, how long it would be before I had to pull the emergency cord and people came running and we realized that she'd been putting it on, playing the part of a living baby girl, an air-breather, one of us. But I had forgotten that she had been practicing. For the last three months she would have been busy taking ever-more-frequent "breaths" of the amniotic fluid. Her respiratory muscles were now fully toned and ready for the task of the next eighty or so years. That tumultuous squeezing in the birth canal had helped empty her lungs of the remaining fluid. All she had to do was remember that the world had changed, and the practiced thing was now happening for real. Fortunately, she remembered that much.

There was no waking in a strange room, wondering what had happened to her. There was hardly any waking at all. Newborns sleep for an average of sixteen to eighteen out of every twenty-four hours, and only a small proportion of the remaining time is spent in a state of alert wakefulness. Paradoxically, the snoozefest that marks our first few weeks on the planet is not the descent into unconsciousness that it is for an adult. In our own brains, the cycles of wakefulness and sleep depend on the thalamus switching cortical circuits on and off in response to sensory stimulation. Although the necessary connections between thalamus and cortex would have been in place from the middle of Athena's time in the womb, the activity in her cortex was still extremely disorganized. Most of the things the newborn Athena could do—breathing, sucking, moving reflexively in response to stimulation—were controlled by subcortical regions, and didn't involve the cortex at all. The cortex wasn't doing much of any use, so switching it off at bedtime made little difference.

When she celebrated her birth, then, by yawning and crashing out, she was only really looking to give her battered little body a break. Neurologically speaking, falling asleep was just a continuation of what she had been doing while awake. In adults, the normal sleep–wake cycle depends on the thalamus getting its switch-throwing into a rhythm, so that those consciousness-supporting cortical connections can be orchestrated in a regular pattern. This daily routine establishes

itself over the first few months of life, partly through the infant's accli-
matization to adult sleep–wake cycles, and partly through increasing
neurological maturity. The adult brain shuts down nightly, like an
office block, for routine maintenance. In the newborn, the cleaners are
wandering around all day long. The supervisor has gone missing. The
technicians are reinstalling software and upgrading the phone system
even as a poor drone is trying to work.

For the neonate this means that, whatever kind of consciousness
she has, it is maintained more or less around the clock. As a result,
her sleeping brain is very far from being cut off from what is going
on around it. EEG studies have shown that newborns' brains, unlike
adults', remain active during all phases of sleep and wakefulness. Not
only are they active, but they are also sensitive to incoming information. One important gauge of such sensitivity, known as the visually
evoked response, is a measure of how the brain's electrical activity
responds to a visual stimulus such as a flash of light. In adults, the
visually evoked response is almost abolished during dreaming sleep,
whereas in neonates it is present twenty-four hours a day. Newborns
seem to be switched on all the time, even when, to the observer, they
seem furthest adrift in dreams.

What does that dreamy consciousness feel like? Like any new parents, we spent a good part of our time musing about what it must be
like on the other side of those pearly eyelids. A famous essay in philosophy, which ends up being skeptical about the possibility of our ever
knowing about the consciousness of another creature, asks, "What
is it like to be a bat?" One of the problems with my imagining bat
consciousness is that bats, with their amazing skills of echolocation,
perceive the world very differently from me. Things matter to them
that my sensory equipment cannot even detect. Athena's way of being
conscious would have been almost as strange, considering the general
immaturity of her perceptual capacities and the disorganization of her
cortex. We were tuned to different frequencies. My efforts to simulate

her consciousness on my own mental apparatus would be like trying to find *The Archers* on Radio One.

But then again, we have so much time in which to speculate. Eighteen hours a day she lies there in one of two fairly distinct stages of sleep. Here she is at four days, swaddled in her white shawl, lying on her back on my knee with daylight falling on her through the picture window to her right. Her eyes are closed. There is a single crease along the midline of her eyelids, which wasn't there when she was born. When she's thirty and complaining about getting wrinkles, I'll tell her the rot set in on Day One. Her eyelashes were invisible three days ago; now they are long and dark. Her mouth is open, her lips encrusted with flakes of milk from the morning's feeds. The close focus of the camera has exaggerated the moony roundness of her face. Her forehead wrinkles briefly, her eyes move behind their lids, and she pushes her tongue against the insides of her lips, then pulls it back, practicing her suction. I say her name and she stops, as though listening. I zoom in and she responds, almost indignantly, to the noise of the camcorder's lens motor; her face twists into a comical frown, one faint eyebrow raised in quizzical disdain. Her smooth forehead is suddenly crumpled. Then she settles again; her lips harden into a duck-bill, which is then stretched out into a lopsided smile. It is far from being a social response, as she can hardly know that I am there. But it's eloquent, telling of well-fed contentment and Elysian dreams. Sometimes she will even whimper with what sounds like pleasure, or make strange wheezes and snorts that don't sound as though they could be coming from a human being. She can do tongues, kingly grimaces, animal impressions without ever having seen an animal. Her breathing can be very irregular. Sometimes her eyes will open slightly and we'll see the whites roaming around under the half-closed lids. She hasn't quite stopped being an alien in a 1950s sci-fi movie. Any minute now, we can't help thinking, she'll climb back into her tinfoil spaceship and the credits will roll.

This is known as "active" sleep, and it is contrasted with the "quiet" stage during which the infant does nothing more than occasionally suck on an imaginary nipple. Given the apparent similarity to adult REM sleep, the watcher can't help concluding that she is dreaming. The fact is, we don't yet know whether active sleep in infancy is a true precursor of the dreaming sleep we experience as adults, or whether babies' neurological immaturity means that these two kinds of lively unconsciousness are essentially different phenomena. The room is quiet, her eyes are closed, so she cannot be perceiving anything directly—which leads me to assume that she must be in the grip of an imagining. Surely *something* is going on behind those flickering eyelids. My insistence that it is adultlike dreaming just underlines how strange her consciousness is to me. She's a bat, and I'm a philosopher. She finds her way in the dark by following the echoes I miss, dozing on the wing, wide-awake behind the mask of sleep.

When she does eventually open her eyes, she might want to close them again straightaway. Her optical equipment, like her cortical activity, is fundamentally different from mine. The lens of my adult eye has become yellowed with age, meaning that the shorter, or bluer, wavelengths are filtered out. Newborn lenses, in contrast, are crystal clear. Getting those eyes back, for us, would be like taking off sunglasses on a bright day. Summer daylight, such as is falling on her through the picture window, would have an almost unbearable ultraviolet brilliance, like a Greek village at noon. In darkness, such as when she wakes for a feed at night, her eyesight will not be much worse than mine. But daytime vision relies on the cone-rich part of the retina called the fovea, which is very immature in newborns. The result is poor visual acuity—the blurredness of everything that isn't between twenty and thirty centimeters from her face—and an insensitivity to contrast. If she had any interest in watching TV, she would see nothing unless the contrast control was turned up all the way. It's this insensitivity to contrast that draws her to big boundaries of brightness rather than more subtle patternings of light and shade. When she looks into our faces, her attention is immediately drawn toward the edges, where the greatest contrasts are. Although it might seem like a neat evolutionary trick that her optimal focusing distance—twenty to thirty centimeters—corresponds to her distance from her mother's face when being held normally, the details of that face don't interest her. She is the gallery-goer who only ever reads the captions screwed to the gold leaf, more interested in the frame than the artwork.

And even if she did look into our faces, she might not recognize what she saw there. Although her cortex remains sufficiently switched on to allow her to learn highly repetitive regularities about the world even when she is asleep, such as the ticking of clocks or the ringing of bells, many of these lessons are forgotten as soon as she opens her eyes. The knowledge that does stick with her is hard-won. Amnesia lurks, ready to wipe the slate clean again at any moment. She won't learn to discriminate the details of familiar faces until around eight weeks, which means that the face associated with feeding may look like a different entity than the face of the person who picked her up a moment ago. Confusion reigns, even in something as simple as watching the world go by. Her inborn mental tool kit might have given her some basic expectations about how physical objects persist in time and space, but that doesn't mean that she will perceive things that way. When objects change position, for example, they won't necessarily impress her as separate entities moving in smooth trajectories. Until she becomes more certain what objects are, it may be that she will perceive them as strings of distinct snapshots, strewn across different locations. If I could look out at the world through her blurry eyes, it would look like a wrecked Disney masterpiece, an animated film from which any number of frames have been torn out.

Perhaps the strangest thing about newborn consciousness is the way that even major channels of sensory stimulation can blend into each other. In his book *The Mind of a Mnemonist*, the great Russian neurologist Alexander Luria describes his subject S.'s experiences of synesthesia, the phenomenon where stimulation in one sensory modality, such as vision, is experienced in another, such as taste. When listening to a high-pitched tone at a volume of 113 decibels, S. said: "It looks something like fireworks tinged with a pink-red hue. The strip of color feels rough and unpleasant, and it has an ugly taste—rather like that of a briny pickle . . . You could hurt your hand on this." When conversing one day with another great Russian psychologist, Lev Vygotsky, S. was heard to remark, "What a crumbly yellow voice you have."

One plausible explanation of synesthesia is that the normal pathways along which sensory information flows through the brain become diverted—leading, say, visual information into the olfactory (or smell-detecting) cortex, or input from the auditory nerve into the touch-sensitive part of the brain. Studies of infants' cortical activity suggest that, far from this being a trick enjoyed only by circus freaks and neurological case studies, it may be a common state of affairs in newborns. In one experiment, visual stimuli that should have been easily discriminable to young infants turned out to produce identical evoked potentials in the visual cortex, suggesting that the infant was not actually distinguishing between them as images. Instead, the different stimuli caused different patterns of activity to bubble up all over the brain: in the olfactory cortex, the auditory cortex, even the sector that controls motor responses. The infant was apparently distinguishing between the different stimuli, but not as distinct images: rather, the stimuli were registering as different kinds of sensations altogether—tastes, sounds, smells. It is possible that Athena's cortex is miswired in a similar way. The smell of her shawl might be a dim flash of light to her. The daylight beyond her eyelids might reach her as a faint hum. She is tasting in color, smelling in sound. Compared with that, dreaming seems positively mundane.

. . .

An hour or so has passed. She has just had a big lunchtime feed. A moment ago she farted so loudly that she still looks in shock from it, and we're joking that the sound waves are still reverberating around the walls. Actually, we shouldn't joke: for her, they are. Her auditory cortex has not yet developed sufficiently to allow it to filter out the echoes that accompany any sound—echoes that none of us hear once we get beyond a few months of age. For the moment her world is a whispering gallery, a chamber of indistinguishable echoes that are almost impossible to locate in space. She is lying on her back on her mother's knee, in that watchful phase after a big feed, and I am videoing their interaction. She can probably tell where her mother's voice is coming from, but, because of the difference in pitch between our voices, she is less responsive to mine. Nevertheless, she turns slowly away from her study of the edge of her mother's face and the frames of the paintings on the wall behind her, and she applies her gaze to me, or rather to the black lump of camcorder in front of my face. To her, with her dodgy wiring, that blackness might be a taste or a smell, or the sound of a chair falling over. Her eyes are very dark and reflective, and it is hard to make out the pupil. She stops for a wriggle, a yawn, and a root, and for a moment her eyes are out of action. Newborns can't watch and move at the same time. It's like that old joke about walking and chewing gum: for a few weeks of our lives, it's true. Then she goes back to fixating on the contrast boundary between her mother's hair and the painted yellow wall behind. All the time Lizzie is speaking to her, making small talk, commenting on her apparent shows of interest. The words are yellow. The wall is a lullaby. There is no center or circumference, no subject or object, no inside or out. It is all mixed up into a single vivid pageant of sensations: not a circus that she watches from some detached ringside seat, but a brilliant carnival parade in which, like a straying tourist in a sea of strange faces, she is caught up and swept away.

And for days, I see her face everywhere. The lunatics have taken over my own telephone exchange. Two mugs of coffee on the table are like her big dark watchful eyes. The neck of the milk bottle as I pour the milk out into the jug is like her mouth, running through the motions of a suck. The bacon in a sandwich is her pink tongue lolling out of white lips. I can even see her face in a SLOW sign painted on the road. The wiring has gone wrong in my own brain. My sensory pathways have been rerouted. I'm a newborn too, washed up on a strange new synesthetic shore.

Four

⌒

THOSE DRIVEN THINGS

Coming to Know the People Who

Shared Her World

You had to wonder, sometimes, if being born wasn't an accident she was trying to ignore. So much of what she did was fetal: those writhing head movements, on axes of rotation that didn't seem anatomically possible; the way she trawled her slow, unblinking gaze across the ceiling, while her arms rehearsed delicate flamenco moves, one wrist bent above her head. Neurologically, her movements were controlled by subcortical feedback loops, the same ones that would have kept her in constant motion in the ever-shrinking rehearsal room of the womb. She hadn't changed her repertoire to fit her new life on the outside. At four weeks, she was really still a beached fetus, vainly practicing her underwater moves while waiting for the tide to come back in.

Her senses, too, were still primed for that suboceanic world. With her visual system still so immature, those blurry hours of wakefulness would have been dominated by the most primitive of her perceptual abilities. Thanks to her well-developed vestibular system, she would have had a feeling of where she was in space. A baby's sense of balance develops sufficiently before birth to allow responses like the

Moro reflex, which causes the newborn to fling her arms out, grasping, whenever her position suddenly changes. Athena felt us, even if she couldn't see us clearly. Her somatosensory, or touch-sensing, cortex would have been educated by her tactile experiences in the womb, so that its surface now represented a map of the different parts of the body where she felt our touches. Holding her quietly in our arms would have communicated more than any amount of visual or auditory stimulation.

Her chemical senses were also well established by these early days, with many of the smells and tastes of this new world being familiar to her from the womb. Women with garlicky diets in pregnancy have babies who show less aversion to that flavor than babies without prenatal exposure. Athena's exclusive reliance on breast milk provided some continuity with the tastes she had known before birth, but her oral explorations soon brought her across other flavors. It's unlikely that these early lessons were truly formative, though. Her first taste of champagne, for example, was too fleeting to shape any subsequent fondness for the stuff. Although important taste preferences would undoubtedly be established later on when she started on solid food, neonatal learning probably doesn't endure long enough to mold the tastes of the adult. We hadn't just gone and created an alcoholic, even with a finger dab of vintage Perrier-Jouët.

All of this sensory activity was going on while her visual abilities were still very immature. There may actually be sound evolutionary reasons for being born with such bad eyesight. Senses like hearing and touch can be primed quite effectively by uterine events, but making sense of the visual world requires direct experience of it. In fact, without the progressively richer input received in the first few months, the brain would never properly rewire itself for vision. By ensuring that the neonate is visually impaired, evolution may have arranged it so that those first lessons are not damagingly harsh. Too much detailed input too early on might overwhelm the system; too little, and the system would never learn at all. The newborn can see what she needs to see, and no more. In any case, the darkness of the womb means that the newborn's vision-processing areas will have had little in the way of input to work with. Because the neonate's visual system has not had the opportunities to be instructed by experience that other systems have had, the time it spends playing catch-up is crucial.

For the first couple of months, her vision would have been a largely subcortical affair. She moved her eyes, apparently intentionally, and did reflexive, lizard-brain stuff like turning toward an object moving on the periphery of her vision. True seeing would require cortical processing. The visual cortex (in the occipital lobe at the back of the brain) is where perceptual features such as color, pattern, and motion are extracted from the input registered on the retinas and ultimately form the basis of conscious perception. One stream of visual processing, known as the "where" stream, leads from the visual cortex to the parietal areas at the top of the brain, and is responsible for the rapid computations that enable us to track objects through space. The other main stream, the "what" stream, leads from the same point in the visual cortex to the temporal lobes, and is specialized to detect those features, such as color and shape, that allow us to identify and recognize objects. In infants, the subconscious "where" stream is first to appear, meaning that babies have the basis for reacting appropriately to objects some time before they really understand what those objects are. If a baby of this age could walk, she would be able to do so without bumping into things. A newborn can track movement in the firmament above her cot with some skill, although her assiduous tracking of the bright objects that dangle above her should not be taken as evidence of recognition. In fact, the newborn's close attention to a visual stimulus sometimes has more to do with a compulsive neural feedback loop than with any genuine show of interest. From about four weeks, infants typically show "sticky fixation," when subcortical instincts to move the eyes toward the periphery of the visual field start to be overridden by developing cortical control systems. Those subcortical reflexes are trying to push her gaze out toward the edges, while the more practically minded cortex is trying to get her to look at what is right in front of her. The result of this neural wrestling match is that the baby is often seen to stare at the same object, or person, for minutes on end. Beware, then, besotted new fathers and mothers. Your beloved newborn may not actually be gazing at you adoringly. It could just be that she hasn't yet worked out how to look away.

If vision was the slowest of her senses to develop, it was also destined to be the quickest to reach maturity. That it could catch up so quickly was largely thanks to an explosion in synapse production at around this time. Imaging techniques such as positron emission tomography (PET), which measures the rate of glucose metabolism in different parts of the brain, show that most of the action in a five-week-old brain is going on in subcortical structures like the thalamus and brain stem. A few weeks later, the picture changes dramatically, with cortical areas such as the primary visual cortex showing the most new growth. At two months, synapses in the baby's cortex are formed at a greater rate than in any other period in development—1.8 million per second, by some estimates. By six months, Athena will have twice the number of cortical synapses that she will have as a college student; twice as many, that is, as she will eventually need. Like the overproduced brain cells in the fetal stage, synapses die away, at the rate of about twenty billion a day, if they fail to make felicitous connections. Neurons compete for precious chemical growth factors, strengthen their connections if they receive the right kind of electrical activation, or lose their synapses if they don't find a role. The brain only keeps the connections it needs, and that depends on the input it receives. The end of the period of synaptic pruning corresponds, in any particular part of the brain, to the end of the period of maximum capacity for learning. We cannot remain bundles of infinite potential forever. We

have to specialize, even if that means a drastic reduction in the range
of things we can learn.

Another profound change concerns the structure of the neurons
themselves. Mature nerve cells are partially covered with a fatty substance, myelin, which forms an insulating sheath around the axon and
gives the white matter of the brain its characteristic appearance. The
formation of these myelin sheaths leads to a large improvement in the
speed and efficiency of communication between nerves, and is at its
peak in the first few months after birth, leading to a massive increase
in brain weight in the first year of life. All that myelin production
demands the intake of great quantities of fats, or lipids—another
reason full-fat milk is an essential part of a baby's diet. Looking at
the extent of myelination gives developmental neuroscientists a clue
to how well different parts of the cortex are talking to each other.
Brain development is not so much about maturation in specific separate regions of the brain as it is about the developing efficiency and
complexity of these myelinated pathways between cortical areas.
The parts of the brain work together as a team, and good teamwork
is always more important than outstanding individual performances.

What did all this mean for Athena's slowly dawning consciousness?
I sit here, imagining. Waking from an unscheduled nap, perhaps, in a
crowded shopping center. Blurred movements and rudimentary color.
No depth to the picture: everything on the surface, like the shifting
images inside a kaleidoscope. A babble of echoing noises, which she
can just begin to locate in space. No sense of herself as anything distinct from this mélange of sensory impressions. Her attention drawn
drowsily to a multisensory, synesthetic pattern that seems to be
repeating, although she cannot be sure. It repeats again, and she is a
little more certain. She is learning, but she doesn't know that she is
learning. A bright light flashes into view above her, and she shrinks
from it instinctively. She feels a faint, radiant, soothing wave of emotion: familiarity. One of the noises swoops close to her, and she smells

the voice powerfully. A firm softness touches her cheek, and she turns reflexively to absorb it into her mouth. Then it is gone again, and it is as though it never happened. She bites sideways at the air, yawning, and blinks her dark-gray almond eyes. She can't move her body; she doesn't even know that she has a body. And yet hands are moving, tiny pink wrinkled hands, reaching up to touch her face. They are wildlife, random bits of passing flesh, and yet they feel like something, as they brush up against her skin—something to do with her. Perhaps she can make them come back, and then she will have the same feeling again. She has a dim sense of wanting to change something, to make it different, but she doesn't realize what is needed. It is just within reach. She would make the connection, if she could only understand how.

I t starts with a voice—that scratchy, leather-scented voice. Familiarity blooms again. Because Athena's ability to localize sound is in a developmental limbo between subcortical and cortical control, she is actually worse at locating the voice's position than she was as a newborn. But her memory for it is good. The sounds people make anchor her in space, give her a sense of continuity even when her visual world is blurred and confused. What voices herald, though, is even more impressive. Something vertiginously vast, looming into view in the top corner of her visual field. A huge moist cloud with edges made of thunder, darkening the scene. It is like one of those alien spaceships that fills the sky in a sci-fi movie, and the mere sight of it connects with something deep and primeval: not a threat to her kind so much as a celebration of it. These aliens come in peace. They are her ancestors, peering at her through the primordial forest leaves. They fixate her with those vast, ghostly lights embedded along their midlines, and she cannot help but return their gaze. She was born to look at them, and that deeply encoded attraction is the bond that has held the species together. No other animals look at each other like we look at each other. As Athena will soon find out, this attention from others can take her, and the people she interacts with, a long way.

Faces have special effects on infants from their very first days. The newborn's poor visual acuity means that she can at first perceive little of a human visage beyond a triad of dark blobs corresponding to eyes and nose. But that primitive pattern is quite enough for the superior colliculus, the structure in the midbrain that takes initial responsibility for face processing. The superior colliculus also finds its work easier when stimuli are in motion, which is why neonates prefer slowly moving faces to stationary ones. If your newborn won't look at you, then you are probably standing too still. As with eye movements and sound localization, these subcortical circuits gradually cede power to cortical regions, with the result that infants' face processing gets worse before it gets better. Less than an hour after birth, neonates show more interest in a simple schematic face showing eyes, nose, and mouth than the equivalent stimulus with its features scrambled. At around six weeks, that preference vanishes temporarily while duties are handed over to cortical control. Eventually, at around two months, the face-recognition systems of the lower temporal lobes become mature enough to take on the task of face processing. At this point the infant can really begin to learn about the distinctive identities of people's eyes, noses and mouths, and chart the varied subtleties of the many different faces that swim into view.

Faces in general are compelling, but eyes specifically have a different power altogether. The human eye is distinct from those of other mammals in that it contains a dark iris and pupil within a relatively large area of white. That simple contrast between light and dark provides infants with conspicuous clues about where people's eyes are pointing. Newborns prefer to look at faces whose eyes are engaging them directly, compared with those where the eyes are looking away. Three-month-olds smile less when an adult they are interacting with turns her gaze away, and cheer up again when the eyes turn back on to them. From about four months, infants can cue in to another person's direction of gaze to follow where that person is looking, as long as it follows one of these periods of mutual gaze. Babies are attuned to the ways in which other people are directing their attention, and their strongest hints come from the windows into the soul.

It is not just a special sensitivity to faces and eyes that hooks young infants into a social world. Although knowledge about body structure, such as the proper configuration of a person's arms and legs, is surprisingly poor until the second year, infants are responsive to the particular ways in which people's bodies move from an early age. Psychologists test this capacity using point-light displays, where it is not an actual human figure that provides the stimulus, but rather an array of lights representing the major joints—shoulders, elbows, hips, and knees—of a moving body. If you attached small lights to your arms and legs and then plunged the room into darkness, you would create a display like this. Even three-month-olds treat this kind of movement differently from other kinds. From electrophysiological studies done at eight months, we know that babies' brains process biological motion in a similar way to adults'. We recognize our fellow humans from the way they walk, as well as the way they look and talk.

This thing that is staring at her is, then, no ordinary thing. Like many other members of the animal kingdom, Athena will have been programmed with certain basic expectations about how physical objects behave: that they remain solid and coherent, for example, and that they act on each other through physical contact. But this object is different. When it moves, it doesn't do so by reacting mechanically to other events and objects; it is self-propelled. Biological motion generates itself, without the need for any external events to set it going. The self-driven things that surround us have special qualities. In fact, some have argued that babies are born knowing that the world is inhabited by two fundamentally different kinds of objects: those that can get around under their own steam (like people) and those that can't.

There can be no doubt that babies are wired to treat people differently. If they can show that special sensitivity, then they have a chance to learn about the other qualities that set people apart. As these social interactions become more sophisticated, the information they can convey will become richer and richer. Just by following where people's eyes are pointing, and the social gestures that accompany their looking, infants can pick up a wide range of knowledge about objects in the world. Much of infants' early learning, it turns out, is determined by their following of another person's gaze.

From my point of view, she is a special object as well. She gives back more, these days, than she did in those first couple of weeks. Cortical maturation and improved muscle tone mean that she has a greater repertoire of social actions. Her first genuine smile gets noted down at about four weeks, although I might have read false signs of the same event in various nonsocial actions, like that one-eyed, sideways gnawing movement she makes in search of an imaginary nipple. Hunger, not happiness, was what she was trying to convey—but what really mattered was that I took her action as having a certain meaning. Just as we start constructing our offspring before birth, so we apply our overactive imaginations to infant behavior long before it is logically sound to do so. If Athena makes a random gurgling sound, which I think sounds like a classic baby coo, then I respond to it with all the emotional dials turned up all the way. I fill it with meaning, and turn that meaning back to her. The emotional stakes are raised: suddenly this *matters*, to both of us. As soon as she can begin to connect my response with the action of hers that triggered it, she can start to close the circle of her own emotions: how feelings lead to responses, and back to feelings, world without end. Infants' social behavior comes to have meaning because we take it as having meaning. We create our babies' smiles before they do.

And Athena is a more competent partner in these proto-conversations than she used to be. The greater sophistication of her behavior means that my feverish imagination has much more to work with than it ever had before. I interpret her expressions and actions with abandon, and reflect them to her with the gaps filled in. She hangs on my every move. This unflinching attentiveness might have a little to do with sticky fixation, a screeching feedback loop between cortical and subcortical circuits, but it means the world to me. To my mind, it is adoration; from that beached fetus of a couple of weeks ago, she has become what I wanted her to be. Like the goddess Athena in the story, she has the gray eyes I imagined for her, and so the story comes true. In time, I am politely relieved of this delusion, as it is gently pointed out to me that all babies have blue-gray eyes at birth. What determines the color of your irises is the presence of pigment cells called chromatophores, which only begin to develop in the first few weeks of life. In the newborn, light passes through the unpigmented front layer of the iris and is reflected with the red frequencies absorbed. The same happens when light passes through a body of water: the longer wavelengths are absorbed, and the water appears blue-gray. The poets are therefore correct: eyes *are* like water pools, especially when they are the drowning eyes of a newborn.

So I bring my own emotional agenda to these meetings. I need things from her, more than she can ever imagine. She absorbs it all. She was born for this; for those minutes or hours every day, she responds to me as though I were the only person in her world. But the flow of emotion is not all one way. She gives as well as receiving. She has expectations of how I will behave, and she reacts if I don't fulfill them. She can recognize a few different emotional expressions, and reproduce the most basic ones for herself. If I were to change my expression suddenly from happy to angry, for example, she would show surprise. If I suddenly made my face freeze up altogether, she would stop smiling, look away, and then try to reengage my attention. She will fight to keep the channels open. We're not saying much, really, except that we love each other, but this is a message we are both completely open to. She is built to talk silently about love, in comfortable close-up. Smooching with a baby is so rewarding, partly, because it is the one thing they can really do.

Perhaps that's why people have found a baby's gaze to be so deep, so containing of multitudes. In Sylvia Plath's "Nick and the Candle-stick," the poet's infant son is "the one / Solid the spaces lean on, envious." In Don Paterson's poem "Waking with Russell," the narra-tor, *nel mezzo del cammin*, finds in his four-day-old son's smile a new meaning for his own life. Similar moments of revelation happen to insomniac parents the world over. In fact, it's no accident that many of these cooey love-ins have a dawn-tinged glow. Sleep deprivation has been shown to have such profound influences on our neurophysiology that it is now classified as an altered state of consciousness. On top of the hormonal chaos, new parents are getting a hit of something mind-bending. Hallucinations are not uncommon; in the sleep-deprived state, many of the normal processes of reasoning become derailed. When we are at our weakest, babies' emotional hold over us is at its strongest. They are wise, and we can only watch and learn.

At six weeks, we took Athena away with us to a hotel for our first city break as a new family. One early morning she woke me with her restlessness after a feed. It was September, and daylight still came early. She lay in the crook of my arm, looking straight at me, about two inches from my face. Her eyes had a gleam of dawn in them, and seemed to radiate an extraordinary peace. She had only just learned to blink. No one had warned me that young infants don't blink, that it takes a few weeks for that spontaneous eye-moistening habit to be acquired. In the twilight her eyes were gray and serene, and she seemed to have opened them wider to look at me, like a lover would. I felt gauche and foolish, as if I had been invited into the bed of a film star and didn't know what to say to her. She was smiling. There was a tiny peak, a sucking blister, on her upper lip. Her lips, the smoothest abalone at birth, had become faintly segmented now, like a grown-up woman's. I took her hand and held it entirely enfolded in mine, and it felt like a tiny spider, minutely limbed, alive with a prickly electricity. She was human, and yet she was a blank canvas. She was a newborn child, and yet she embodied all that a human being could ever be. Like the goddess in the story, she seemed to have come from a place outside this world, to teach me how my life would unfold. I had thought that she was the ephemeral one, who needed to be conjured up from thin air through sheer force of imagination. But it was I who now felt threatened with extinction, reassuringly diminished by this brush with immortality.

Five

WHO'S PLAYING
THAT PIANO?

Acting, Reacting, and Gaining Control

It is a bright autumn day. Athena is four months old. From the scrap of a thing I videoed at four days, she has become a chubby-cheeked infant, the sort our government baby brochures promised us. She is almost completely bald on top, but at the back her hair is long and wispy. She is wearing a pink sleepsuit with the word "Itsy" printed on the front, and she is propped up against a darker pink cushion on the sofa bed in the room we call the study. People come and go. She can tell them apart now. There is a tall person, whose clothes open at the front at mealtimes, and an even taller one, who has no such talent. They speak in rushed monosyllables. The breast one is in a hurry. Athena watches with one eyebrow curled in puzzlement as the breast one leaves and then immediately comes back in. She is in a piece of avant-garde theater. It is something by Samuel Beckett. Not-Breast is sitting at the desk, making marks on a piece of paper. The Teletubbies are looking for Po.

Breast finds what she had mislaid and goes out through the door.

It becomes a two-hander. Athena, the quiet one, is almost completely immobile, her limbs made useless by incoherent routings from motor cortex to musculature. Not-Breast is quite capable of moving but, with the exception of the painful paper-gouging of his writing hand, he is simply choosing not to. The sofa bed has been extended for a nonexistent guest, and all the toys in the house are laid out on a white duvet. Athena lifts the rattle in her hand and roots at it, shaking her head rapidly from side to side before contact, like an attacking Rottweiler. She gets no comfort from it, and tries instead to suckle at the cushion she is propped against. The cushion is dry and rough. She looks at the door. The vanishing of Breast is associated with it somehow. She has no real sense of how that soft, perfumed object persists in time, but she can connect the door with her vanishing, and that's enough to keep her interest, for now. Associations that she couldn't have made, even a few weeks ago, are now marking paths through the chaos. At a hundred twenty days of age, she has the necessary tools: vastly improved perception of space and depth, greater visual acuity and color vision that is as good as any adult's. Her neonatal synesthesia has receded, and things are starting to appear as they really are. She is going to learn her way out of this, like the eagle-eyed hostage who eventually spots the key to her escape. If she could just get some control over these wobbly legs, she'd be on her way.

Not-Breast looks out the window and sees a bright windy day. He glances at the new baby carrier propped up on the floor on its own aluminum motorbike stand. He thinks of the snowsuit that will have to be picked up and turned inside out, the scarves that will have to be tucked in, the zips negotiated. He closes his eyes and then opens them again, but all of those things are still there.

He swivels around in his chair and speaks to the immobile one.

"Shall we go for a walk?"

They do not move.

. . .

She wasn't actually paralyzed, of course. If the right stimulus presented itself, she could lurch into action with surprising speed. But those movements were not under any organized direction. As cognitive scientists put it, the forces behind them were all bottom-up, driven by external stimulation. She needed some top-down control. Like most of her early accomplishments, that would come from cortical maturation. As a newborn, the surface of her motor cortex was still largely undifferentiated. Signals would bleed into it from different parts of the brain altogether. Smells could cause a leg to kick, a hand to flutter. Colored lights would set her off like a dancing flower. She was a human sound-to-light machine, a weird bit of disco apparatus converting perception into motion. You could leave her on her mat, fed and changed and warm, and she would perform like clockwork. It was up to us to interpret the gestures and expressions, to say that a certain grimace looked like snooty disapproval, or that those graceful writhing movements made it look as though she were practicing tai chi. We, the observers, were safely convinced by the illusion of our own free will, the sense that our actions were ultimately under our control. Athena, in contrast, was a passenger in a mysterious machine, waiting for connections to be rewired even as she was traveling. There was a steering wheel, but it wasn't connected to the wheels. The brakes had been tampered with. It wasn't that her muscles were too weak for the task—she had the brawn, even if she couldn't always connect it to the brain. She wanted to be moving around under her own steam, but she couldn't quite bring her musculature under her brain's commands. Until a few weeks of synapse formation and pruning had corrected the wiring, those top-down processes would not be ready to assume control.

If the breakthrough was slow in coming, it was because an extraordinarily complex motor system needed to start pulling together in all sorts of sophisticated ways. As an adult, her gross motor actions, such as head and limb movements, would be instigated in the primary motor cortex at the top of the brain. The primary motor cortex has been likened to a piano keyboard, across which the brain's commands play like so many nimble fingers. Like its neighbor, the somatosensory cortex, the surface of this part of the brain constitutes a detailed map of the rest of the body, such that an electrode placed in a particular location will cause a Frankenstein-like twitch in the corresponding limb, finger, or toe. Naturally, this clever routing takes time to develop. She needed to form synapses in the fibers of her corticospinal tract, the neural bundle that leads down from the primary motor cortex and along the spinal cord to the motor neurons, which stimulate the body's muscles. These fibers would then need to become myelinated before they could reach their full transmission speed. One outcome of this dependence on maturation was that she gained control over the muscles that were closer to the neural heart of things, like those in her torso, before she gained control of her periphery. Motor control is also established in a head-to-toe direction, so that she had command over her face muscles, say, before she could do anything equally complicated with her toes.

Generating gross motor actions was only part of the story, though. She didn't only need to be able to produce the neural commands that would have her musculature dancing to her tune; she also needed to be able to feed back information about how she was moving, and how her body was currently configured, to the control processes that generated the movement in the first place. The area of the brain mostly responsible for the fine-tuning of movements, the cerebellum, makes up only about a tenth of the brain's volume but contains about half of its neurons. The cerebellum is where the various sources of information about the body's position become integrated, and its complexity means that it needs to keep developing for some time after birth. When it came to putting together a sequence of actions as complicated as

walking—a milestone that, for Athena, was still eight months away—
she would need all of these systems to be functional. Paradoxically,
she would have had the basic command structure for walking, known
as a central pattern generator, from the days when she was practicing
stepping movements in the womb. The central pattern generator for
bipedal motion resides in the spinal cord, and it is an heirloom from a
distant evolutionary past. We have the instructions for walking long
before our higher-level control processes mature sufficiently to know
when and how to implement them.

There was a piano keyboard, but who was going to play it? If I
make a decision to raise my right arm, I can be confident that a moment
later I will see it moving in the expected direction. Some have argued
that this feeling of consciously willing an action is actually an illusion,
caused by an overimaginative interpretation of the association between
a conscious thought and a physical action. It's not just our babies that
we construct; we construct our own behavior, seeing intentional control where there may in fact be none. I do have voluntary control over
what I do—I'm not a clockwork toy at the mercy of deterministic
forces—but it may not have anything to do with conscious thoughts
like "Raise your arm." Something is planning my actions: if not "me,"
then something in the system that my mind, brain, and body combine
to make.

For a young infant, though, that rich interpretation of the links
between conscious thought and action is probably out of reach. For
one thing, planned behavior requires the development of the executive functions, which reside primarily in the prefrontal cortex right at
the front of the brain. These systems do not begin to develop until
halfway through the first year. If the motor cortex is like a piano keyboard, voluntary actions need a pianist: someone who can tap out a
string of commands according to an organized plan. Until then, the
infant's movements are little more than responses to stimuli in an
ever-less-blurred sensory world. For a while, Athena's actions are

programmed by sight as much as anything else. She is like some gullible shopper, entirely in thrall to what she can see in front of her. That blue floral-patterned curtain, for example, in the bathroom next to her changing mat: she can't *not* reach out and touch it. Irresistible though these actions may be, they represent a breakthrough in the emergence of voluntary control. Athena might be a sucker for the first thing to be put in front of her, but she is at least responsible for producing the action. It might be compulsive, but it is hers.

Crucially, that also puts her in a position to start learning about the effects that her actions cause. Her developing control over fine movements, such as the emergence of a pincer grip at around eight months, will mean that the kinds of manipulation she can do will become more sophisticated, and so her opportunities for learning will become richer too. Some aspects of voluntary control turn out to be more tricky to master than others. Spend any time with an infant who is not yet mobile, and you will find yourself passing new playthings to her that she cannot reach on her own. Beware, though, if you expect the transaction to be reversible. Babies are happy to take objects from you, but they are less cooperative about giving them back. As in other areas of development, terminating an action requires more advanced powers of self-control than initiating it. Grabbing hold is relatively easy; the hardest part is letting go.

Reaching for objects was one thing; what she really wanted was to be eating them as well. Partly because chewing on things reduced the pain of teething, her desire to consume soon put all other desires in the shade. Her mouth became the aperture of a new sense, a way of testing out the stuffness of stuff. For Lizzie and me, it was also a surefire indication of which of our home contents were the most dangerous. Forget the brightly colored toys built to British safety standards: she was only really interested in things that could potentially kill her. She would wake from sleep and, like a zombie in Toytown, immediately lunge for the nearest object: a propelling pencil, a muslin square, someone's hair. At six months, when she was big enough to sit up in a high chair, we took to playing a game called Tidying Up. She sat on her elevated blue-gingham throne, throwing toys on to the floor as quickly as I could pass them to her. Sometimes she would chew on them first. I was never quite sure what the rules were, but speed seemed to be of the essence. We fed her trinket habit willingly. As she got older she would show her boredom with the things we'd given her by waving them wildly at the end of an outstretched arm, as though asking, *What am I bid for this piece of rubbish?* I would hand her a hi-fi remote control, or a pair of glasses, just to keep her happy. That was better: something unsuitable for children. When it came down to it, Dad knew how to have fun.

So that was also the end of my own immobility. The better she was able to knit perception and action together, the more quickly I had to move. The universe tends toward a state of maximum disorder, and children are there to speed the process along. Everything that mattered ended up on the floor. If it really had been a Beckett drama, we might have saved ourselves the bother and taken to the floor permanently, never rising above, say, knee level, where everything she dropped or threw down would be within constant easy reach. I could have had a crooked stick, like Malone in Beckett's novel *Malone Dies*, to retrieve items lying just beyond my circle. I didn't have a crooked stick, so I had done what I thought was the next best thing: I had put down the sofa bed in the study and scattered its duvet-soft surface with toys. She couldn't fall anywhere: there was nowhere to fall to. Every so often I would break off, midsentence, from what I was writing, turn around, and feed her a new toy. She would take it, gnaw on it halfheartedly, then cast it aside. She wanted small parts, choking hazards. This bland, made-in-China junk would not satisfy a young girl's thrill craving.

It may have made her a handful for her mother and me, but this was Athena's way out of her helplessness. She needed a piano player, and she got one, at least partly, through this frenzy of half-voluntary, half-reflexive action. Being controlled was a way of gaining control. She was also getting a new way of finding out about the world, by acting upon it. Her visual cortex could now use slight differences between the images on the two retinas to produce a stereoscopic, three-dimensional representation of space. This new expertise in depth perception meant that she could use her eyesight to guide her reaching. Instead of waiting for objects to be handed to her, she could accurately acquire them for herself. The possibilities of solo play extended before her. As she became stronger at bouncing on her haunches and propelling herself forward on the bed, her circle of influence grew wider. She could reach new places and previously unreachable things. She could observe how an arm movement was progressing from moment to moment, and adjust her hand's trajectory to maximize accuracy. The flailing grasps of her early life were replaced by coordinated movements in which a hand position was locked on to a target with military precision. Even moving targets could now fall under her influence. Experiments with six-month-olds have shown that babies launch their reaching movements toward the point where they expect to meet a moving object, rather than toward its observed starting point. Infants are not famous for their foresight, but in their rudimentary catching behavior we already see forward planning at work.

Reaching for the unreachable, hoisting herself up on her jelly legs only to collapse in a heap once again . . . to an observer, it looked like perseverance beyond all hope of reward. But Athena's sensorimotor curiosity probably had some sound motivations behind it. For one thing, being able to act upon the world brought her closer to the social partners who were shaping her learning. The more she could do, the more she could collaborate on. Through her own actions, and those of her actions that she could align with others', she had new ways of learning about the world outside. The blur of synesthesia had given way to a truly organized sensory integration, allowing her to match knowledge about an object gained through touch, for example, with information delivered by her eyes. What she saw in front of her was no longer a blind trigger of behavior so much as a problem to be investigated. For the first time, her curiosity had some power behind it. She didn't have to wait for knowledge to come to her; she could go out and get it for herself. She was becoming a scientist.

Six

CLOSING THE CIRCLE

Object Lessons

At ten months, Athena was already the outdoor type. One after-noon in June, in the middle of that bright, breezy spell that in our part of the world passes for summer, we were walking by the river that runs through the valley below our house when we saw a swan flap past over the water with a low whistling sound. Athena turned to follow it out of sight, astonished by the miracle that was clattering past at eye-level. We were on the stony beach where I often unstrapped her from the baby carrier and let her paddle, dangling her between my two hands. The river was shallow here, and lined with blond pebbles. I told her the name of the thing we had seen, and waited to see if she would repeat it. A crease deepened between her eyebrows. I crouched down to her level, as if that might get me closer to her thoughts. The swan had black trailing legs covered with scaly gnarlings. The whis-tling sound must have been those shanks cutting through the air. As I hunkered down on the stones and propped her collapsible frame upright, I said the word for a second time, and caught the fluttering of her heart against my hand. She was used to our little tutorials. I named the components of the world for her and she listened, patiently, perhaps quietly amazed that one man could pretend to know so much, but for now, at least, giving me the courtesy of her attention.

"What about that?" I said. "Did you see the swan?"

She stared at the far bank, still thoughtful. For a moment I thought the white flash of lightning was still with her. But then I saw that her attention had been hooked on something else, a scurrying in the undergrowth, or perhaps the simple absence of anything that might now detain her. I was watching her forget. I had this word, *swan*, which I wanted to offer as currency, in fair exchange for her rethinking the thought. But there was nothing in her mind for it to match up with. She could not think about things that were not there. When the swan had flown off around the bend in the river, it was flying out of her consciousness. My talk about it, when the object wasn't there in front of her eyes, was wasted breath.

The next day we were getting our shoes on, preparing to repeat the walk. As I fiddled with the straps of the baby carrier, I tried again to get her thinking about the sights of the day before. There was more at stake than a question of infant memory. There was a question of Velcro, gravity, and impossible fastenings: I needed her to *want* to get into this baby carrier. I said it—"Maybe we'll see the swan again"— pretty sure that the words would mean nothing to her, but somehow hoping language could have its effect in different ways, like the chatter of foreign voices on the radio can affirm something you'd be hard-pressed to explain. As I crouched behind her to buckle on her shoes, she leaned forward between my arms, peering down at my fingers like someone checking quality on a factory assembly line. When one shoe was buckled on, she bent forward and tried to tug it off with both hands, as though she had spotted a defective item and it was her duty to make sure it went no further. She showed the same diligence with her purple cardigan and the sun hat I tried to pull down over her head: they were both wrong, dangerously faulty, had to be removed and done again. I slotted her feet-first into the baby carrier, where she could not reach anything except her own head, which she grabbed with two hands and twisted, as if trying to unscrew it. Now only her eyes were visible, looking up at me over the top of the padded casing. She had slept for two hours before lunch, which should have left me more than enough time to see off the last few pages of Kant's "General Remarks on the Transcendental Aesthetic"—but I was carrying a weight around with me, a dragging sense of uselessness that made the words swim in front of my eyes, as if they had come loose in the fluid in which the years had preserved them. Instead of using my few precious moments of quiet to get somewhere with the *Critique of Pure Reason*, I found myself waiting for her to wake up, to sit up suddenly, automatically, stare at me as though I were a stranger, and give me some reason to continue existing. Now, as I swung the baby carrier on to my shoulders and felt the silent heft of her on my back, it seemed as though the weight that had been dragging me down all morning had found a counterbalance, and I had a feeling that things would be better once we had crossed the road into the village and walked down to the old stone bridge, where we could pick up the path along the river.

My progress with Kant had been slow, to say the least. All I wanted to do was read his famous *Critique* from start to finish—and all I meant by reading was letting my eyes pass over the words one at a time, stabbing at individual blisters of meaning, and hoping some of their wisdom would enter my brain by osmosis. Understanding any of Kant's philosophy would have been a bonus. I had splashed out on a beautiful new edition from Cambridge University Press, with an introductory commentary by two American academics. It took me most of April to read the introductory commentary. By the time I reached Kant's own introduction, it was May. I was a hundred fifty-five pages into a book that I hadn't even actually started reading—of which, at best, I could manage to pass my eyes over ten pages in a day. In June I had excitedly begun the Transcendental Aesthetic, and told myself, "At last, I'm reading the *Critique of Pure Reason*." Then I stopped and did something else. I hadn't expected it to be easy, but neither had I expected the real Kant, when it finally emerged from the introductory preamble, to be so impossible. Meaning was everywhere and nowhere. I had to stop and get the measure of each sentence, like a batsman sizing up a field, before I could even think about tackling it. I found myself reading each sentence three times: once to find out where the verb was, once to try to scratch out some semblance of its message, and once to try to pick up some of what I'd missed. My ten-page-a-day rate was beginning to look impressive. These days, I was lucky if I could manage two.

Kant's purpose in the *Critique* was no less than to lay out the foundations for the possibility of objective knowledge. On what basis, he asked, can we claim to know facts about the world? I had the strange sense, as you sometimes do with great books, that Kant was asking this question for my benefit alone. Scientists need to know what sort of facts we can be certain about: how to distinguish the real from the not-real, the rocks of data from the vanishing sand of theory. But so do ordinary people. We need to know whether to trust the evidence of our senses or the persuasions of our intellects, whether we are right to believe that the earth is round, that lemonade is made of atoms, even when our experience tells us otherwise. Objective knowledge: the truths that hold true no matter where you are standing. We need to understand truth if we are to believe what the scientists tell us, and the scientists need to understand it before they can tell what messages can safely be given to the world. It all seemed to hang on what it meant to have knowledge about reality. If Kant could tell me what I could be certain about, I might find some certainty about other things as well.

By the time we reached the river, Athena was asleep. Even if yesterday's swan-sighting had stayed in her mind, that mind was now enjoying downtime. There's a myth that a dead body is heavier than a living one, the bundle of twitching nerves and blooded flesh that lived and breathed only moments before. Something similar applies to children.

It had gotten to the point in our walks along the riverside where I knew she had fallen asleep, just because of the extra weight I seemed to be carrying. When she woke up, she would look out on a scene that had no continuity with the one she had fallen asleep on. Kant's question was more relevant to her than to any of us. What could we say about a baby's understanding of objective reality? Where was Athena going to get her knowledge of the world? She had been here, grappling with it, for ten months now, and her grip was still shaky. Even I, a reality-rooted adult, sometimes doubted the ground beneath my feet. How much stranger must it be for her?

In 1936, the Swiss psychologist Jean Piaget tried to answer the question of how children come to have knowledge of the real world. Trained as a biologist—an expert in the mollusks of Lake Neuchâtel at the age of fifteen—he was convinced that human intelligence is an example of the biological phenomenon of adaptation, the constant modification of the organism's life systems to fit the environment in which it finds itself. Babies' minds are structured to deal with the reality of the world they encounter; at the same time, this mental organization is constantly updated to deal with the new information that life throws up. The result is a succession of ever-more-sophisticated knowledge structures, which children can employ, like little scientific theories, to make sense of their world.

Famously, Piaget illustrated his theory with detailed observations of his own children. At twenty days, Laurent is offered a crooked index finger instead of the nipple. He immediately sucks it, Piaget writes, but rejects it after a few seconds and begins to cry. Second attempt: same reaction. Third attempt: he sucks it, this time for a long time and thoroughly, and it is Piaget who retracts it after a few minutes. The finger is assimilated into the baby's existing knowledge structures. On the same day, Laurent accidentally touches the nipple with the inside of his upper lip, and at once adjusts his lips and begins to suck. He cleverly modifies his way of acting on the world to take account of the unexpected position of the nipple. Later, baby Laurent will use the same principles of adaptation to develop even more sophisticated ways of knowing. These will include the ability to think about an object in its absence, to adopt the perspectives of others, and to think logically about simple reasoning problems; and ultimately to do the sort of hypothetical thinking that characterizes scientific thought.

In Piaget's view, this relentless process of adaptation is the driving force behind human rationality. All later intellectual achievements can be traced back to these early adventures in the sensory world. The most basic knowledge, the lesson that Piaget thought infants spend at least the first year of their lives learning, is that there is a world of objects that exists independently of one's own self. At the river that day, Athena seemed to me as though she lacked that knowledge. The world was as it appeared to her. There was no absolute reality out there whose existence had to be inferred from the evidence of her senses. There was just whatever was in front of her eyes. When one of us left the room, that person ceased to exist. When a toy fell off the tray of her high chair, it was gone forever. A jumble of toys in the corner of the room was not a collection of separate objects; it was colorful background, part of the sensory wallpaper. She couldn't think to go over and pick it apart. When I reached over and selected, say, a shape-sorter for her to play with, I was performing magic: it was the act of bringing an object into being. When that toy was finished with and had dropped from view, it may as well never have existed. Out of sight, out of mind: babies take the saying literally.

A few weeks earlier we had tried a more formal test of her understanding of objects. Here she is, sitting in her high chair, chewing on a colorful napkin ring. Lizzie has put two identical blue-and-white-striped napkins down in front of her. In full view of Athena, Lizzie hides the napkin ring under one of the napkins: call this Location A.

Athena has no difficulty retrieving it, and holds it up for the camera with a satisfied shout: Bah! Lizzie repeats the process twice, each time hiding the object at Location A and allowing Athena to find it. Then comes the crucial part of the test. Once again, everything happens in full view of the baby. This time Lizzie hides the ring under the second napkin, at Location B. We look to see where Athena will search for it. Even though she has seen where the ring has been hidden, she makes a telling error: she goes back and looks under the first napkin, at Location A. It is as though she is unable to appreciate that the ring is a thing in itself, something that has an existence independent of her own perception of it. Instead, her search behavior is guided by an out-of-date rule, which has not been modified in the light of the new evidence. The little scientist seems to be saying to herself: *In the past I got a reward when I lifted up this napkin, so I'm going to lift it up again now.*

According to Piaget, this striking (and universal) error proves that knowledge of objects has to be constructed gradually over the first year or so of life. The infant starts out with innate reflexes, such as the grasping and sucking reflexes demonstrated by Laurent at twenty days, and then has to get to work modifying these primitive ways of knowing. It is not that objective reality has to be constructed according to social conventions, as some postmodernist thinkers would like us to believe—rather, it is the infant's knowledge of that reality that has to be built up, as we build up our knowledge of physics or geography. For Piaget, there is a real world out there, and Athena had to learn about it. She couldn't stay adrift in the fetal dream forever. But how was she to learn? She had the evidence of her senses, of course, but all they could deliver was a blurring flow of sensations. To come to the understanding that the world was made of real things, independent of her own perception, she needed something more. Knowledge of reality cannot be derived from pure experience. Our minds must somehow be prepared for acquiring that knowledge. The question is:

what sort of knowledge can we be born with? Before we even set foot
in it, what can we possibly know about the world?

The question of what we can bring to our understanding of the
world—how our knowledge of reality can be structured by
some preexisting organization—was precisely the question Kant was
asking in the *Critique*. The point of the Transcendental Aesthetic,
which I had been slowly trying to absorb that morning, was to show
that our understanding of the most important entities, such as space,
time, and causation, cannot come directly from experience. Rather,
we must bring these entities *to* perception: the human mind is fundamentally organized so as to impose these structures on the world. For
example, Kant discusses the idea of causation. Consider a boat moving downstream past a jetty upon which you are standing. You can
choose to look at the boat and then the river, or at the river and then
the boat. You can do what you like with your own perceptual abilities. You cannot, however, choose to see the boat first downstream
and then upstream. You cannot choose to see it floating off into the air
and disappearing into the clouds. This is because there is an aspect of
perception, its objective aspect, that is independent of the act of perceiving. There is a real world out there. The perceived motion of the
boat is *caused* by the actual motion of the boat, a fact that is beyond
your capacity as a spectator to change. The perceived motion belongs
to the subjective aspect of perception, while the actual motion remains
resolutely an objective aspect, immune to any alterations the viewer
might make to his point of view.

According to psychologist James Russell, the ability to distinguish between these two aspects of perception is the starting point
for infants to distinguish themselves from the world. Piaget saw the
newborn infant as existing in a muddle of needy selflessness, unable
to draw any boundary to the limits of her own experience. For the

newborn, everything is self: there is no separate, independent reality. The first opportunity for infants to make this crucial self–world distinction comes when they learn that there are bits of the visual field that stay the same however they try to look at them. I can look where I like; I can stand on my head and see the world upside down—but I cannot turn the world upside down. By trying and failing to change the way the world looks, infants learn about the objective existence of that world. Because they have a built-in understanding of causation, infants also learn which changes in the flowing pageant of perception are their own work. With improving knowledge of their own body movements, they know what they have done—which feet have been kicked and which hands flapped—and so they can determine what they have caused.

As psychologists, we looked forward to seeing this process in action for the first time. At eight weeks, Athena spent much of her time on her back on her activity mat, looking up at the soft animals that dangled above her. Her sky was filled with zodiacal creatures, suspended from the firmament on strings. These were the air-guitar days. I would play Tom Waits songs on my old electro-acoustic, and she would play along, windmilling her right arm across her left in great wide circles, unicycling her feet as if trying to push herself higher for a better view. For three-quarters of an hour she would jam along, her concentration never faltering, through my entire repertoire of kindly whores and maverick Chinamen, freight-yard hoboes and sad-luck dames. Even when I wasn't playing, her arms and legs were constantly in motion. With all this zoology dangling above her, it was only a matter of time before an animal was sent flying. Colorful life-forms would be swinging, inches from her face. Until now she had paid no attention: all this was just part of Athena, absorbed into the universe of her undifferentiated self. But one day, after landing a punch that set Zoë the Zebra pogo-ing, she stopped and looked at what she had done. She pulled a distinctive face, which always reminded us of the English comedian

Frankie Howerd: lips pursed around a bloodless O. She had swung that fist, and now a thing was moving that hadn't been moving before. She had made this difference. She had had some impact on the world.

What she had done was simple, in a way. Beginning with accidental movements, which happened to have interesting, perceptible effects, she had begun to close the circle of her own actions. She made something happen; she perceived its effects; she learned something about the limits of what she could do. Some of these circular actions, termed "primary circular reactions" by Piaget, had her own body as an object. At three weeks, for example, I would see her stroking the back of her head, apparently enjoying the connection between the action, the sensation in her fingers, and the feeling it gave her on the sensitive skin of her nape. Thumb-sucking, to give another example, is a lesson in selfhood: what you are and what you can do. But she wasn't only learning about the limits of her own experience. In the next stage, that of "secondary circular reactions," these actions became directed at the physical world. The accident with Zoë the Zebra could well have been the starting point for her first truly intentional actions on that object: movements that, to start with, were blindly triggered by the perception of that particular thing, but that would soon lead to an understanding of it as an entity in its own right—how it bent to her actions, in some respects, but also how it remained resistant to them. She was learning about herself, but she was also learning about the world. She discovered both at the same time, through the same kinds of explorations.

It was a lesson that would have profound consequences. One thing it did was allow her to draw a boundary line between the world of hard facts and the realm of her own experience. This was a Kantian lesson. Athena had started to carve out what was objective from what was not. In November 2004, an advertisement for a satellite television company promised that a new viewing system allowed you to pause, and rewind, live TV. Not strictly possible, of course: the point of live TV is that it is immune to button-pressing. Babies have to learn that. They have to learn that reality can't be paused, fast-forwarded, or switched off. While their eyes are open, they're watching a live broadcast. They can't whiz forward to watch the ending before it has even happened: they're in this for the whole show.

We reached the river and walked along until we found the stony beach. I heard a clucking sound behind me and realized that Athena had woken from her snooze. I slid her out of her baby carrier and let her press on the stones with her soft-shoed toes. The feel of hard objects under her feet triggered automatic stepping movements: these smooth mini-boulders were something to be scaled, an obstacle to get across. I felt her heartbeat tap out the story of her excitement. The swan was still in my head. Despite my doubts about her understanding of object permanence, I thought I'd try asking her again whether she remembered it. Now that she had the context in front of her, the sights of the riverbank and the shimmering water, maybe remembering would be easier.

"Do you remember the swan, Athena? The swan we saw yesterday?"

I watched her head turn to follow the river. She made a chewy, hard-lipped *bah!* sound. She was staring intently down the river, her blond-wisped head held impressively erect, at exactly the spot where the swan had vanished from view the day before. It might have been wishful thinking, but I thought I had my answer. Her face was turned upward, signaling distance, and there was a spark of happy recognition in her eyes. I had been mistaken about her blankness yesterday. She *had* remembered. After ten months she seemed to have learned a little about the world's regularities and obstinacies, how objects persisted even when your back was turned, how they had lives that were separate from your own. Things had started to split away from her own actions and perceptions, and that meant they could enter her thoughts in a new way. She could represent them in their absence, and call them to mind through imagination. With her improved powers of memory, she could now think about things that weren't there.

And because she could do that, she could get started on something entirely new. She could begin to refer to those absent objects, using the labels she picked up from the rest of us. She could take my word, *swan*, and tie it to a thought. Now that she knew about reality, it could be a topic of conversation, not just her own private intellectual problem. Suddenly, this was a reality that could be shared.

Seven

WHERE'S THE BEAR?

A Word for Everything

She wove language from the plainest of threads. Before she could talk, she could spin lengths of undifferentiated sound, just by voicing an outbreath and letting the noise push out on a flow of exhaled air. By eight weeks she could shape her mouth to make a contented *ur-ur*, expressing satisfaction at the way the world looked and the fact that she was at the center of it. Her growing awareness of reality meant multiplying objects of desire, new ways for her material ambitions to be thwarted. There was a gutsy, frustrated *errghh*, which seemed to say, *I want something and I can't quite get it from here.* At other times her speech, like her crying, was simply an affirmation of her own existence. She learned to widen her mouth and push out a throaty pterodactyl squawk, alarmingly loud, not so much *Feed me!* as *Look at me!* As with the dancing animals she was learning to control at will, she was testing her own powers, exploring the limits of her ability to make things happen. The message was simple: I'm here. I can do this. Don't ignore me.

Until now, these had all been variations on the same basic theme. Lacking any degree of tonal range, she had to rely on rhythm and phrasing to color the limited sound that she could produce. The break-through came when she realized that she could do something with this pleasurable flow of excitation over her vocal cords. Changing the shape of the aperture it was escaping through, such as by making use of her growing tongue control, changed the noise that came out into something remarkably like adult language. When she moved her jaw, often breaking off from chomping on her knuckles with her budding teeth, she was biting off chunks of speech, leaving a trail of chewy, pensive vowels and syllables. She was finding different techniques for manipulating the sound source, eloquent new degrees of freedom. In fact, she had exactly what our primate cousins lack: an articulatory apparatus sophisticated enough to create the subtleties and nuances of speech. For all their propensities for learning sign language, chimps and bonobos can't even get started on human speech. They're not built for it; they simply cannot shape their tongues, lips, and other parts of their mouths into the right contortions. It turns out that they lack part of a particular gene, known as *FOXP2*, which is involved in the fine-tuning of those subtle articulatory movements we need for producing speech. In humans, mistakes in this gene lead to great difficulties in producing intelligible spoken language. Without the right version of *FOXP2*, the simplest string of words would be a tongue twister.

She may not have advertised it, but our firstborn was already an expert in human phonology. Babies the world over show an innate capacity to distinguish the hundreds of basic sound units that make up all human languages. A new speaker needs to know only a fraction of these in learning her mother tongue. In Russian, for example, there are two *i* sounds, transliterated as *i* and *y*, which make the difference between the words *sin'* (blue) and *syn* (son). The distinction between the two vowels means nothing to us English speakers: the Russian phonemes form a single phonemic category in our language. Conse-quently, mature English speakers are deaf to the distinction. The sur-prising thing is that young infants, innocents in language, are not. In one study, American six-month-olds could discriminate speech units from Hindi and Salish (a group of languages from Western Canada), but showed far less discrimination in judging non-native language sounds at one year. A recent study looked at infants' actual brain responses when exposed to native and non-native consonants. While discrimination of non-native language sounds declined as the infants got older, their sensitivity to consonants in their own native language increased steadily. These findings have been taken as evidence that babies' neural networks become steadily more attuned to the patterns of their own language (a process known as "neural commitment"), while knowledge of any unnecessary language sounds is tuned out. Indeed, there are good reasons for them to narrow their focus in this way. By specializing in a few important categories of sound, the boundaries between those categories become sharper, and the infant's perception of them more efficient. In language, as in many other areas in which synaptic pruning channels us into particular developmental paths, you have to go backward to go forward. At twelve months, Athena had already had to sacrifice some of her potential to become a native speaker of Japanese or Russian. Because she was still well within the critical period for learning language—estimated to last for the first six or seven years of life—she could still reverse the decline with the appropriate exposure. If she didn't get the right input within that time, her brain would simply tune foreign phonemes out, as an adult's would. She might master those languages in later life, but she would already have lost her built-in advantage.

Her first step in language acquisition, then, was to shuck off her unnecessary phonological knowledge. How did she learn which phonemes were going to matter? She did it by listening to the language that was spoken around her. It was this experience, after all, that pushed her toward English rather than the hundreds of other languages she might potentially have learned. But phonemes are shape-shifters: their acoustic properties change, chameleonlike, depending on what background they are heard against. A tone of 440 Hz is always the A above middle C, no matter what context it appears in, but there is no such neat set of acoustic properties that defines a phoneme. The exact sounds of the hard vowels in English depend on the age of the speaker, the accent, and what phonemes surround them on either side—compare a Londoner and a Yorkshireman saying "bubble bath." No computer program ever written has been able to master the learning of phonemes from the rapid, variable, and messy flow of human speech. Babies probably rise to this challenge by responding to statistical regularities in the speech they are exposed to. They learn which sounds occur most frequently, and are able to group them into the forty or so phonemic categories they need for putting them together into words.

If carving the speech input into phonemes is a tricky business, deciding how this flow of sound is to be sectioned into words is a task apart. The trouble is that spoken language does not come in easy, bite-size chunks, but instead forms an unbroken stream with no silences between individual words—ask any adult second-language learner who has ever tried to follow the blur of conversation in their new, nonnative tongue. As with their learning of the relevant phonemic distinctions, babies rely on sophisticated statistical reasoning in working out where words begin and end. In the particular language they are becoming neurally committed to, certain sounds go together with some frequency, while others are never to be found in the same breath. By learning these regularities, infants can begin to pick out the individual patterns of sound, which correspond to some of the half a million words found in English.

They can get a long way down this road simply by following the rhythm of the speech they are exposed to. One way in which babies tune themselves for their native language is by learning its characteristic rhythmic patterns. In English, for example, most words are pronounced with the stress on the first syllable. Slavic languages, such as Russian, tend to stress the second. Infants pick up on this regularity and place their word boundaries accordingly. In one study, researchers measured how long English-learning infants, aged seven and a half months, spent looking at colored lights associated with different speech stimuli. By looking at how infants' head-turns betrayed their preference for certain sounds, the researchers concluded that babies could fairly easily come to recognize words with a strong syllable followed by a weak one (such as *hamlet*), but they were much worse at detecting a weak/strong pattern (such as *guitar*). The team concluded that, at this age, babies rely almost exclusively on prosodic, or rhythmic, cues. Slightly older infants showed an ability to learn these more difficult weak/strong patterns, suggesting that, by ten or eleven months of age, they can use cues other than pure prosody when carving the speech input up into words.

To a certain extent it was the rhythm of her language that first convinced us that Athena was saying some of these words back at us. The findings from these infant head-turn studies suggest that she would have been well attuned to the rhythmic properties of our speech. Furthermore, her innate talents for imitation meant that it should have been a simple matter to wrap her own vocalizations in a similar packaging. At this stage, it didn't matter that her utterances had no meaning—at least, not in any conventional sense of the word. We *took* them as having meaning, and for the time being that was enough. "Laggy loo!" she proclaimed one day in her sixth month, as she broke off from playing with something plastic and chewable. We took it as an expression of wistful optimism, of life's ability to promise and foreclose at the same time. We could imagine it as a refrain from a seventeenth-century ballad:

> *Times are hard! Laggy loo!*
> *Food is scarce! Laggy loo!*

We interpreted freely, and we overdid it: most parents do. We were wired in to the sound of our own offspring, demonstrating that skill, so astonishing to nonparents, of recognizing our own infant's particular cry in a family gathering or busy, child-crowded supermarket. When our offspring was uttering, we couldn't help but respond. What many parents perhaps don't realize is that their fanciful interpretations form the basis of invaluable linguistic lessons. By responding to them *as if* they were making sense, long before they actually are, parents are scaffolding children's language acquisition, turning their infants' utterances back to them with the outlines straightened and the gaps filled in. We took *laggy loo* as language because it sounded like language. It might have been junk but, like a scrapyard collage, it made a picture. She was only sketching in rhythm, but she was speaking to us.

We soon saw the fruits of our careful overinterpretation. Just as she had learned that certain grimaces and proto-smiles were taken as having social meaning, Athena realized that her noises had certain effects on us. She only needed to say her versions of our names—*Mama* and *Dada*—to secure reactions that were something to behold. Language did stuff; it had functions, predominantly social ones, whose effects were plain to see. In learning how to do things with words, she was getting a grip on what linguists call pragmatics. Our insistence on treating her vocalizations as though they were meaningful ensured that, even if her intentions in wielding a word were not entirely clear to her at first, they soon would be.

By this stage, however, the very overinterpretation that may have given her a foothold into language was proving an obstacle to scientific inquiry. Gripped by the same hysteria that attended her first steps, we were in a first-word frenzy. Everything was a first word. We couldn't help delving into the pile of dribbly approximations and pulling out what we were convinced was the real thing. This was our only child; we didn't yet know what a first word really was. Like die-hard fans sighting Elvis, we saw the signs everywhere, and fell over ourselves in the race to be first to report the milestone. Marital rivalry is never so strong as when it comes to recording the sole heir's achievements. It was not uncommon for one of us to announce proudly, at the end of a day at home with her, that she had reached some thrilling new stage in her development, only to hear the other announce that she had been spotted doing the same thing weeks ago. Even worse was the thought that a stranger might witness these breakthroughs in walking and talking. How many guilty parents pack their one-year-olds off to child care with the feverish, telepathic command: Stay on all fours and say nothing, at least until I get you home?

In reality, of course, there are no first words. As in the ancient Greek paradox where no single grain makes a heap, and yet a heap is formed anyway, there are just ever-closer approximations, a negotiation of meaning within a messy to-and-fro. She had been making a *da* sound, and repeating it, since about six months: was that *dada* a word? It certainly seemed referential when, at nine months, she said it crawling toward the study where she knew I was working. But these easy-to-pronounce baby words for close family members are very similar the world over; we should play safe, and reject *dada* as another random pattern in the tea leaves. A parent is on more solid ground, surely, with something further from home. Her next obvious first word, a whole two months later, was *bear*. But it sounded a lot like *bah*, and there had been plenty of *bahs* already. The lesson seemed obvious: these "first words" that we were trying so hard to pinpoint were going to say more about us, her parents, than they would about her.

Perhaps her receptive vocabulary would be a truer test. At eighteen months, infants recognize around three times as many words as they can say. We said the word *clap* and looked to see whether she could obey the command: at ten months, she could do that fine. The strictest test would be knowing and saying. If she knew the word from both sides, on its way in and on its way out, then we would feel confident that she had made a genuine addition to her vocabulary. The trouble was, her receptive and productive vocabularies didn't match up so neatly. She could respond correctly to words that she would never dream of saying, and she wouldn't always point appropriately to objects whose names she had already been using happily.

It didn't matter, of course, beyond our having something to boast about to other parents. If she pointed to a duck and made a *dah* sound, we would congratulate her: "That's right, it's a duck! Clever girl!" Any uncertainty on her part would surely be short-lived. Next time, she would know what sound we wanted her to make, and knowing the meaning of words is, in large part, knowing what your audience wants of you. It used to be thought that word acquisition was simply a matter of learning the associations between objects in the world and the sound labels you hear being attached to them. Nowadays, psycholinguists recognize that reading the minds of your social partners is just as important. For Saint Augustine, writing about his childhood in the fifth century, the intentions of his elders in naming objects for him was evident in everything they did—for there is a kind of universal language, he wrote, consisting of expressions of the face and eyes, gestures and tones of voice, that can show whether a person means to ask for something and get it, or refuse it and have nothing to do with it. In other words, Augustine learned words by reconstructing the intentions—the mental representations of meaning—of the people who were using them. Humans stand alone in their capacity for this kind of mind reading. The fact that they are not built for talking is not the only reason chimps and bonobos don't learn words. They fail because they don't tune in to the speaker's intentions in anything like the same way. As we were about to have proven to us, there are other, characteristically human linguistic abilities that stack the odds even higher against our hairy cousins.

Not long after her first birthday, Athena had a grasp of three of the four essential components of language. She had phonology: she had whittled down her inborn encyclopedic knowledge of language sounds to specialize in only those forty or so phonemes she would need. She had pragmatics: she knew how to package sound to cause effects in people, thus showing her understanding of language as a social tool. She had semantics: she was building a vocabulary of object names, verbs, pronouns, and adjectives that was essentially the same as ours. All of these achievements had been made possible by the application of certain general cognitive skills, such as imitation, concept learning, and mind reading. The final component, putting words together into ordered, meaningful strings, was going to call on special talents. According to some powerful arguments from the science of linguistics, she could only meet this challenge because she had been born with a certain basic, universal knowledge about how language worked, about what kinds of things nouns and verbs and agents and objects were. This was blood knowledge, not schoolbook knowledge. It had prepared her for the task of building sentences before she had ever heard a word spoken, and it would mean that she could do things in language that no one had ever done before.

It should have been simple: take the ideas you want to express, choose the corresponding words from your rapidly expanding lexicon, and put them together.

At sixteen months, a toddler's vocabulary is a snapshot of her preoccupations. Athena had animal names, which, in our petless home, were mostly acquired from storybooks: *bear, cat, dog, duck, rabbit, bird.* She could designate household objects—*keys, car, spoon, bag*—and furniture, parts of the body, clothing, and food. Less common were action words, like *dancing* (their lack of concrete tangibility means that verbs usually lag behind nouns in early vocabularies). Then there were the connectives she used to express relations between these ideas: *there, that,* and, of course, *no.* The negative was her sword of righteousness, the billowing standard of her disapproval.

She would march me around the house, a piece of half-chewed bread held aloft like a martial cross, and point out all the things I wasn't allowed to do. "No!" she would bark as, exhausted from keeping up with her demands, I tried to break away to do something better suited to my pace of living. When she came into our bed in the mornings, we couldn't move—literally—for the strictures she imposed on us. We had to lie still, like volunteers in some naked-multitude artwork, and keep our limbs exactly as she arranged them. Even the flow of air could mess up her careful plans, which meant that we were often required to cease breathing altogether. "No! Dad-*dee*! No!" It was like having a cuddle with Hitler.

For a while, the big news was *gone*. The difficulty with representing absence is the very lack of any entity in the world to hook the word on to. No matter how willing you are as a parent, you can't point to something that isn't there, which means that the usual point-and-say mechanism of word learning cannot work. Some have argued that this is a case where progress in language requires progress in cognition: you can't use the word until you've got the concept, and you don't get the concept until you've reached the end of the road of object understanding. Certainly, most children get *gone* around the time they pass the last of Piaget's object-permanence tasks. Athena was using it happily at sixteen months, to designate an empty plate, a missing toy. Just as the arrival of the concept of zero transformed the science of mathematics, so her object-filled world was enriched by the representation of not-being. She had a word for something that wasn't a thing at all, an arrow for pointing at absence.

Her favorite book was *Set and Match: Wild Animals*, a board book with magnetic animals that could be fitted into different wildlife scenes. One day the panda was missing. She pointed to its outline on the jungle diorama and said "gone"—familiar talk from our budding laureate of loss. Then she pointed to the other animals, one by one, and said "no gone." Two words, with different meanings, put together to express one thought. It was the first time she had put two concepts, and two corresponding words, together in her own way. In linguistic terms it was the beginning of syntax, the sequential structuring of utterances that guarantees their specific meaning.

Back then, she may just have been sticking words together like Lego bricks. She constructed telegraphic utterances such as *boots off, all gone,* and *Mummy phone,* any of which might have made as much sense in the alternative word order. To express more-complex ideas, she would have to pay attention to the fact that the meaning conveyed by combinations of syntactic elements, such as nouns and verbs, depends on the order in which they are combined. To paraphrase Eric Morecambe, it was no good having the right words in the wrong order. Disappointing as it always seems, *I love you* doesn't necessarily mean *You love me.*

Often the correct order was easy to determine. When she tumbled on to the duvet saying "all fall down," she was simply lifting a pattern from the nursery rhyme. What excited us about *no gone* was that she was putting words into combinations she had not heard us use, or at least not with any frequency. She couldn't simply be repeating, parrot-fashion, bits of speech she had already heard. She was creating new language, in ways that couldn't have been copied or learned in any usual sense of the word.

Research in developmental psycholinguistics has shown that toddlers are sensitive to these grammatical categories from very early on. In one classic study of children's syntactic development, Lois Bloom observed her daughter Alison saying *mommy sock.* "Mommy's sock," perhaps—and sure enough, one context in which Alison made this utterance was when she picked up that item from the floor. But in a second usage, the utterance commented on Alison's own sock, which was being fitted on to her foot by her mother. What Alison was now trying to communicate was something more like, "Mommy is putting my sock on." In the first case, the syntactic relation is that of possession; in the second, it is an agent (Mommy) doing something to an object (sock). In each version of the utterance, the same two words had very different syntactic properties, and Alison seemed sensitive to them.

One day Athena and I were in the bath, enjoying our usual routine of tipping jugs of water over Daddy's hair. "Tip hair wet," she announced as she prepared me for another drenching. She had an action word, *tip*, directed at an object, *hair*. To the object she was attaching an attribute, *wet*, which was causally connected to the action. She didn't put the cart before the horse and say *wet hair tip*. Nor did she make *hair* the subject of the action by putting that word first. She seemed attuned to the syntactic value of her words and was using them appropriately. This was not a parroted phrase like *all fall down*; she had most likely never heard anyone use these words in this arrangement. She had created a more or less grammatical utterance by combining words she had never heard combined before. In saying *tip hair wet*, Athena was being a creative pioneer.

The implications were clear. We language-users cannot simply be learning a response that goes with a stimulus, like Pavlov's dogs learned to salivate upon the sounding of a bell. We can use language in this systematic, or "combinatorial," way because we have a set of rules, the grammar of our native language, for combining the limited number of words in our vocabulary in unlimited ways. Furthermore, children don't learn these rules in any conventional sense. In the bath, dousing me with water, Athena had no idea what an action word or an adjectival attribute were, and I wasn't about to teach her. I didn't need to. Children acquire the rules of syntax without any formal instruction by their caregivers. We corrected what she was saying if it was untrue, but not if it was merely ungrammatical. She was acquiring syntax far removed from the iron rod of a reinforcement schedule, and she was doing it remarkably rapidly.

Syntax wasn't learned, then: it grew. According to one interpretation of these facts about language acquisition, I was not watching experience inscribe its lessons on a blank slate: I was witnessing a multifaceted, preordained marvel rising spectacularly into shape. There was not much for me, or Lizzie, or life to do except set certain basic parameters (push her toward English rather than Cantonese, for example) and watch the pattern unfold. The very term "language acquisition" was a misnomer: you can't acquire what you already have. The observations in my notebooks were the record of a maturation process, not a story of learning or education. From this point of view, her growing up had more in common with botany than with developmental psychology.

The discovery of an innate, universal grammar had far-reaching consequences for the cognitive sciences. Drawing analogies between syntax processing and other mental abilities, nativists like Steven Pinker and Jerry Fodor argued persuasively that we were bundles of neatly circumscribed instincts, or specialized information-processing modules, whittled into shape by Darwinian natural selection. Instead of a lump of infinitely malleable wonder-stuff, we were told that we had a Swiss Army knife between our ears, ready to flip out the appropriate utensil for any cognitive, social, or emotional task. Just as we wouldn't try to peel an apple with the corkscrew bit, making language needed no other intellectual faculty than a Language Acquisition Device and its subservient submodules. It did exactly what it said on the tin—and for other tasks there were other tins: for causal reasoning, ethical judgments, reading the minds of others, and many other capacities that had traditionally been seen as being shaped exclusively by culture and learning. If there was any role for environmental influences in the maturation of these modules, it was in setting parameters, turning the dials on systems that had already been installed.

But although these ideas quickly permeated popular culture, most of those who studied children's development realized that this form of nativism was too extreme. Instead of proposing innate knowledge, a more sensible balance seemed to propose innate structure: a brain

designed for certain kinds of learning, a baby born with a predisposi-
tion to receive content, if not the content itself. It was a message that
was finding support from the science of brain development. Genetic
instructions gave the developing brain a great deal of prespecification,
but experience was needed to make the system work properly. A new
brand of molecular genetics was showing us that genes themselves,
those supposedly immutable blueprints for biology, were profoundly
influenced by the contexts in which they functioned. Athena was
born to use language, but it wasn't something that merely happened
to her: it needed other parts of the cognitive jigsaw to be in place. She
had to build it, through her own efforts, just as she had to build her
knowledge of objects and people from the biases and predispositions
she had been born with. Nature had given her the basics. Now it was
up to her to put them to some use.

E ach Peach Pear Plum, I spy . . ."
    "Bear!"
    It is early morning, and everyone in this Cretan village is asleep.
We have escaped for an early autumn getaway, still clinging to the pre-
parental privilege of taking vacations outside school holidays. It is my
shift for looking after her. To avoid disturbing Lizzie, we have undone
the shutters and come out on to the balcony in our nightclothes. A
whitewashed parapet shelters us from the breeze that is scouring the
sea in the bay below.
    "Is that a bear?" I say. "It looks like a bunny rabbit to me."
    She picks at the image with an index finger. A few weeks ago I
would have left the mistake uncorrected. But, at fourteen months,
she is using the label confidently, if a little too promiscuously. In her
struggle to match our grown-up words to her small-scale experiences,
the odd bit of corrective feedback can't do any harm.
    "Athena, you find the bear."

She turns the pages, flicking through the board book with slightly cross-eyed concentration. She finds the picture she wants—the Three Bears from the Goldilocks story, setting out on a hunting adventure— and says the word again: "Bear." Where previously the contents of her consciousness dissolved as soon as their objects slipped from view, she can now hang on to them in their absence. Her memory has improved, but so have her techniques for encoding information. The labels that language gives her are fixation points upon which the objects of per- ception can be anchored in her mind. In this simple game we are playing, she can hold on to the label I have given her, and use it to direct her search, even before the object of that search becomes vis- ible. Objects are permanent for her now, and they retain some repre- sented existence even when they are not physically present. Her mind is a mirror held up to the world, rather than a sand blotter that absorbs everything obliviously. She can now act on the idea of a thing, rather than the thing itself.

"Bear," she says, pointing to another bunny rabbit. This error in applying the word is not a confusion between objects so much as a failure to draw the boundaries of the word in the right place. In her eagerness to apply the new labels she has acquired, Athena "overex- tends": she stretches them to cover too broad a class of objects. She sees bears everywhere: in the animals of her toy farm, in her Dorling Kindersley *First Words* book, even in her mother's face. When she pointed to Lizzie and anointed her with her favorite label—*Bear!*— both seemed to appreciate the humor. It may or may not have been an intentional joke (it was certainly taken as one, which meets half of the challenge of joke-making), but it was a natural extension of her scat- tershot bear-spotting. The fact is, there are a lot of bears around, in her board books, on her Chinese-made pajamas, in her spinning-top merry-go-round. Some might wonder why children's environments are so repetitive: the same bright colors, the same farmyard-and-savanna wildlife. But when you are learning to apply labels to objects, it helps if those objects recur with some regularity. Precisely which things we choose to furnish a child's world with is probably not important; the repetitiveness undoubtedly is.

"Now, can you find the . . . road?"

I hold the book open for her, expecting her to point to the road in the frontispiece picture, which is where we always start our joint sessions with this Janet and Allan Ahlberg classic. Instead she raises her hand and points to the road below our rented apartment. The road in *Each Peach Pear Plum* is the same kind of thing as the road below our balcony. If you have a word, and use it correctly, you get something for free: a concept.

"Kair. Ditch."

"Is that right?"

These are words I can't interpret, and I probably don't hide the fact too well. My platitudes only frustrate her more. She pushes the book out of the way and tries to raise herself with little puffy grunts of protest. She wants something that isn't immediately gettable. This is a breakthrough, of a sort: it is an idea that is upsetting her, not the thing itself. It is striking how determined she is to use language, even when other ways of satisfying her desires would be much simpler. We see her struggling to ask for something when she could just as easily go over and grab it. This is one of the few areas in our lives where we humans quite happily take the path of most resistance.

"Go on. You show me."

She pushes up from my lap and takes a few unsteady steps. This vertiginous balancing act is another thing she has been compelled to do when other options, like crawling or bum-shuffling, were undoubtedly easier. She has been walking now for a couple of months, but Crete has been a breakthrough: all those whitewashed steps in hilly villages for her to goose-step up and down, endlessly. After one week here, we all have the leg muscles of fell-runners.

"Kair! Ditch!" she says again.

I watch her toddle over to the clotheshorse where our towels are drying. She is wearing her short pink pajamas with the rocking horses on them, and her feet are bare. The Cretan sun has turned her skin faintly gold, her hair almost invisibly white. Walking is still new, but her other bodily movements are strong, quick, and subtle. Those anxious joyrides, careering around at the helm of her own body, are a thing of the past. She is in control of this machine now.

"Pah!" she says, in what sounds like triumphant dismissal.

We have only been able to bring a few toys with us, but we managed to find space for two of the cars from her Happy Street toy town. She bends at the knees to pick up the red one, and straightens herself in one smooth movement.

"Car," she says.

"That's right. Now can you find me the *blue* car?"

"Bue," she repeats, storing the idea.

She drops the red car with a clatter and makes a quarter-turn on a wobbly heel. She finds the blue car and clasps it to her mouth. She looks at me, checking my reaction. As well as giving her a new way of thinking about what she is chewing, language has broadened the range of things she can do socially. I'm not sure that she has accurately recognized the color—red and blue are, after all, the only colors on offer—but the word, self-expressed, seems to have given her some extra grasp on what she has to do.

"Can you find me something else that's blue?"

She gazes around, slightly forlorn. This is more difficult. I'm asking her to forget about how the label relates to an object, and think instead how it relates to an attribute of the object. I am always struck by how hopeless toddlers are at colors. For philosophers, the experience of redness, or any other vivid perceptual quality, is supposed to be the overwhelming, undeniable fact that makes the subjectivity of consciousness so tricky to explain. It is because it is subjective that it is so hard to formulate in words. You can't *describe* redness, or daylight, or the smell of freshly stirred paint; you can only know it, or not. Perhaps the color strikes her with all of that subjective immediacy, but pinning a word to it is just too difficult.

"Look, Athena! There's your friend!"

Her name is Anna, and she lives in the apartment across from ours. She is German, and about a year older than Athena. Last night, in the taverna, she and Athena did a bit of cagey toddler socializing around *Count with Maisy*, Athena's colors-and-counting board book. Then the cats came, and Athena screamed and had to be picked up. She is wary of Anna because she is strange and big and doesn't know the same words that Athena knows, but also because she is associated with those scourges of the taverna, those shadowy creatures that come out of the night and curl around your legs without warning. At this age, Athena's fearfulness is extravagant. She is afraid of vacuum cleaners, hair dryers, and all their noisy machine cousins; she is afraid of most things that move. Dogs, flies, even fast-moving clouds can set her off whimpering. It makes navigating the world a fraught experience, sometimes, but it shouldn't surprise us. She is trying to learn to predict how things will behave, and these things break all the rules.

"Come in, Anna," I say, beckoning her over.

The little German girl takes a tentative step on to our balcony.

"Athena? Do you want to show Anna your car?"

Athena stands up and faces her visitor, still apprehensive. I encourage her—"Go on, don't be afraid"—and she holds the car out, with one arm outstretched, as though feeding a crocodile. Her bright new teeth—four on top, two below—are gritted in an underbite grin. Her cheeks, like her lips, are plump, pink, and wet. The Mediterranean sun has mixed a deeper azure into her eyes. She has a harsh crease of concentration on her forehead, where a contemplative frown has squeezed out all the color. She seems to be weighing the possibilities of this encounter, but in a place that is private to her, where she cannot be overheard. I want to say that she looks thoughtful. Anna is there, fended off by a force field of shyness. She is one of those special, driven things: mostly unknowable, but strangely responsive. The kind of object that watches you. Athena takes another step forward. Ideas flow by, but they now boomerang back to her as well, warmly familiar. Memory keeps them on strings. The mirror reflects the world. Big child. Car. Clotheshorse hung with colorful towels. Blue sky, scented breeze. Each Peach Pear Plum, I spy . . .

Eight

⌒

UM . . .

Language and Thought

She was a thinker before we even set eyes on her. At her nineteen-week scan, she struck a pose that it was hard not to interpret as contemplative: her big, eerily transparent head bowed, one silver-boned fist pulled up under her chin. Many fetuses do this: it turns out to be a standard posture for those passing time in the womb. As the sonographer turned the gelled scanning probe over Lizzie's abdomen, rotating the fetal Athena on the screen like the prototype of something, a new model not yet launched on the world, we wondered what amorphous thoughts might be occupying her, glooping up through a brain that was still little more than a folded neural tube. What couldn't be doubted was her absorption. To our eyes, she looked rapt, engrossed. She was *The Thinker*, in fact, in Rodin's famous depiction of internal struggle, the shiny, chin-punching bronze reproduced in countless Western living rooms—and, it seemed, in a few Western wombs as well.

It wasn't just the similarity of her pose to the famous statue that looked meditative. Nowhere near being a snug fit into the walls of the uterus, she took the opportunity to kick, somersault, and stretch in a space that was hers alone to enjoy. She fluttered around the screen like an image from the early days of motion pictures, a Victorian flick book in animated chiaroscuro. When she stopped, we inevitably read it as meaningful. It looked thoughtful, intended, a decision to stop convulsing in order to do something else. *What next?* she seemed to be saying to herself. *A triple backflip?* Thought, by definition, is an unobservable. We never see or hear it; we can only attribute it. If a creature's visible movement stops, we assume the action must be switching to the inside. If our baby-to-be wasn't flailing, she must be thinking.

Rich interpretation, of course. The fine detail of the sonograph gave our imaginations a little too much free rein. In the ultrasound photo we took away with us, she has one arm crossed over her turned-away face, as if to say, *Leave me alone, I'm trying to work something through.* She was a swooning, kohl-eyed heroine from silent cinema, and she was lost to me. I could see her heart beating, but I couldn't see inside her head. I never would, of course, but her unknowability seemed more poignant when I could count the ventricles of her brain. She would never be so transparent, and so opaque.

Much of her first year after birth was a silent movie, too. As a few brilliant chimps might tell you, humans are generally slow to attribute intelligence to creatures who can't put those thoughts into words. Pre-linguistic babies are different, because they at least have the potential for language: their capacity for expression is only months away. But what to express, in that first bewildered year? It wasn't a question of whether she was conscious: I knew she had the brain structures to make that a possibility, and it would have been hard to imagine that this alert little baby could not have been at least minimally aware of what was going on around her. It was more a question of whether she was doing anything with that consciousness. We saw her looking thoughtful, all dark-eyed, chubby-cheeked contemplation, and we jumped to our own conclusions, just as we feverishly interpreted her social actions and her first forays into communicative speech. But it could have been wishful thinking. Did her inner life really have any structure? If you could have listened in to those primordial thoughts, would you have heard anything more than expressions of bafflement? For sure, she was responding to stimuli, getting better at organizing her knowledge of them, receiving object lessons about the regularities of the social and physical worlds. It seemed a little too generous, though, to suggest that she could really have been thinking things through.

Then, magically, the faders went up. As language kicked in, it was as though we had been watching a film in which the sound track had been damaged, and suddenly we could hear the accompaniment that had been intended all along. Perhaps a better analogy would be an old TV with a dodgy volume potentiometer: language gave it a bash, and at last we could follow the story. The most striking thing, perhaps, was that there *was* a story. When we saw her talking herself through an episode of shape-sorting, for example, or repeating my invitations to find the bears in *Each Peach Pear Plum*, we weren't just listening to wordplay or expressions she had parroted from us. We were hearing something of Athena. Language didn't only give her ways of naming things for us, of sticking the contents of her consciousness into place with handy labels. It also allowed her to channel her thoughts into a medium through which they could be communicated. How significant was this, as a milestone? Was she finding words for thoughts that had already been there, or was she getting the capacity for thinking anew? Was language translating thought, or creating it?

To settle for the latter would be to make a strong claim. For a start, it would deny intelligence to all nonhuman animals, and perhaps even to human aphasics and mutes as well. Inferring stupidity from muteness was a medieval pastime: we wouldn't want to see the same injustices done to our prelinguistic children. Even before language comes along, babies can do lots of things that we would want to call intelligent.

The question remains, though, whether there are any intellectual challenges for which only language can prepare you. According to one influential view of the relation between language and thought, there are certain kinds of thinking that can only happen if you have the right linguistic resources to draw on. A notorious example is the Inuit people's four hundred different words for snow. We non-Arctic types can't think about the subtleties of snowfall, the argument goes, because we don't have the linguistic palette for expressing the thoughts. Similarly, the "linguistic relativity" hypothesis proposes that infants will not be able to think about certain conceptual distinctions made in their language culture until they have entered into that language culture. Vocabulary gives you concepts, not the other way around. Words carve up the world, and our brains follow behind.

Fans of linguistic relativity have had a hard time of it in recent years. For one thing, few of the apocryphal stories about the thought-shaping powers of language have actually been substantiated by empirical research. It turns out that the Yupik and Inuit-Inupiaq languages spoken in the Arctic Circle have a grand total of about a dozen words for forms of snow and sleet, roughly equivalent to the number in English. If language does have any crucial role to play in thinking, perhaps it will show its influences earlier in development. In one experiment, psychologists Susan Hespos and Elizabeth Spelke set out to investigate a linguistic contrast unfamiliar to English speakers. In Korean, a distinction is made between "tight-fitting contact" and "loose-fitting contact." This distinction may sound arcane to Anglophone ears, but in Korean it is part of the furniture. According to the linguistic relativity hypothesis, speakers of the language that makes the distinction should be more sensitive to it (as it applies to a pair of shoes, for example) than speakers of the language that doesn't. Furthermore, speakers of no language—five-month-old infants—should have no handle on the distinction at all.

Hespos and Spelke tested these predictions using a technique known as "dishabituation." If we are exposed to a repeating stimulus, such as the hum of a washing machine, we soon get used to it. If that stimulus then changes (for example, by transforming into a spin cycle), we start responding to it again. Developmental psychologists make use of this basic phenomenon as a way of finding out whether babies can distinguish between two similar stimuli. If they notice the transition from one stimulus to the other, they "dishabituate," or start responding again at the level at which they were responding before. In their study, Hespos and Spelke looked to see whether prelinguistic five-month-olds would notice (dishabituate to) the transition between the two kinds of stimuli: for example, a tight-fitting event (a cylinder placed within a narrow tube) changing to a loose-fitting one (the same cylinder placed inside a capacious tub). It turned out that babies from both language groups were sensitive to the distinction: they didn't need the Korean language to help them acquire the relevant concepts. In many ways, babies are doing what they do with phonology. From an initial sensitivity to most phonemic distinctions made in the world's languages, they whittle away until they have just those distinctions that they need. Similarly, Hespos and Spelke argue, infants start off being able to think about a broad range of subtly differing ideas. This knowledge might ultimately be fine-tuned by language, but it is not created by it.

Studies such as these seem to show that infants have more of the basic building blocks of thought than we have traditionally given them credit for. For instance, Hespos and Spelke's five-month-olds already seemed to be showing quite sophisticated understanding of how objects fit together with other objects. Where Piaget insisted that the understanding of objects was not really established until the second year of life, studies using dishabituation and preferential looking have shown evidence of much earlier understanding of how objects behave. For example, infants show surprise when an object seems to pass right through another object that they have previously seen to be behaving in solid ways. They seem to have certain core expectations (shared with other animals) about how objects will persist through space and time, and this is a form of thinking that is *specific* to objects: it can't be applied to any other domain of reasoning, such as thinking about people or abstract entities.

Spelke has argued that the most complex of our cognitive capacities are assembled from just these kinds of primitive building blocks, or what she calls "core knowledge systems." Four such knowledge systems have been identified so far, for representing objects, actions, numerical relations, and spatial information. Building more-sophisticated knowledge systems involves combining your varieties of core knowledge, and adding further knowledge gained from experience. Learning to count, for instance, means putting your understanding of the permanence of objects together with a basic ability to represent numbers. Although these knowledge systems are innate, and have developed in response to specific evolutionary challenges, they are not quite the dedicated information-processing modules beloved of the nativists. Some nativists want to propose hundreds or even thousands of highly specialized computational devices, which together account for the most valuable of our mental capacities. For Spelke, the Swiss Army knife between our ears is a simpler entity, with only a few blades in total. This simplicity, and the fact that our innate endowments can be built on by subsequent experience, offers an answer to the very old question of whether our minds are the products of nature or nurture. For Spelke, nature provides the building blocks, and experience does much of the rest.

Thought before language, then. If Spelke is right, many of the basic components of intelligence are present even before newborns look around at the world for the first time. And even when words and concepts emerge roughly simultaneously later in development, as happens with *gone*, the evidence is that thought gets there first. Those who espouse a nativist view of language would say that it can be no other way. If we want to propose a module specialized for nothing but language processing, then it needs something to work with. The device might be able to talk, but it cannot come up with anything to talk *about*. This, for most nativists, is a ready-made argument that there must be a language of thought, or "mentalese," in which we do our thinking before packaging it into words for wider consumption. I might be typing English into my computer, but my computer is not thinking in English. My mentalese is the equivalent of my computer's machine code, the program that keeps it operating seamlessly, far removed from the messy ambiguities of natural language.

Thought, though. It's hard to imagine that Rodin's rippling bronze was being torn apart by mentalese. Hamlet's inner wranglings had more than a flavor of language about them, and not just because Shakespeare wanted them to be overheard. Although much of our thinking has nothing to do with language—chess players, for example, seem to rely almost entirely on spatial reasoning in solving their problems—the most casual introspection reveals our heads to be full of words. In one kind of study, volunteers are equipped with little beepers, which clip to their belts and go off at random intervals. On hearing the signal, participants are asked to record, without any further deliberation, what is going on in their heads. Up to 80 percent of these reports involve the experience of thinking in words. If language is just for communicating thought, why are our private thoughts (which are intended for no one but ourselves) so full of it? Language cannot create thought, but perhaps it can transform it. Athena's new facility with English might not have made her a thinker, but it might have made her a new kind of thinker. With words to play with, she might be raising thought to a new level.

A thena is seventeen months old. It is January, and we are relaxing in our living room with the fire glowing. She is wearing an orange T-shirt and green cardigan with dark blue detailing. Although steady on her feet, and capable of dexterous, focused movements, she still looks more like a walking baby than a little girl. Her hair has never been cut: it is blond, silky, and straight on top, finely curled around her ears. She has set up her little wooden table and she is going to do her puzzle. There is a board with cutout shapes for twelve colorful pieces. The train has been missing for as long as we can remember, but we still have the fish, the bee, the car, the sun, the teddy bear. The animals all have cheesy, sheepish grins and wobbly outlines, drafted, like most of her toys, in faraway China. "Pah, pah," she says (for *puzzle*), picking up the board from the floor. With Lizzie's help she gathers all the pieces and sits down.

She has one piece already in her hand: the horse, which she places in its horse-shaped cutout in the top right-hand corner. "Horse 'nere." *Horse in there.* She picks up the duck. "What's that one?" Lizzie asks. "Duck. 'Nere." She places it in the correct slot, but it won't settle down and she glances up at her mother with a little gasp of frustration. Then it clicks into place, and Lizzie responds: "Good girl." Parental involvement in these routines is as much about emotional support as it is about intellectual. Positive stroking keeps her focused on the task, and, ultimately, gives her a way of managing her own emotions, independently of Mum's tireless encouragement. Athena has found the cat. "What's that?" Lizzie asks. "Cat . . . Miaouw!" Their minds meet across a little colorful concept; they are sharing attention. Athena is captured by the immediacies of the objects in front of her, while Lizzie's focus is more strategic. She wants to get things named, make connections with Athena's other known facts. She wants to elaborate. This is not about getting a job done—no one is *really* interested in whether the puzzle gets finished—so much as taking time to think things through in collaboration with another person. Thinking starts off like this. The solitary cogitation depicted in Rodin's sculpture is an end point, not a beginning. Thought has a social life. It connects people, and parents have a big role in ensuring that the channels stay open.

"What's next?" Athena turns over a piece from the pile at the top of the table. She names it—"Dog"—and, in response to Lizzie's invitation, imitates its woof as well. Now she reaches back to the stash of pieces that, like playing cards in a magic trick, are all turned face-down. "Hun," she says, mispronouncing *sun*. But she hasn't yet seen the sun, or picked it out from the encrypted pile. She is instigating a plan, to make the sun her next conquest, and she is expressing it in words. *Hun* does not mean, *There's the sun*; it means, *I'm going to do the sun next, wherever the pesky thing might be hiding*. True to her word, she sorts through the pile and finds it. It is a distinctive piece, the most difficult of all to place: an archetypal smiley orange face with a mane of yellow rays. It is these rays, and the crinkly, asymmetrical outline they make, that pose such a puzzler. "Hun." She grabs it from the pile and holds it up, twirling it under her fingers by the little yellow plastic knob. "Yes, you've got to twiddle it around like that, haven't you?" her mother says, referring to past sunny tribulations. It is upside down. She twiddles it. "Keep going. Turn it round." Athena smiles and jiggles her legs impatiently, provoking laughter. She looks at Lizzie, bidding for help. "You need to turn it all the way around." But Athena has had enough: she drops the piece, pulls the table toward her, and sits down determinedly on her pink chair. Sitting down: another hallmark of thought. *We're going to sit down and sort the problem out.* This is going to take serious concentration.

"Can you put the teddy bear in?" A good suggestion, as it's the piece right under her nose. But Athena is still thinking about that troublesome sun. "Ha, hun," she says, looking at Lizzie. It sounds as though she is just repeating the object's name, and all Lizzie does is sympathize: "Yes, it's pesky, isn't it?" Athena gets on with the less-problematic teddy bear. Then it's "Ha, hun" again, but this time she is holding the piece out in obvious supplication. *Help*, she has been saying. *Help me with this sun.* It turns out to be an early multiword utterance, fitting in the chronological record somewhere between *no gone* and *tip hair wet.* "You want me to help?" The affirmative: "Neh." Having made sure that the request has been noted for later, she turns to the fish, which also won't fit easily. "In," she says imploringly. "Hard." This is partly a request for help—*Can't you see that this is hard?*—but it is also a note for herself. She is commenting on the task, and her own problems with it, and the intended audience is none but Athena. Lizzie offers the help she has been hinting at, and this time she places it easily. There is a high, celebratory raising of the hand as she pulls it away, the sporty flourish of a slam-dunking basketball player.

No time to feel smug, though, not with impossible suns still at large. This time she tries a little human persuasion. "Hun!" She holds it high and shows it off, twisting her body underneath it like a game-show bimbo, as though it were the prettiest thing in the world. She leans forward as far as she can and sees whether the full-stretch posture gives her any more luck at fitting it. "Um, bit hard." "It's very hard, that one," her mother agrees. Athena twirls it poignantly under her fingers for a moment, as though let down by something loved and trusted. Her disappointment is short-lived. "House!" she says, flitting inconstantly to the next piece. She tries the bee slot: "No?" Then the house slot, just alongside. "Yeah!" She poses the question silently, and answers it herself. Is that the right slot? No. Is *that* the right slot? Bingo!

She continues with her seduction of the sun. Perhaps if I drop it on the table repeatedly, it will succumb! Perhaps if I twist my head and peer at it from sideways on? All right, then, I'll try the telephone. "Halloo?" There has been plenty of talking into the real phone, on the rare occasions when she can get her hands on it. Ever since she managed to dial 999 as a twelve-month-old, triggering brisk returned calls from uniformed types who had better things to be doing on a Sunday morning, we have tried to keep it out of her reach. This one is made of safe, noncommunicative plywood, and it gives her something else to do before worrying about the sun again. The bee and the car go in fairly easily. Now only two slots remain: sun and train. She points to the train-shaped hole, cocks her head, and looks at Lizzie quizzically. "Yes," her mother replies, "the train used to go there but we can't find it, can we?" "No," Athena says, shaking her head quite a few more times than she needs to. Because their executive functions are still only weakly developed, infants typically perseverate on simple actions like these. Just as they find it more difficult to let go of an object than to grab it in the first place, they find it harder to terminate an action than they do to initiate it.

In the end the sun gets the better of her. She attacks it full of confidence, her lips extended in a comical, chimpish pout, and utters an incantation as she twists it in its slot but somehow fails to line up the rays. Then, finally, she loses patience. She scrubs the puzzle board vigorously across the table, as though willing it to clean up its act. Lizzie has one last go at balancing the sun on the brink of in-ness, so that the smallest judicious nudge would give Athena some sense of vicarious satisfaction. Athena's response is to pick up the board and stare at it in its vertical position, as though it were a canvas that, in the end, she just wasn't quite satisfied with. Then she tips out all the pieces and starts again.

There was nothing unusual about these five minutes of Athena's life. Some version of this negotiated, shared thinking goes on whenever a reasonably sensitive adult sits down with a toddler and a jigsaw puzzle. In situations like these, caregivers aren't just keeping infants' thinking afloat while they wait for some slowly maturing intelligence to take over. They are actually shaping and structuring that very intelligence. Thinking, in the sense in which we usually mean the word, is something that happens between people. If we can manage it by ourselves later in life, it is only because we have previously had someone close by to do it with us.

The idea that social interaction can shape thought can be traced to the great Russian psychologist Lev Vygotsky. Born in Gomel, in modern-day Belarus, in 1896—making him an exact contemporary of Jean Piaget—Vygotsky's intellectual goal was nothing less than a new science of how biology and culture interact to shape humanity. A Jew growing up in pogrom-torn imperial Russia, the young Lev Semenovich's academic career depended on a couple of lucky breaks. Jewish children's admission to university was controlled by a strict quota system, and it was only because Vygotsky got the better of hundred-to-one odds that he made it into higher education at all. A second stroke of luck was that his academic career unfolded during the heady days of Leninist intellectual freedom, before censorship and purges changed the Soviet intellectual landscape irrevocably. In other respects Vygotsky's short life was a battle against crushing hardships. Writing in her own old age, his daughter recalled how her father's 1934 masterpiece, *Thinking and Speech*, was composed at the table she shared with him for her homework, in a two-room apartment stuffed with an extended family. Vygotsky succumbed to tuberculosis in the year of his great work's publication, after a career in psychology that had lasted a mere decade.

Although his work ultimately fell foul of Soviet censors for being too concerned with the bourgeois degeneracies of an individual's consciousness, Vygotsky's thinking about the mind borrowed two important ideas from Karl Marx's philosophy. The first was that human thought develops out of social processes, or, as he put it, the drama that occurs among people. The second was that mental endeavors are mediated by tools. Just as we would not try to put up a shed without screwdrivers and wrenches, so we would not apply our brains to a problem without making use of certain devices for assisting thought. For Vygotsky, the most powerful of such devices was the language we learn at our mother's knee. With words, we can work with things that are not there. We can represent reality to ourselves, as we represent it to other people in social interactions, and use those representations as the rough workings of our thinking. When words get into our heads, they bring bits of the world with them. For Vygotsky, it wasn't the possession of language itself that separated us from other animals: it was what language allowed us to do.

One thing language lets us do is take control of our own behavior. Back in our fire-warmed living room, the camcorder is still purring. Since she brought a clattering conclusion to her first attempt, Athena's renewed application to her puzzle is proving to have a rather different feel. For one thing, Lizzie's role in the interaction has been reduced to that of management consultant, the troubleshooter who gets called in when things go wrong. The rich, mutually sensitive dialogue of a moment ago has been almost entirely appropriated by Athena. She is doing the elaborating for herself, such as making police car noises to accompany the placing of the car. She doesn't need Lizzie to bring her attention repeatedly back to the task; she can keep her own self focused. And through it all she is talking: naming pieces, stating their destinations, asking questions and then answering them on her own. We are witnessing a new kind of thought taking shape, transforming itself from a shared, social activity into Athena's dialogue with herself. As thinking continues to move inward—as it becomes "internalized"—she will be able to conduct these dialogues of thought completely silently. Like a pensive adult, she'll do it all in her head. Language will still be mediating her thinking, but it will be a new kind of language, the sort that only she will hear.

We will never know about her inner speech, of course. Her thoughts in later childhood will be as unknowable as her cogitations in the womb. But, earlier in life, this process of internalization betrays itself by its own incompleteness: in the self-directed speech that is still on its way inside. We hear her talking herself through a problem, taking on the same roles of questioner and respondent that she has fulfilled so enthusiastically when the problem is shared, but this time to achieve her own solitary goals. This kind of noncommunicative language is known as "private speech." Piaget, who was the first to document the phenomenon, saw children's self-talk as a manifestation of their egocentrism, or inability to take other people's points of view into account when conversing. In a famous disagreement between these two great minds, Vygotsky saw it very differently. For him, private speech represented internalization in action, a midpoint in the transition from the social exchanges of early collaborations toward the silent dialogue of verbal thought. If private speech dropped away in later childhood, it wasn't because children were getting better at communicating, but rather because that speech had become more fully internalized. Private speech becomes inner speech. We still talk to ourselves, but we do it all upstairs.

Studying children's private speech has turned out to be one of the best ways of testing Vygotsky's theory. In a typical experimental study, we ask children to solve puzzles that we know will stretch them mentally, such as moving colored balls among three sticks in order to match a similar configuration on a model. We videotape children solving puzzles like this, of varying difficulties, and later analyze their speech to see whether it is social (directed at another person) or private (meant only for themselves). From this coding process, we can obtain a measure of how much our volunteers are talking to themselves.

The results suggest that Vygotsky was right about the importance of this kind of speech for thinking. Children who use more private speech solve the puzzles more quickly and accurately, and these associations persist even when you take into account children's age and IQ. Talking out loud helps young children think better. Do teachers know? One recent survey of American primary schoolteachers suggested that they have some inkling of the potential benefits of this kind of speech, and for the most part do not try to discourage it. Generally, though, educationalists have been slow to incorporate findings such as these into their policy making. There are implications for adults, too, especially those who might worry that talking to yourself is the first sign of madness. Any concerned self-chatterer might draw heart from recent findings that private speech is a common phenomenon in adulthood, and may serve exactly the same purposes in people who have left their school days long behind. It has often been assumed that internalization is a one-way street: once it has happened, it stays happened. It now seems much more likely that the process can be reversed, and that challenging mental conditions can cause our inner speech to bubble up as private speech whenever the going gets tough. Hamlet said it out loud, after all, and he was a man who knew about tough goings.

Vygotsky's theory of private and inner speech is sometimes dismissed as a typical case of airy-fairy social determinism, Marxlite talk about the social construction of reality. In fact, Vygotsky was a biologically minded cognitive scientist who would never have dreamed that language might *replace* those evolved building blocks of thought described by Spelke and others. Indeed, it is becoming clearer that language plays its role by knitting together the outputs of these independent knowledge systems. By plugging them in to each other, language can combine the components of our thinking into powerful new arrangements.

As an example, take an ability that you might think would have nothing to do with language: the knack of finding your way around an unfamiliar space. Navigational skills have been studied extensively in animals, and experimental research points toward some evolved module for computing geometry. If rats have it, it is likely that humans do too, and indeed the evidence from infant cognition is that a "geometric module" would qualify as one of the basic mental capacities postulated by Spelke. Imagine that you are blindfolded in a very large room, trying to find the exit. A sensible strategy would be to find a wall, stick to it, and start walking, keeping the wall to one side of you until you stumble across a door. Your geometric module is what allows you to compute your own orientation in relation to the wall and keep it constant: to keep it on your right, for example, if it starts out that way.

It turns out that rats can do something similar. In fact, in another experimental situation that requires making use of one's geometric module, they perform exactly as humans do. In this experiment, participants are placed in the middle of a large rectangular room. The room is completely white: walls, ceiling, floor. The volunteer sees an object being hidden behind a white cloth flap in one of the corners. Because the fabric of the room is completely uniform, there is only one way of mentally marking the location in which the object has been hidden, and that is in terms of the configuration of the walls around it. A hiding corner in a rectangular room can either have a long wall on the left and a short wall on the right, or a short wall on the left and a long wall on the right. There are no other possibilities. The volunteer is then disoriented (for humans, that means being blindfolded and turned around slowly in several revolutions) and then invited to search for the object. Because the only information they have is the configuration of the walls, subjects tend to look equally in two diagonally opposite locations, where the arrangements of the short and long walls are the same. Half of the time participants will be right, just by chance, and half of the time they will go mistakenly to the opposite corner of the room, where the walls (short on the left, long on the right, for example) are similarly arrayed.

Adult rats and adult Homo sapiens are indistinguishable in this task. Their geometric modules see to it that the object's location is correctly encoded, given the only information that is available to them: the arrangement of the long and short walls. Crucially, the geometric module can *only* make use of that kind of information. If other, nongeometric cues are introduced, such as color, the geometric module draws a blank. It was designed by natural selection to work with geometric information: it can't compute anything else.

Generally speaking, rats have no difficulty making use of nongeometric information like color. What they cannot do is make use of
such information at the same time as computing geometric relations.
Their geometric modules cannot talk to their nongeometric ones. To
test this, Spelke and her colleague Linda Hermer-Vazquez introduced
a nongeometric feature to their white-walled room. They painted
one of the short walls blue. Color is nice, but it has nothing to do with
geometry. This time there was enough information for human participants to find the object easily: they could integrate the geometric information (say, short wall on the right) with the nongeometric
information (the blue short wall, not the white one). Rats could not do
this, and neither could human toddlers. Both groups of participants
seemed to lack the ability to integrate these two sources of information, to tie the workings of one computational module in with those of
the other.

The missing link, Hermer-Vazquez and colleagues hypothesized,
was language. To test their hunch, they repeated the experiment with
adult human participants, plus an important new condition. On some
of the hiding trials, volunteers were asked to perform a second task
while playing the hiding game. This secondary task, known as "shad-
owing," involves the immediate repetition of an auditory stimulus. In
one version, volunteers had to shadow a recording of speech, and in
another they were asked to shadow a rhythm. Speech-shadowing tasks
are known to block the systems that process language, thus effectively
eliminating inner speech. In the rhythm-shadowing condition, language processing remains intact. Having a plan to disrupt their participants' inner speech, the researchers wanted to know whether this
particular secondary task would affect performance in the blue-walled
room. If you stop people from talking to themselves, do you stop their
modules from talking to each other as well?

The answer, they discovered, was yes. In the speech-shadowing
condition, but not the rhythm-shadowing one, adult participants'

performance dropped to that of toddlers or rats. The researchers concluded that language must play a role in communication between independent processing modules. Cognitive archaeologist Steven Mithen, who looks at how ancient patterns of tool use and behavior give clues to the evolution of our minds, has likened those modules to the side chapels of a Gothic cathedral. Direct communication between separate side chapels is impossible: they are independent, discrete spaces, sealed off by careful workmanship. Each side-chapel, however, has an aperture into the main body of the church: cross the nave and the ideas can flow. If this metaphor is accurate, our modules have the possibility of talking to each other indirectly, through some mental equivalent of crossing the floor. By making use of this shared space, dedicated processing modules, which on their own seem rather limited, can play a wider role in the life of the mind.

Vygotsky's claims about verbal mediation can therefore be recast in a twenty-first-century light. Language comes along when infants are already being fairly intelligent about the world, and demonstrating those predispositions for reasoning about objects and physical relations that have served the species well in its evolutionary history. The trouble is, those specialized knowledge systems lack a way of talking to each other. They have developed for very different biological tasks, and they lack a common language. According to philosopher Peter Carruthers, language is that common language. It mediates between the components of a semimodular cognitive architecture, and glues together the parts of a mind that would otherwise be too diffusely specialized. It should be no surprise, then, if acquiring such a language revolutionizes children's thinking. It's not only what language offers in communicating with others: it's also what it gives you in communicating with yourself.

When Athena was eighteen months old, I had a close-up view of this revolution. As words colonized her thoughts and spilled out in running commentaries on her own actions, the enigmatic thinker of infancy became more knowable. The point was not that language was necessary for her to become a thinker, but that language transformed whatever intellectual capacities were already in place. When the two lines of development come together—when communicative language combines with mute, animal intelligence—some time in the second year of life, something extraordinary happens. Whatever thinking Athena was doing before language, it was disconnected, biological thinking. Language put it all together. When the faders went up on her consciousness, the story finally began to cohere.

Nine

⌒

ALL BY MYSELF

Emerging from the Mirror

She would wake in the night, saying no to something in a bleary whisper. I would find her adrift in the double bed we had installed for her, as though sleep had overcome her in an outsized place, and she were taking a fairy-tale nap in a house of giants. If I couldn't settle her easily, I would carry her back across the landing to our bedroom, where she would fall asleep quickly, her moonlit cheeks puffed up on my pillow, little fists clutched around handfuls of her mother's hair. I would be on my own strange orbit, devastated by prospects that would scarcely have detained me in my waking life. Grief was a planet I would slingshot around in the early hours, a galactic outpost so toxic that it was only safe to go past it in a state of suspended animation. Athena's night-waking stripped me of that protection, woke me to a blast of regret from which I would ordinarily have been shielded by sleep. Not even she, the precious child asleep beside me, could lift me out of this. I wanted to make her a defense against these vicious bouts of despair, a little blond charm I could turn to whenever this horror swung into view. But she couldn't be those things. I had asked too much of her, and all she could do was roll back into the sleep she had fallen from, leaving me on my own.

I would get up and go downstairs to the study. If the moon was bright, I would use its light to flick through my notebooks. There was so much there: pages of observations, snippets of dialogue, all the magpie gleanings of our time together. Two years had passed since I had started writing in here. I had not worked—gone out in the morning and earned money—in all that time. Staying at home with her had made this possible, but I could not stay at home with her forever. I would switch on the desk lamp and read a page at random, a few paragraphs of brief notes, scribbled in a hurry as I snatched time off from looking after her. I had wanted to capture her while she was still there to be captured, while there was still a trail to follow. It was the proof of how much I needed her, and how much I wanted her to need me. It's a shock that I guess many parents feel, when the wise, patient counselor they have been longing for all their lives turns out to be a kid in diapers. There was a gap in my life, and she was filling it, because she couldn't—yet—turn around and tell me that she was not up to the job.

I sat in the moonlight, thinking about the desperate images I had awoken to. They had come from somewhere that had nothing to do with rationality. They were dressed up as cognition, but they were warm with body heat. I could still feel them, in the pit of my stomach, in the nerves in the backs of my legs. If I needed it, it was more evidence that there is no such thing as cold reason. The more we study how the emotional pulse of the brain is entangled with the neural pathways of rational thought, the more this becomes clear. Neuroscientists have hypothesized that many of our most logical chess moves of the mind actually come down to myriads of little unconscious emotional calculations, which push our judgments one way or another without our really being aware that they are doing so. The myth of affectless thought is the same myth as the one that would keep mind separate from body. Your thoughts about a thing are driven by your feelings about that thing; without feeling, you would not bother thinking anything at all.

This hour of the wolf, then, showed me that I was only telling half of the story of Athena's developing intelligence. If we are to have any chance of explaining how thought comes about, of having a causal account of its formation, then we need to ask what motivates it. We must, Vygotsky wrote, identify the needs, interests, incentives, and tendencies that direct the movement of thought in one direction or another. It is not just what causes thought that betrays the hand of emotion; it is what thought goes on to make happen. We can't understand how thinking affects behavior unless we recognize its emotional underpinning. The great psychologist's conclusion was simple, although its implications are only beginning to be explored by cognitive scientists. Just as every idea corresponds to some object in the world, so every notion that passes through our minds contains some remnant of our feelings toward that thing. If thought has a social life, it has an emotional life as well.

To understand Athena's thinking, I would have to understand the emotions that drove her thoughts from place to place. With the same spreading doubt I would feel, a year later, when I quizzed her about her memory in the Old Vienna Coffee House, I sensed that the question would sound absurd. Young children's wants are all on the surface. They can be read like open books. For Freud, a toddler was little more than a self-propelling id, a wobbly support system for a cauldron of barely suppressed desires. An infant wanted food, and he grabbed it. He found certain shiny, dangerous objects interesting, and he went for them too. He could not show concern for abstract ideas, or things that were not immediately present to his perception. This was another reason, perhaps, that I could find no toddlers in fiction. To satisfy as a character in a novel, you have to have an organized set of motives, secrets, desires, shames. You have to care about something, if the reader is to care about you. Small children, the theory seems to go, can't be that complicated emotionally—unless you want to ascribe to them those cryptosexual yearnings that make many psychoanalytical writings seem so far-fetched. Whatever makes them tick, it ticks loudly enough for everyone to hear.

I wasn't satisfied with this characterization of a toddler. Athena could be willful: we knew about tantrums, and we had as little idea as most parents how to deal with them. But her emotional life was far more complex than the battle of an all-consuming will against those shadowy Others who held the power. It could not fail to be, given how enmeshed she had been in social relationships since the day she was born. Freud's ideas about the emergence of ego and superego, those higher powers that develop to control the seething pressures of the id, stemmed from an assumption that babies are little autists, cut off from a social world. As those who have studied infants' social responsivity have shown, nothing could be further from the truth. If Athena had learned anything so far, a big part of it had been made possible by her emotional engagement with us. Her actions toward objects, her attention to different aspects of the world: all of these supposedly pure cognitive abilities were sensitive to the emotional vibes that were going around. How her caregivers were feeling influenced how she felt and, since much of her learning happened in a social context, that affected what she learned. My notebooks were full of examples of situations where she threw a glance at me to check the safety, accuracy, or permissibility of what she was intending to do. Getting smart was a matter for the heart as well as the cortex. Although it would rarely make much sense to separate them, thought and feeling would never be as closely intertwined as they were then.

Whatever she wanted, it wasn't a case of her will against the world. She grabbed at what was there, for sure, but she also grabbed at things that weren't. At least some of this must have been due to the cognitive advances she had made. Language had given her a way of transcending appearances, of crossing distances in her imagination, and she was acquiring the new medium of verbal thought in which to think those absences through. When, around her second birthday, she saw the tiger in Regent's Park Zoo, she was scared of it: you could see that from her frowning, sideward-glancing vigilance as I carried her on my shoulders right up to the reinforced glass that held the sleeping tiger at bay. But she was also scared of it the next day, when I asked her about it. With memory and language, emotions could cross boundaries of time. You could even be afraid of something that had never happened, as she showed one day when, walking with me in the forest, she yelled a warning to some hikers far ahead who seemed to be in the path of a speeding mountain bike. She was probably mimicking my own nervousness around roads and other channels of traffic, but she seemed aware of the possibility of danger. Loud noises, such as those made by the vacuum cleaner and by her parents as they called for each other through the house, probably terrified her for lots of reasons, but at least one might have been that they heralded awful events to come. Fear gave her a line into the future. When she eventually came to understand the concept of *tomorrow*, it would be at least partly because she was afraid of it.

It was through these manifested habits of feeling and thinking that we saw her personality cohere. Athena was building a self out of her fears and favorite things, the gradually crystallizing lists of things she liked and didn't like. What was more, she now understood enough about how the world worked, and about how her actions had their effects, to be able to take some control over it. Enhanced memory and a developing prefrontal cortex had raised her to a new level of consciousness, in which she could judge her own capabilities relative to a goal represented in her mind. She could stop merely reacting to stimuli and start organizing the world to fit her own specifications. She knew what she wanted, and how much her own efforts were capable of achieving. She could start doing things for herself.

. . .

W hat Athena wanted, more than anything else in the world, was a soft-boiled egg. But then she had wanted a soft-boiled egg, with toast soldiers, every morning for the last week. When there are no other options worthy of consideration, it hardly counts as a choice at all.

"Athena, what do you want to do today?"

She glanced up at me. "What we doing today?"

"Well, that's what I'm asking you."

"I want to . . . go to the forest."

It is August, a few weeks after our zoo visit. The forestry park that lies ten minutes' drive from here has an adventure playground that will fill the hours until an early lunch. If I can get her bathed and dressed in good time, I should be able to fit in a few moments' work before we leave. I take her upstairs to the bathroom, slurp in some of the bubble bath that changes color when it hits the water, and get the taps going. She's getting too big to do this comfortably but, when I'm on my own with her, bathing à deux is the only way. If I left her on the outside of the tub while I was in it, I wouldn't be able to trust her not to let herself out of the bathroom, go downstairs to the kitchen, and start fixing us a snack. She shows her usual contempt for the potty and instead wants to get in among the suds. Her little body has the slinky tautness of the underside of a puppy. The skin on her ribs is pale and translucent, with the occasional faint thread of a blue vein. She half-bends and splashes water daintily around herself as though it were expensive perfume. As I climb in after her, she is ready with the jug of water for hair-washing duties. One thing that's guaranteed to make a toddler squeal with glee is the sight of a grown-up's head, close up, in an unusual orientation: seen from the top, where little eyes usually never get to see, or upside down on a bed, or poked through the rails of a banister. Athena would have my head off my shoulders, if she could; it would be her favorite plaything. I exaggerate my reaction to her tipping the water over me, blowing it out in high-pitched raspberries and sputtering as though the drenching were a complete surprise. When she thinks I'm wet enough she starts dabbing soap on to my cheeks, lathering it up in one cupped palm and then fingertipping it on in little circles, like a sculptor applying finishing touches. This is all done with a prim, pleased-with-herself expression; the roles are reversed, and now *she* is the proud parent, wanting everyone to know how good she is at this. I put up with it until I can decently make an exit. As usual, the water is several degrees cooler down at my end, and anyway she needs the space I have been occupying for rearranging the shampoo bottles on the windowsill and then wrist-flicking them into the water, simulating the last moments of the *Titanic*.

I dry her in two big towels and fix her diaper on the floor of the bathroom. We play a favorite game: she pretendingly names a bit of her that hurts (head, tummy, ear) and I have to kiss it better. She's learning the parts of a person. My next task is to get those parts of a person into acceptable clothing. I fetch some green trousers and a yellow T-shirt that seems to match. Allowing Daddy to dress her was a weakness that she has consigned to history; these days, she does it all by herself. She certainly has the fine motor control necessary to lay out the items of clothing and open them at their hems, but getting her own self oriented in relation to them is trickier. Our fussy adult conventions—garment label at the back, trousers before shoes—seem unpersuasive to her. The signposts of right and left, back and front, are even stranger. In the bath a few weeks ago, I asked her if she could wash her own ears. Keen as ever to be doing things for herself, she lifted her washcloth to one ear and rubbed at it vaguely. I asked if she could wash the other one. She kept the washcloth clamped to the same ear, raised her free hand to the other ear, and fiddled with that, equally uncertainly. Then I explained that the trick was simply to put the washcloth in her free hand to do it. Her response was to make a full 180-degree turn, still with the washcloth clamped to one ear and one empty hand clamped to the other. To get to the other side of her body, she had to turn her whole body. She wanted to bring the ear to the washcloth, like Mohammed moving the mountain, rather than the other way around. She couldn't make the shift while keeping her own body fixed in space. When she brushes her teeth with one hand, her idle hand flaps around in synchrony, as though it wanted its own toothbrush, and perhaps its own set of pearly whites, to keep it busy. It is probably a question of executive control, a prefrontal cortex not yet dominant enough to close down one unnecessary side of the action. But it is also partly an uncertainty about just how big this thing is, how far it extends, and how its behavior can be streamlined by shutting down those moving parts that aren't strictly necessary.

In the kitchen she helps me make a cup of tea, standing on the butcher's block, taking the lid off the tea caddy, and selecting a bag. If I can get her settled down in front of *Teletubbies*, I should be able to squeeze some work in before we leave for the forest. I prop her on her little pink chair before our portal of inanity, a color portable with a screen no bigger than my computer's. I prop myself in front of my computer and start work. She puts up with the Teletubbies until what we call the boring bit: when one of Laa-Laa and friends' tummy-fuzz clarifies into a short realistic film about middle-class children doing middle-class things. Athena finds the boring bit as repulsive as I do, and has started retuning the TV. Perhaps I should have strapped her down in her car seat. I fetch her a bottle of milk, hoping that will anesthetize her. I hold her as she suckles, pressing a perma-kiss to her crown as I did when she was tiny, and she is almost the same weight as my remorse. How can I love her, when I want her to shut up all the time? The pang doesn't last, and I soon start key-tapping again with my one free hand. I can block out the guilt like I block out the sound track. It washes over me, like Laa-Laa's singing.

What I can't block out is her attempt to reprogram my computer.

In lifting her on to my knee, and showing her the new tinkering opportunities laid out on the desk, I've made the fatal error of redirecting her attention. Being a toddler must be like wearing a suit of armor in a room full of magnets: clangingly attracted to everything, and hard to shift once latched on. What's so exhausting is having to adjust my goals, my pace of doing things, to accommodate hers. I thought it might be a nice collaborative thing to do to pull up a blank document for her to type into, but she's more interested in making the CD drive pop in and out, and seeing how many precious documents she can lasso with a few incautious swipes of the mouse. I can see my own unfinished chapter winking at me from behind the window she steadfastly refuses to populate. Frustration builds. I pry her hand from the mouse, and she starts to cry. Suddenly she's tired, clingy, and doubly determined. She grabs the keyboard and seems about to pull the computer over. I have to unpick her fingers and support her body as it collapses in rage. I pick her up as soon as I've made the computer safe, but she is inconsolable. I look around for something to distract her, a bird on the fence outside, a wood louse crawling along the carpet, but she is betrayed. I have been trying to understand what makes her tick, what motives push her from action to action, but, in my efforts to understand her, I have lost sight of her. I have been asking what she wants, and it is staring me in the face. She wants the one thing I am unable to give her: my complete, constant, undivided attention. I have refused her the object of her greatest desire, and that means trouble.

As she rages, things become simple again. In psychoanalytical theory, these dramatic challenges to the toddler's will are how the ego—the social face of the self—starts to scream its way into existence. Those moments of inconsolable betrayal are also the moments when parents face up to how little they understand about their offspring. Ever since she was a baby, I had been trying to figure these moments out. I would hold her, her soft-sinewed body writhing in my arms, her mouth a hot wet vent of hell. I could hardly cling on to her: she would be fighting against my grip with every muscle. "What does she want from us?" we would whisper, awestruck by this devilish prodigy. "What does she want us to do?" What made her tick was never such a critical, and unanswerable, question. I want to record how she looked, in her perfect, oblivious rage, but I've wiped it from my memory. It's evolution, probably, that programs us only to remember the good bits: natural selection for selective memory. Like most parents, I've ended up with almost blanket amnesia for the screaming in my ears, and that even louder internal scream, coming from deep within me, saying, I can't do this, I can't cope, I want this to stop.

Today's tantrum offers me a little more in the way of options. She has a greater capacity for violence now, more muscle-power with which to hurt me, and much more understanding that she is doing so. I, on the other hand, have had time to get to know her; I have better ideas on how to distract her from her outrage. I carry her up the stairs, sssh-ing her as we climb, and tango her into our bedroom, where there is a wardrobe with a full-length mirror. By reflecting her rage back at her, perhaps I can help to objectify it, and she can conquer it by giving it a name. She can leave her crying self in the mirror and come back to me in wonderment. It's an old game, one we have played since she was born. Why is the baby in the mirror crying? Is the baby sad? Is the baby hungry? Oh, what shall we do about the baby in the mirror?

Infants are fascinated by mirrors, of course. Charles Darwin noted that his baby son Doddy, at four and a half months, would repeatedly smile at his own reflection and that of his father, appearing to take them for separate beings. For Doddy, as for the fictional culture that banned all reflective devices in Borges's famous story, mirrors multiplied the contents of the world rather than reflecting them. We probably experience the same confusion when we catch sight of our own reflection unexpectedly, and take a moment to realize what the image represents. That moment of "mirror surprise" has been likened to the psychiatric condition of dissociation, when sufferers, shocked in many cases by emotive memories of a trauma, temporarily become absent from who they are. For a moment we are strangers to ourselves, and the thread of consciousness is broken. For an adult, returning to this state of primordial confusion can be a striking, even life-changing, experience. Doddy, in contrast, would have had little in the way of self to be a stranger to. He wasn't yet aware that he had one single, indivisible presence, and so he couldn't have been surprised to see it multiplied in this way.

Two months later, Doddy's understanding of mirrors had taken a step forward. Facing the mirror in front of his father, he now seemed to realize that his father's reflection was connected to the person standing behind him. When Darwin made a face in the mirror, Doddy turned to look at the man, not at his reflection. We saw Athena doing something similar at the same age. We would sit her on the bed and stand to one side, so that she could see us in the mirror but not herself. She would raise her arms and throw herself forward, reaching, as though in prayer. When we waved, she would give her characteristic double-handed wave in return, a cross between a communicative gesture and an exuberant attempt at taking flight, raising both hands high and then batting them down on the duvet on either side. Then she would turn to look at the figure reflected, confirming it against its image. She understood something about the mechanics of reflection, that what you see in the mirror is not an extension of the world but a special version of it. She was far from having a full understanding of it, but the looking-glass world was becoming real.

Knowing that she understood something about mirrors made her reaction to her own reflection that much more interesting. Here she is at the same age, being held up close to the wardrobe mirror. Her eyes are wide. She stares at her reflection and then darts a couple of glances into the corners of the mirror, as though establishing the limits of this weird version of reality. Then she reaches forward excitedly, patting at the glass with both hands. There is a gleeful shout, a smile of pleasure, but her eyes are still active, looking the reflected stranger up and down in what could almost be taken for suspicion. She stays rapt like this for quite a while. She may be noting the connection between her own actions and those she sees reflected: when I bat my hands forward like that, the baby in the mirror does it too. From the inside, from the sense that she has of her own body's movements and position, she has information about what she is doing; and now the mirror reflects the same information back at her. She can imitate its imitations. She recognizes that this specular creature has something to do with herself, and no one else. At the same time, she knows that it is not *her*; it exists in a different location, flat against our old walnut-wood wardrobe, and it does its corresponding at a distance.

Then Lizzie changes the game in a critical way. She has secretly smeared a tissue with some rouge from her makeup bag, and is now dabbing it gently on Athena's nose, leaving it with a conspicuous red dot at its tip. The operation complete, she turns Athena back to her reflection. Nothing changes in Athena's reaction. She shows the same interest in the baby in the mirror, but she pays no attention to the mark on the baby's nose. She does not yet recognize that this is an image of her, only her, and no one else. There is still not yet a clear *her* that can be represented. Psychologists have termed this the "proto-narcissistic" stage, calling to mind the mythical youth who caught sight of his reflection in a pool, and fell in love with it. That kind of love cannot follow if you truly recognize the other person as yourself, but Athena is still susceptible to it. She is a little Narcissus, delighted with the chance to imitate her reflection with such a perfect contingency, but not yet able to identify with its image.

She will not take this next step until several months later. At fourteen months, faced with her reflection in the same mirror, her first action is to say her own name. This next stage of mirror self-recognition, known as "identification," coincides with the beginnings of the use of language in a self-referring way. The baby in the mirror is Athena. She names her, gives a little embarrassed chuckle, and makes a big sigh, as though, after all these patient months of waiting for her self to turn up, it has finally done so. She glances at the mirror's edge, then sings a brief, funny tune to her reflection. She touches the glass, but this time the gesture is about communication rather than exploration. She reaches her arms wide, trying to embrace the whole of the image, then leans forward and gives it a kiss. Poised with her red-blotched tissue, Lizzie tries the rouge test again. Her nose newly spotted, Athena looks back at her image, glances away, then does a double take, gazing back at herself with more purpose. She looks at her mother, touching her nose, then turns to the mirror again.

"Look!" she says, with genuine surprise.

"What is it?" Lizzie asks.

Athena looks back at her with a big grin. The test has become a game. She bats at the spot in the mirror, then touches her own blotched features. She is doing something quite remarkable: seeing herself as others see her, and somehow identifying herself with the image. More than that, she is mapping specific parts of that image—its nose, in this case—on to the parts of her own person. She is showing that she understands the image *as* an image, a representation of the thing rather than the thing itself. On top of that, she understands that the image is real, not a fantasy or hallucination. For French psychologist Henri Wallon, this was a vitally important step in the growth of the imagination. After experience of the mirror, the world that the child experiences is no longer a purely perceptual one; it is one that contains representations. Once reality can be represented, it can become transformed through imagination into anything at all.

Something similar happens when Athena sees her image in a video recording. Here she is again at age two and a quarter, a couple of months after the tantrum about the computer. She is gazing at herself in the mirror of our camcorder, whose view screen I have clicked around so that she can watch herself as she is being filmed. This is guaranteed to delight her, although, like some megalomaniacal movie star, she wants to be behind the camera at the same time as being in front of it, so that much of my footage is of the side of her head as she tries to wrestle the camera from me. Her expression is proud, with just a trace of the wonder she showed when first confronted with this high-tech version of Wallon's mirror. Self-identification has repeatedly been linked with the expression of feelings like pride and embarrassment; as the child passes the rouge test, these emotions are not far behind. They are social emotions, which only make sense if the individual can see herself as others see her. Embarrassment, for example, suggests that there is some mismatch between how she represents herself and how she sees herself in the mirror. "Do I really look like that?" we tend to say when we show our clumsier sides in someone's home movie. This could only happen if there were some representation of self that could be disappointed by the harsh reality of the technologically reflected world. If you don't care about yourself, mirrors can't shame you.

It is not just the occasions when the mirror image disappoints us that can bother us. Trouble can also follow when we look too good. For French psychoanalyst Jacques Lacan, whose ideas were probably heavily borrowed from Wallon's writings, the mirror presents the child with an image of the perfect, integrated self, which the infant, painfully aware of her own lack of coordination and power, cannot live up to. As many film theorists have argued, Hollywood does something very similar. The immaculate humanoids who fill our movie screens challenge the ego by showing us an ideal image that we can't measure up to. We flock willingly to the cinema, and yet films are traps that ensnare our feeble egos and create a crippling sense of alienation. It all comes down, the Lacanian would say, to our anxieties as infants, during the stage in which we struggle to reconcile the perfection of our mirror image with the fragmentary experiences of babyhood. The "flutter of jubilant activity" that Lacan described in the baby's response to her own mirror image could actually be the source of the modern cult of personality. Just as our minds are starting to reflect the world, the mirror is there, unforgivingly, to reflect us.

"Who can you see?" I ask her, triggering the recording with my thumb.

"Me!"

She used to call the image by her own name, as though the mirror-Athena were still not quite the same as the real little girl. When we look back at the videos after a lapse of time, she still fends the image off behind a proper noun. If the contingencies are perfect and immediate, as in the rouge test, she can understand how the reflected image maps on to her own body. When she is looking at a version of herself in the past, though, there is always the slight suspicion that she might be looking at an impostor, a replacement Athena who just happens to be wearing her clothes. The flow of time gives her Capgras syndrome, a profound suspicion about her own otherwise familiar identity. She has a self in the present, but not yet in the past.

"And what is your name?"

"Seena Bear-hoe!" she declaims, pronouncing the last syllable of her surname with an odd Icelandic aspirated vowel. She tries to grab the camera from me, wanting to embrace the image as she tried to embrace the mirror.

"And where do you live?"

She gives an answer that might bring an obliging delivery van to within about fifty miles of our house.

"And . . . what did you say you found in your shoes this morning?"

She looks down and pulls a funny face. "Kangaroos!"

The mirror is a window into imagination. It reflects the world as it is, but also as it might be.

"That's right, you thought you had kangaroos in your shoes this morning. And what did you say you found in the garden yesterday morning?"

"Crocodiles!"

"And how many crocodiles were there?"

She starts counting: ". . . four . . . five . . . *six*!"

"And . . . would you like to go to a place where you can see some real kangaroos and crocodiles?"

She nods vaguely, distracted by her plans to relieve me of the camera. She still thinks we're pretending.

"Athena, do you know where Australia is?"

She frowns, showing the treble-clef eyebrow of my dad, and his sister, and me.

"Where?"

"It's a country a long way away. Would you like to go on a big airplane and live there for a while?"

"I like go to Adrayer. I like go on big airplane."

"They have kangaroos there. And crocodiles."

She nods. The embellishment isn't needed. She is already sold.

"I like kangaroos. I play chaseys."

I'm almost disappointed, in a way, not to have any explaining to do. And yet Athena can hardly fail to be accepting about this news. Brimming with autonomy she might be, but her plans for her own future are not yet developed enough for this upheaval to affect them. I think about whether I will finish my chapter in Australia. Perhaps I'll put on a spurt and finish what I am writing. But then I will have to start living, and that's no good. I feel that airy-hearted, nerve-pulling unease, the chasm between where I am and where I want to be. I have my own mirror crisis to deal with, my own ideal, self-constructed image to live up to. There is one cure beloved of all who are trying to escape themselves, and I'm about to take it. Wherever I am, I will soon not be here.

Ten

⌒

THE SHINING THREAD

A Self That Endures

Project yourself into the future—that party you've got scratched into your diary, the beach holiday you'll take next year—and a thread goes with you. A self can feel like such a singular fixture, hugging one's here-and-now like a twenty-four-hour undergarment, but actually it's a string, looping back and forward in time to knit together our past and future moments. In contemplating a forthcoming journey, we don't just make a physical connection with the human being who will be passing through that airport and hailing that taxi; we make a mental connection, imagining the sights and sounds, the varied emotions of arrival. It takes a leap of imagination before we make the leap of substance. In foreseeing herself in Australia, Athena needed some of that thread-self. There was that little person, in the image of the future she had conjured up; there was something that it was like to be that little person; and it would be the same as what it was like to be *this* little person. A self is a Tardis, a time-machine: it can swallow you up and spit you out somewhere else. Athena needed some understanding of herself as a center of experience that persisted like her body persisted, with a future as well as a present. She needed to be a time-traveler.

This journeying in time went backward as well as forward. In casting herself forward into Australia, she was drawing on the same self-threads she drew on in telling the story of her life so far. In order to do the first-person storytelling that is autobiographical memory, she needed an equally rich connection with the subjective quality of experience, that something-that-it-is-likeness that made her experiences so ineffably her own. I knew that, at two and a quarter, she was only on the threshold of that capacity for reliving events that would allow her to center herself in her own memories. Competent at recognizing herself in a photograph or a mirror, she still reacted to our home movies as though she were watching the biopic of a stranger. Just as mirror self-recognition required her to make a connection between her subjective experience and what she saw reflected at her, identifying with the stranger in those missives from the past required a grasp of something much more subtle than physical resemblance. It called for a meeting of minds, the confluence of the thoughts and feelings of her present with those of her past.

Understanding one's past and future experiences, it seems, hangs on understanding the mind that can have those experiences. Psychologists have begun to wonder whether this is the critical ability that distinguishes the amnesic infant from the toddling autobiographer. Having a "theory of mind," as the terminology goes, could be the quality that allows us to star in our own memories. It may also be a capacity that is uniquely human. Although some nonhuman animals show skill at both mental time travel and mind understanding, they are the exceptions rather than the rule. In the search for the unique endowment that makes human civilization and culture what they are, the focus has shifted from language (once thought to be the human gift to surpass all others) to theory of mind: from knowledge of syntax to knowledge of one's own and others' mental worlds. Becoming a person involves accessing that knowledge about how human beings work. For a mind shaped by the rhythms and unpredictabilities of social life, acquiring that insight would be a profound achievement indeed.

In the end, it was about learning a language—or, rather, learning two languages. From the earliest days of infancy, Athena would have been sensitive to the different ways in which living and nonliving things behaved. People came and went with regularities that belied an underlying grammar, a purpose to their actions that made sense if you knew what kind of thing a person was. The behavior of objects was also structured, but it followed different rules. Inanimate objects were suckers for gravity and a general tendency to end up scattered around the floor. People, on the other hand, pulled tricks like speaking suddenly after minutes of silence, staring at a page for hours with only occasional exasperated sighs to show that they were still alive, or stopping mid-motion, looking thoughtful, and then heading off in the opposite direction. The rich pageant of visual perception posed a translation problem. Why did things move as they moved, and why did people move differently? What were the rules of behavior?

It seems that infants' early sensitivity to these two kinds of behaving gives them a foothold in understanding the different causes behind biological and nonbiological motion. Young babies know that biological motion is special, but they also seem to understand something of what is special about it. Those driven things behave differently because they have something driving them: specific mental causes that are unobservable and yet, with the right knowledge, can be inferred. Studies of young babies using techniques like dishabituation and preferential looking have revealed a very early, and possibly innate, sensitivity to these mental causes. The trick, in these various studies, is to make inanimate objects behave like animate ones. In a standard experiment, infants watch computer-generated dots moving around a screen. In some sequences the dots behave in typical object fashion: for example, cannoning into and bouncing off each other like snooker balls. In other sequences the dots appear to be moving with intention, like objects with minds of their own. One larger dot, for example, might be seen as "chasing" a smaller dot around the screen. Infants as young as twelve months react differently to these different stimuli. Psychologist Paul Bloom has argued that young infants are "dualists": that is, that their thinking is founded on a fundamental distinction between things with minds and things without. Non-minded objects go about their business blindly, slaves to the laws of Newtonian mechanics. Minded objects, on the other hand, act with intention: they have someone at the wheel.

This developing sensitivity to the minds behind behavior was, for Athena, a passport to a new social world. Minded objects behave differently from nonminded ones, and it is to minded objects—people— that we turn for comfort, food, and conversation. Wise infants know who their parents are: it is to them that they yell their needs, not to the fridge or the TV. Rather than settling on the infant in one fell swoop, the understanding of other people as intentional agents goes through some clearly defined stages. First, at around six months, babies know enough about animate motion to be able to make predictions about how those motions are directed at goals. If they have previously observed a human hand reaching for an object, they expect the hand to continue reaching for the object, and show surprise when they see the same behavior performed by an inanimate object, such as a garden claw. They seem to appreciate that these animate actions are directed toward a specific goal: in this example, obtaining the reached-for object. A few months later infants understand that minded objects will persist in reaching for their goals in the face of initial failure, and they also understand that such failures are not part of the plan. Just as some things don't happen when they are supposed to, so stuff sometimes does happen that isn't meant to. Understanding intention brings with it an understanding of accident: to understand how plans go awry, you need to understand the plans. In one study, nine-month-old infants showed frustration when an adult teasingly withheld a toy, but not when the failure to pass on the toy was accidental—for example, as a result of the adult dropping it. The infants seemed to acknowledge an intention to pass the toy, even though it wasn't successfully acted upon. They allowed the adult the old excuse: I didn't manage to do it, but I tried.

Having a goal, even one that remains unfulfilled, gives intentional agents a strange connectivity with the world. If I think about the bottle of beer that is in the fridge, there is a connection between my mental event—my thought about the beer—and the thing itself. My thought is *about* that object: it has what philosophers call intentionality. Intentionality has caused cognitive scientists more than a few problems in trying to explain how mental states go about their business. If thoughts were only ever connected with other thoughts, then explaining them might be simpler. The trouble is, thoughts cast their line much further, into the world of physical objects, and beyond, into the realm of things that only exist in the imagination. I can think about that bottle of beer (an object that exists, but resolutely outside myself), but I can also think about a unicorn (an object that doesn't exist at all). How can my thoughts have such unreachable targets? How can a mental event be about anything?

What Athena needed to understand was that other people's thoughts were directed at something outside themselves. More than that, she needed to understand that another person's "aboutness" was not necessarily the same as her own. We didn't all want the same things, and we weren't all tremendously interested in that beetle she had spotted crawling across the carpet or the speck of fluff she had picked out of her bath. Understanding that other people's minds are directed in this way was surely the first step toward understanding how minds point in different directions. It was also a first step toward sharing that aboutness: hooking up with another person's directedness and, by pointing the way we were pointing, sharing the content of our thoughts.

Much of that was done by the adults around her. We went to her rather than she to us. If infants get a chance to line up their mental radar with others, it is largely because caregivers spend much of their time making it easier for them. In the first weeks of infancy, our meeting of minds was simply about looking at each other. Athena was interested in our faces, and, as her visual acuity improved, gradually less interested in their edges and contrast boundaries and more interested in the features at their center, particularly our eyes. When she did latch on, we were ready to return her gaze. The conventional bids for attention that drive social interaction—coughing conspicuously or saying a person's name—weren't going to work, and so we waited for her to make the first move. From the day she was born, we had been trying to catch her eye. This was what developmental psychologists have termed "primary intersubjectivity": those sophisticated, emotionally rich wordless "conversations," exchanges of smiles and happy vocalizations that follow the same rules of turn-taking as later linguistic exchanges—and, for that matter, the rules of love. I smile, and you smile back: it's how getting to know you begins.

We spoke a language of love, but it lacked nouns. It was about each other, but it wasn't about any actual *thing*. We needed some substance to our conversations, and we got it from solid objects. Things gave us grist, something to talk about beyond ourselves. One milestone we were looking out for was the emergence of what baby-watchers have called "secondary intersubjectivity." At around nine months, infants' attention typically shifts from dyadic interaction, where the interactional partners are focused on each other, to exchanges where both partners' mental directedness takes the same object. These interactions are often called "triadic," structured as they are around the triad of infant, adult, and physical thing. The word *thing*, in Old Norse, means "meeting"; it's where our minds go to make friends. Infants are interested in objects; adults are interested in infants being interested in objects; infants soon pick up that the big people around them are sharing their attention. Where the task had previously been to attend to the other's attention to oneself—to watch you watching me—it was now about tuning in to their directedness to the world. It has been argued that these primordial sharing situations are the context in which we really start finding out about other minds. Social interaction becomes a way of learning about the world, but also of learning about the minds that make social interaction possible.

What these interactions really throw into relief are the differences between people's minds. Because our proto-conversations now have a concrete topic, as they didn't when we were simply gazing at each other, these differences in perspective are that much more obvious. Here is Athena at eleven months, trying to suck the germs out of a wooden jigsaw piece. "Is it tasty?" I ask her. She takes the soggy cartoon dog from her mouth and inspects it in close-up. Tasty? She had just been thinking about its satisfying texture on her gums. Or perhaps its blue-spotted yellowness. Or the way her tooth marks have abraded the dogginess of its shape. All that matters is that she sees it differently from me. We are attending to the same object, but we have different perspectives on it. In that moment of slippage between the thing and a person's *representation* of the thing, children's understanding of mind finds a powerful new focus.

The metaphor of slippage may be a useful one. In their 1963 book *Symbol Formation*, Heinz Werner and Bernard Kaplan described how the primordial sharing situation creates one of the foundations of the successful use of language: the understanding that the symbol of a thing (the word *dog*, for example) is different from the thing itself. Generally speaking, toddlers can have difficulties understanding the representational nature of pictures, symbols, and words. As late as age two, Athena would avoid touching a picture of a crocodile in a book, for fear that it might bite her. Even adults occasionally have problems separating the representation of a thing from the thing itself. Try writing down a sentence describing the imagined death of a loved one, and see how long it takes before you are compelled to erase it. The point is that, despite their emotional power, words are only representations of states of affairs. The word *dog* does not bark or shed hair, but it does slip easily into a sentence. Werner and Kaplan argued that the experience of labeling objects in the primordial sharing situation, and of hearing the different labels that others apply to the same thing, is essential for the child's uncoupling of a symbol from its referent. Using symbols, in linguistic interaction, is the glue that binds us socially, but it seems that understanding how those symbols function in the first place requires a social context.

If this is true, then your experience of those sorts of social contexts should relate to your ability to use symbols, and more generally to appreciate that the world can be taken in different ways. Psychologist Peter Hobson has picked up on Werner and Kaplan's insights to explain why children with certain developmental disorders, such as autism, show characteristic problems with mind reading and symbol use. For some as-yet-unknown biological reason, children who later develop autism are born without the full repertoire of social skills that allow babies to engage in dyadic interaction and proto-conversations. As a result, these kids never get to enjoy the kinds of interactions that provide such useful lessons about other minds. Although Hobson's hypothesis is unproven, it makes a welcome contrast to those neuroscientific theories of autism that pin the disorder exclusively on to genetic and biological abnormalities, such as prenatal brain damage or excessive exposure to testosterone. In Hobson's theory, autism *develops:* not because of any failure on the part of the parents, but because an innate abnormality in social interaction colors the kinds of social experience the infant can have.

Adults are not to blame for autism, but when things develop smoothly they do take prime responsibility for constructing interactions centered around objects. Infants have their part to play too, showing a motivation to share their aboutness that gets many an interaction moving from the small person's side. Babies are great at showing. Let an infant discover an interesting toy and you can be sure that she will let you know about it. At nine months, Athena took pleasure in showing me any trinket that took her fancy: the plastic ball from a shape-sorter, a bit of thread she had picked off the rug. Later in childhood, showing has an ice-breaking function that can get all kinds of new intimacies off the ground. In the most satisfying way possible, it extends the hand of friendship at the same time as emphasizing the facts of possession. "Do you want to have a look at my toys?" she asks me one morning, after she has spent a heavy-breathing five minutes stuffing the pockets of her dressing gown with wooden farm animals. How many other times could she only be encouraged to make a new social foray if she had a favorite toy to take with her, a pocketful of cash in the currency of things?

Psychologist and primatologist Michael Tomasello has proposed that it is this motivation to share intentionality that distinguishes humankind from other socially adept animals. Chimps and bonobos can do all sorts of things that demonstrate their understanding of others as intentional agents, but they never show any motivation to share their aboutness. Give a chimp an interesting object and she will scurry away to play with it on her own. Chimps do not show, nor do they point out, objects to their fellow chimps just for interest's sake. Nor, for that matter, are they great teachers: perfectly capable of learning from each other, they nevertheless are unlikely to deliberately set out to impart information to their peers. The sight of a huddle of chimp students sitting around a chimp teacher is quite simply unknown. (That inspirational teacher of yours from primary school was a master, or mistress, of shared intentionality.) It is not just that

Athena *could* share her aboutness, but that she *wanted* to. Language is crucial too, but without that primordial motivation to share the contents of our minds, it is unlikely that human-style social interaction would ever get off the ground.

For all these burgeoning skills, Athena still wasn't a mind reader. She understood that she shared the world with creatures driven by intentions, and she was constantly propelled into social interactions by an urge to share her own aboutness with others. There were limits to that understanding, though. Many of her terrible-two tantrums stemmed from her temporarily forgetting that we were minded beings. Instead she seemed to act as though we were mannequins whose actions could be physically manipulated, by tugging an arm or trying to wrestle walking feet in a different direction. Like all preschoolers, she made the converse mistake as well, attributing intention to objects that most certainly had no mind at the wheel. Talking to toys as though they are alive is cute; thinking that a car isn't moving because it "needs to wake up first" offers a more telling insight into children's confusions between animate and inanimate beings. Again, adults are not immune to these errors either, as anyone who has ever called a computer "stupid" should admit. But animism really runs riot in childhood. Kids see spirits everywhere, intention where there is actually only blind physics. If attributing intention is a key skill for acquiring a theory of mind, it is one that takes time to find its right targets.

What was really holding her back, though, was a more profound hindrance. She seemed to understand that other minds were boxes whose contents were different from her own. But she couldn't yet see into the boxes. She couldn't represent their contents, and use that understanding to predict what people would do or say, or explain why someone had acted as they had done. She could share intention, but she couldn't share subjectivity. She couldn't know what was going on for another person: what they believed, what they wanted, what they were thinking about. People still moved in mysterious ways. And just as she couldn't represent another person's thoughts, her own mind was something of a mystery to her. She knew things, but she didn't know how she knew them, or understand that there had been a time when she had not known them. She couldn't quite get the lay of the mind she inhabited now, nor of the mental states she would be experiencing when she stepped off that Malaysian Airlines flight in Sydney. Subjectively, emotionally, her future was a mystery, because her present was a mystery. On the path to acquiring a true theory of mind, she still had some way to go.

We had taken a six-month lease on a house in Turramurra, in Sydney's hilly northern suburbs. Pristine white sedans, piloted by grumpy-looking Chinese Australians, backed silently out of carports overhung by spindly eucalyptus. There were manicured lawns and swimming pools. Sulfur-crested cockatoos screeched into the palm trees that towered over our small garden, gorging on the palm fruit and shitting a copious purple-brown. The gum trees were chameleonic, capable of all kinds of approximations to humanness, from pom-pom-tossing cheerleaders to wizened old shamans. It was January, and the air had a scent of bush fires.

Blue sky, white cars, gum trees: I too was time-traveling. I had come to Sydney as a backpacker, driven across the world not so much by a desire to see it as by a mortal terror of committing to a career. When, twelve years later, the chance came for Lizzie to take a sabbatical, we thought of this place. I had fallen in love with it, as I had never fallen in love with a city before, and I wanted to reclaim my parallel existence there. We had found a place for Athena at a local preschool, which would leave me plenty of time to finish the work I needed to do. If I couldn't do that, then I could swim and—a secret ambition, sharpened by the unlikelihood that I would ever have one of my own—learn about the maintenance of a swimming pool. For a brief time I would be master of one of these playthings of the rich, which for a brief time would be as good as being rich myself.

We anticipated that Athena would travel well. As she had already proved on flights to Spain and Crete, she was patient in airports and on airplanes, and endearingly willing to give herself over to new, foreign-speaking routines. I remember being struck by this emergent reality: that this was her personality, this was what she was *like*, for now if not for always. It was humbling that this little person's openness to new experiences could translate into a preparedness to take flight to the other side of the world. She was between nursery schools, so there was no great wrench away from friendships. I somehow knew that the coming months would be a time of breakthroughs, of milestones surpassed: swimming, socializing, toilet training. At two and a half, with her strengthening grasp of her own subjectivity, she was old enough for this not to be instantly forgotten—at least, I wanted to believe that she was. As usual, we caught ourselves trying to enrich her experience, to sow the seeds of some precious and unique memories. It was part of the extraordinary power that we felt as parents, that we could do something that would change the way she remembered her life.

What did Australia, or any kind of nation or nationhood, mean to her? She saw the map of the country, with its distinctive terrier's-head shape, in our *Rough Guide*, and she responded to it by name: "Adrayer." Her understanding of where she fit in to this mythical place, though, was complex and fragmentary. Shortly after our arrival in Turramurra, she pointed to the picture of the Harbour Bridge in the same book and said, "I go dat Adrayer." *I'm going to go to that Australia.* How to break it to her: *You're already here?* It seemed that she was using the proper noun generically, like we call a vacuum cleaner a Hoover. For her, it signified any kind of foreign place, not necessarily the one she was in now. In other respects, she seemed very clear that she had already arrived. Sometimes, in a vulnerable moment, she would lose patience with our house in Turramurra and say, "I want to go to the yellow house," meaning our home in County Durham. She knew that she was somewhere, and that it was not the place she was used to. I tried to press it home, to ensure that she could not be in any doubt about the enormity of what was happening to her. The videos from those days embarrass me now. Every extract of footage begins with a question: "Athena, where are we?" or "Athena, what are we doing now?" So much for letting her work things out for herself. Our trip of a lifetime had turned into one long oral examination.

Her reaction to the reality of where we were wasn't always what I had hoped for. When we took a train to Milson's Point and she looked up at the real Harbour Bridge for the first time, I thought she looked gently underwhelmed. How I wanted her to say, with a self-aware excitability way beyond her years: "Wow, Dad, the Harbour Bridge! I can't believe we're really here!" Instead it seemed to strike her with a quiet inevitability, as though we had somehow magically talked this iron marvel into being. After all the planning and discussion, the famous bridge and opera house could hardly fail to materialize. We had sung them up from the earth, brought them into existence through sheer force of will. When you are still learning the rules of minded and unminded behavior, imagination can have this power.

She had no such preconceptions about 8 Solander Close, Turramurra. She charted the two-story house with its utility room and laundry, its trampoline and sandbox, with eager, functional sorties. She listened to our warnings about spiders and their dangers with genuine concern, and sent us regular dispatches from the sandbox on the minibeast situation. Our house had no TV. No Tweenies, no Maisy Mouse, no Elmo. No *Teletubbies* to feed her Dipsy-mania. We thought about buying a cheap portable, and then realized that we were enjoying the silence too much. Athena didn't seem to have noticed. She became hooked instead on jigsaw puzzles, of which the owners of the house had furnished us with plenty. We went to Grace Brothers in

Central Plaza and bought her Ravensburger creations of ever-increasing complexity: twenty-eight pieces, then sixty-three, then a hundred or more. It reached the point where both of us had to lend a hand with her jigsaw challenges. Early mornings last forever when there are no cartoons to fill the spaces. We could have tiled the Euclidean plane, that summer, in the hours between six and nine.

At nursery, she had a social life to restart. She was already a veteran of child care, having done two or three days a week at her nursery in England, beginning just after her first birthday. As her attunement to other people's states of mind had improved, so too had her socializing opportunities. Parents often worry when their toddlers spend their first few sessions at nursery playing entirely on their own: are they turning into sad little loners, or worse? In fact, those concerned mums and dads are just witnessing a developmental progression. Child's play might seem aimless and haphazard, but it has goals: building that tower, putting on that puppet show. Because young children cannot yet see into their playmates' minds, they cannot link up with their intentions. They are like a team of builders who can only work from their own individual sets of plans. The result, as any visitor to the younger rooms of a preschool knows, is lots of little solo players working in parallel. Truly collaborative play requires children to be good enough mind readers to be able to represent a shared goal and know when their partner is deviating from it. In terms of building civilizations, chimps don't achieve what we achieve for many reasons, but not least because they lack the urge to share their blueprints.

She was in the Wombat Room. The babies were Possums. When she was a big girl she would be a Koala. The native animals of Australia gave her a ready time frame, a structure for understanding the ages of man. She got her first sense of human juniority and seniority from marsupials and monotremes. Next year she would be an Echidna. Echidnas wore undies, every boy and girl of them, and no longer needed sticker rewards for using the loo. Her forthcoming Echidna-hood may have been her invention (unless we moved here permanently, there would be no Echidna Room for her), but it was something she could get a handle on. It was her first taste of sixth-former envy, but it also gave her a road map for her own life. She might not yet be able to guess how it would feel, but she knew how it would look and how it would carry itself. A bigger Athena was out there, waiting, in undies. When it came to waving good-bye to this part of her past, it would be that Echidna Athena who would be putting up her hand.

Non-nursery days were Daddy-days. Here is a typical morning in late summer: the February rains have abated and it is scorchingly hot again. Qantas jets in their distinctive red-and-white livery incline against a blue sky. We're at the table in our dining room, making twice as many Vegemite sandwiches as we will actually need for our trip. At just gone two and a half, hunger is a condition of being. Even the shortest trips out of the house need to be planned around the ready provision of food. I could stay at home and look after her in the kitchen, perhaps with the fridge door propped ajar, but getting out into the snack-rich city is an easier option. Looking after her at home is exhausting now, because her agenda is so irreconcilably removed from mine. She was hard work as a baby, of course, but there was none of this ambition about what she could make happen, this newfound certainty about the way the world ought to be. Balance on these stones. Stand on my teddy bear's head. Daddy, you go to sleep *there*. Traveling limits her options, and therefore restores to me some semblance of control. Besides, we're in a beautiful city and the sun is shining. Dawdling indoors can wait for rainy days at home.

"Where shall we go today?" I ask her.

"Sindy."

"Okay, Sydney." I slice two more pieces of bread for her to trowel with butter. "But where exactly in Sydney?"

She puts the knife down and responds in a singsong, do-I-really-have-to-explain-this-again voice.

"Watson's *Bay*."

"You want to go to Watson's Bay?" I enthuse, thinking of the beer garden at Doyle's. "For fish-and-chips?"

"For shopping," she says, firmly.

She makes a grab for the little jar of Vegemite like a cricketer would fling a hand out for a catch. She doesn't apply herself to a task so much as attack it; every call on her time has to be dispatched swiftly, as though it were stopping her from doing something else. She eats with the same impatience, wincingly snatching at each mouthful as though she had to get the spoon in and out of her mouth as quickly as possible. What's the hurry? What has she heard about the passing of time? Does she know more about it than I do?

"There aren't any shops at Watson's Bay," I reason.

"We going to Watson's Bay today?"

I'm disarmed. "If you like. It's your day. Where do you *want* to go?"

"Um . . . not sure."

"Well, take your time. I wouldn't want you to make any hasty decisions."

She looks up at me with a wide-open, buttery frown. Never give a child a choice, the parenting books tell us. I'm beginning to think they have a point.

"I think I like to go to playground."

I think . . . Like most of her developmental milestones, this one will pass without fanfare. She has just put into words something that is known only to her: a thought. The mental states that drive behavior are now a topic of conversation. My sarcasm might be lost on her, for the simple reason that she can't reconstruct the real intention behind my words, but at least she now has the language to describe, and have conversations about, those intentions and thoughts. If she has a word for the thing, understanding the thing itself might come more easily.

"Which playground? We know lots."

"On the ferry."

I smile, showing her that I understand. These early conversations can be one-sided, too focused on Athena's agenda or mine, but here we have a meeting of minds. She knows she has put the thought into my head, the plan she wanted to share. Already, we've left Chimpland behind and are into the unique social world of humans.

"Okay, the ferry playground. Come on, let's pack this bag."

I leave her smearing her arms with sunscreen and go into the kitchen to fill her sippy cup with water. A few months ago, in our last English summer, the application of sun cream would have been a greasy ordeal. Now she has the skill and, apparently, the sensual motivation to do it herself. Anointing herself with Factor 40, like washing, is also one of the few things she will do slowly. She is never more fastidious than when she is polishing her cheeks with a washcloth. The removal of stickiness with an impregnated wipe is a pleasure to savor. Even as a baby, a single Wet One would keep her happy for half an hour or more.

I hear her scream and jolt back into the room. A rainbow lorikeet, one of those color-splashed mini-parrots that look as though they belong in a pet shop, is trying to hop in through the open window. I shoo it away and slam the window shut. Once, I thought her fear of cats and dogs would be short-lived, but it has generalized to anything with fur or feathers that moves around under its own steam. Animate motion is fine as long as it comes from a human being; from anything else, it is a horror movie.

"I bit scared," she says, rubbing her shiny arm absentmindedly.

And so the conversation turns to feelings as well as thoughts. Toddlers talk about affairs of the heart surprisingly early, and some time before they fully understand emotion as a driving force in human behavior. Feelings represent another spectrum along which minds can differ—what scares me might not scare you—and so conversations with folk who don't necessarily feel the same way are full of lessons in other people's aboutness. It might be a lesson too far for

Athena, though. She is looking anxiously out at the palm trees, wondering where the killer lorikeet has gotten to. How strange all this wildlife is: the magpies with their evil stares and haunting, fluting calls, the sentinel kookaburras, the cockatoos with their leathery eyes and odd, smashed-in faces. Zoologically speaking, she has been raised in an English farmyard. Her storybooks are about ducks and kittens, and the fields outside her window contain the knowable quantities of sheep and cattle. Cows are kindly old aunts. Ducks are scatty chancers. What personality traits would you ascribe to a numbat, or a bilby? What on earth is an echidna, aside from a three-year-old in undies? We plunge into the classics of Australian children's literature, but I can see she finds them baffling. At least *Possum Magic* has food in it. And what does Grandma Poss do when she needs to reverse her vanishing charm and make the little possum, Hush, visible again? She reaches for a Vegemite sandwich.

We get a lift to the station and buy a Daytripper ticket for me. Athena enjoys the pleasures of public transport—inserting the ticket into the electronic reader, pressing the bell button on the bus—for free. On the train she wants to stand on her seat, her hands and nose pressed against the window, and sing a song about a teddy bear. She has sticky tips of Vegemite in her hair from the sandwiches she has already helped herself to. She is wearing a butter-stained red T-shirt and a pink dress ruched around the middle. Today is forecast to reach eighty-six degrees, but a peach gingham hat will see off the summer sun.

Our first stop is Town Hall, and the walkway under the QVB that leads to the Little Girls' Toilet. Others navigate Sydney by the tourist-brochure landmarks; our compass is marked by the poles of excretion and food . Never mind the opera house and the MCG: Australia should be famous for its public toilets. On the second floor of Grace

Brothers in Central Plaza, there is a parents' room with a toddler-sized loo that is never less than spotlessly clean. One place we stopped at, in Port Douglas in the north of Queensland, even had a grown-up-sized loo placed alongside the smaller one, so that parent and child could strain together in blissful company. Those who complain that parents are potty-fixated should, of course, try looking after a toddler who is toilet training. My claims on such an obsession are weaker than most, because this is one thing that Athena is taking in her stride. She left England in diapers and landed in Sydney in underwear. The parenting industry goes to some lengths to glamorize the mucky end of the alimentary process, with its Disney-branded training pants and days-of-the-week underwear. It needn't bother. Pooing is a pleasure that cannot be enhanced by advertising. When toddlers get down to it, they really get down. We have had some of our best conversations with Athena on the throne, her flow of discourse only interrupted by moist-browed, flush-cheeked pauses. "I do two wees and two poos," she announces, sitting down to another bout of stinky bliss. She celebrates it, sings its praises, frequently for an entire public convenience to hear. More embarrassing is her insistence on commenting on her fellow occupants' activities. She thinks she's alone with me in those cramped white stalls, but of course the man next door, upon whose grunting she is commentating loudly, knows otherwise. Once again, she is tripped up by the question of how people come to know things, how perception shapes the contents of minds. She seems not to understand that, if she can hear a person, that person can hear her. Social life is a hall of mirrors. At any moment, you can be caught out by how another mind reflects your self to you.

After easing her bladder, it's down to the lower ground floor for lunch at the food court. If we're there by eleven forty-five, we can beat the crowds of office workers. After a few revolutions of the room, she decides (as she usually does) that she wants Chinese Rice, and so we share a five-dollar Korean special with two plastic forks. Then it's back to the Little Girls' Toilet to clean up, and onward to the fifth-floor toy department. "I going do the bills!" she announces, pulling a toy calculator onto the floor and pressing the buttons carefully, and once again I have the alarming sense of witnessing my own obsessions reflected back at me through her. But wait: she's *telling* me about her pretense. That means she must understand that I cannot see through it on my own; that it is, in other words, what philosophers call "opaque." When pretending, she is the boss, and whatever she says goes. If she wants a wooden brick to be a car, then that's the way it is. Because my beliefs about the situation don't necessarily coincide with hers, I need to be led into the game. Even in this simple play routine, there is an acknowledgment that my aboutness is different from hers.

With other children, though, I suspect that she is more struck by similarities than differences. I notice how she will stop and stare at them in shops, as though she can't quite believe that there are other creatures like her out there. She is drawn to them as though they were members of an alien race, seeking solidarity or safety in numbers. Sometimes they are more like dogs, sniffing around each other, sizing each other up but rarely initiating an interaction. Socially speaking, she simply does not know how to start the ball rolling. For this small person there is no such thing as small talk. It might be shyness, but it is also an unfamiliarity with social conventions. She doesn't yet know the grammar of getting to know you. Like the physical objects she learned about in her first year, people are refractory, largely immune to her own actions. Without an ability to see inside those other mind boxes, it is hard to see how you can have anything in common.

Next it's a train to Circular Quay. The playground she referred to earlier is at Balmain East, and to get there we need the Darling Harbour ferry. We sit on a bench on the jetty, watching the one-footed pigeons fighting over crumbs. Around us, yellow-and-green ferries peep three times and reverse out into the bright harbor. At the cruise terminal, a huge white access gangplank descends from the second floor and ends in midair. We watch a floating crane pull in to one of the wharves farther along. She looks down at the green water and asks what would happen if she fell in. "I would cry," I say. "For ever and ever." She thinks about this. She has seen me cry, but she can't imagine me doing it for ever and ever. She can hardly imagine tomorrow, let alone eternity. "You cry for ever and ever?" she says. "Make you sad?" "I'd cry *because* I was sad," I reply, underlining the causal point. We do things because we believe certain things, and because we feel certain ways. Mind: it's the engine of human behavior. Mind-blindness, as a result, must make human behavior pretty strange.

"I want Vegemite sandjidge," she says.

"You've just had lunch. Besides, this is our ferry."

We watch the boat docking, and men in shorts and sunglasses tossing rope lassos on to coir-polished bollards. I hold her hand as she crosses the portable footbridge on to the ferry and chooses a bench along the side. She's tired and wants to snuggle in. To the south, behind the city skyline, a bank of dark cloud signals one of those pushy, aggressive New South Wales rainstorms. The waves rock her in my arms. I watch her fall asleep, her eyes roaming behind closed eyelids, her upturned face open to some beneficence from above. Her eyes tighten as she loses her way, then flicker open, glancing around sightlessly. Consciousness is everything; all we can ever know or experience comes to us through this brilliant portal. There is nothing outside it, and so losing it is losing everything. Perhaps that's why she resists sleep so fiercely, why she rages against the dying of the light; why, on waking, she will deny that it ever happened. I slipped up, she seems to be saying. I took my eye off the ball. Don't hold it against me.

She comes to in an enclosed space. There are the backs of people's heads, and a big sheet of glass with grayness behind. Her head is on her Daddy's lap. The fingers of her right hand pick up the soft convolutions of a coat, which has been laid over her as she slept. Something has changed, but she has no memory of how it was before, and all that registers is a diffuse sadness. The red plastic seats are rocking; her father is rocking. Then she remembers: she is on the big boat that was going fast across the water. It is the light that has changed. She is inside now, and it is raining.

An old lady is watching her. She is sitting across the space between the two banks of seats, pointing her eyes at her. Athena closes her eyes, so that the old lady will not be able to see her. It is so easy to make yourself invisible. Then she opens her eyes again and sees that the old lady is still there. She has white hair and a brown face. She is as old as Nanna, which is as old as Jesus and the dinosaurs.

"I'd like one of those cuddles." The old lady stretches her hands out. "You coming?"

Athena swivels around on the seat and snuggles in closer to the warm lap that has been supporting her.

"What's your name, sweetheart?"

She says it clearly, but still the old lady asks her again.

A-the-na. Big people have to be spoken to so loudly. Now the old lady is reaching into her handbag and opening her hand to reveal a colorful marble.

"Do you like magic?" she asks.

Athena nods. She recognizes the word, but she doesn't really know what magic is. People seem to know all about her without her ever having seen them before. It's all magic to her.

"Do you want to come and see?"

"It's all right," her daddy reassures her. "You can have a look."

Shyly she gets down from her seat and takes a step toward the lady's seat. The old lady hands her the marble, which looks like a yellow-and-green eye.

"Now, hide it in one of your hands. Don't tell me, now!"

Athena cups the marble in one palm with both hands held wide open. Gently the lady closes both sets of fingers for her. She then says um and ah several times and screws up her face. She is sad because she wants her marble back. Athena opens both hands again.

"Now watch," the old lady says.

She takes the marble, pops it into her mouth, and swallows it. Just like that! Athena looks back at her daddy, who looks very surprised. The lady takes a deep breath and puts a fist up to the side of Athena's face. She feels something hard and warm against her skin. "There," the lady says, pulling the marble out of Athena's ear and blowing on it. "Now, *you* show me some magic."

Athena is speechless. Maybe the lady will just go away, or maybe her daddy will say something to the lady. The lady looks nice but she is making Athena feel scared. She hears a bump and feels the boat shake. She looks at the lady, who yells, "Balmain East!" Then they are going. She follows her daddy toward the steps, then turns to wave good-bye. People are strange. You never know what they are going to do. You never know what to do once they have done it, but you know you are supposed to do something.

"Looks like we've just missed the rain," her daddy is saying.

She slips on the wet jetty and starts running up the slope. In the playground there is a pirate ship you can climb up. Her daddy is a shark and she has to run away from him. He is not a very good shark, though. He keeps stopping to look out at the big ships docked across the water and write things in his black book. She is the pirate captain sailing for Sydney. She will live in this Australia in a house with her mummy and daddy, and she will have a birthday party and she will be an Echidna and her name will be Francesca. Things will keep happening and it will feel happy and sometimes sad, and then she will be a boy and as old as Daddy and then she will be a lady and as old as the old lady on the ferry. The future is all these things that are going to happen. She can see everything, from up here.

Eleven

BELIEVE ME

Telling the Truth About Other Minds

A re you sure you brushed your teeth?"

"*What?*" Her tone suggests a resentment at being disturbed, rather than an apology for mishearing.

"I said, are you sure you brushed your teeth?"

We're sitting on the wooden sun-lounger next to our winter-blanketed swimming pool. Athena is having a pretend picnic with her sandbox toys and is periodically serving me delicacies in a cracked plastic bucket. It is a cold afternoon in May, and the sky over Turramurra is marbled like the iris of an eye.

"I told you a million times. I *brushed* my *teeth*."

"It's just that . . ."

It's quite right that she has told me. But I know, and she has recently come to know, that telling doesn't make the told thing true. In fact, it's because she has told me so insistently that I am asking her again. When you understand something about the differences between people's minds, you learn how talk can put a picture of the world into a place where it has no right to be. At two and three-quarters, Athena understands the power of words to shape a belief in another person's mind. She has learned how to lie.

"It's just that I didn't see you do them."

"I tell you something," she says. "I brush my teeth in the *maw*-ning."

How Australian we all are now. The first time I heard her twist the vowel of *nine*, I foolishly thought she had acquired a twang of West Country. She was pretty much accentless when we left, and so there were no hard Durham vowels for the new way of talking to fight against. I had only just gotten used to the fact that she would grow up speaking differently from me, a southerner, and now here's a new reality for me to absorb. If we were to stay here, apply for citizenship, and emigrate, she would grow up sounding like any regular Aussie kid.

"You brushed them when Daddy wasn't there?"

"Uh-huh."

Of course Daddy wasn't there. The lie wouldn't work otherwise. She now knows that she must *hide* the deceptive act from me. If I witness events for myself, then my own processes of belief formation—the mechanisms that take in sensory information and sculpt a representation of the state of the world—will expose any fibs she might throw my way. If I see it with my own eyes, it makes no difference what you might tell me otherwise. The proof of this new understanding came a few days ago, when we were getting ready for one of our outings into the city. I could tell that she had something on her mind: she had that guiltily absorbed expression that I've only just started to see on her, the weight of thoughts that need to be hidden. Until now, she has blithely assumed that anything that goes on in her head is on public view—look at how she talks to others on the phone, for example, describing her ongoing actions with no acknowledgment that the other is blind to what she's doing. Now, though, she is beginning to understand that her thoughts are her own. Keep them quiet, and no one need ever know.

She went into the kitchen, telling me to go on upstairs without her.

I stood on the stairs and watched her in the mirror, which gave a partial view of the drawer unit she was heading for. It felt wrong to spy on her when her command of the dark arts was still so unimpressive, but I thought it was an important lesson for her as well: you're not the only one who can indulge in deception. I watched her go to a drawer of the unit and take out a resealable polythene sandwich bag, a favorite plaything in which, for a few weeks now, she has been secretly stashing her most precious trinkets. Then she caught sight of me. Her first reaction was to try to salvage the attempt to mislead me, by quickly tucking the bag out of sight behind her back. She had not only tried to manipulate my beliefs by sending me on upstairs without her (and thus blindsiding me), but she had also tried to continue the manipulation by hiding the bag from my view. It was an enacted version of her verbal porkies: she was representing the world as it was not, and hoping I would adopt that erroneous representation for myself.

Small wonder, then, that children's early skills at deception have been taken as precursors of a true theory of mind. Understanding how a belief is shaped by perception, and knowing what to do to instill such a belief in another person's brain, shows not just an understanding that other minds differ, but also a grasp of *how* they differ: how their contents might diverge from one's own. Athena knew that, if she stopped me from seeing something, I couldn't form a true belief about it. I would be unknowledgeable as well as unsighted. When our interactions turned to collaboration rather than conflict, her sensitivity to my ignorance could have more positive results. When she was not yet two, we needed Jake (one of her beloved Tweenies toys) for a pretend tea party. I headed off to the living room, believing him to be buried in the pile of toys in the corner. "In nere," she said, pointing immediately toward the study. *In there.* She seemed to appreciate that I had a mistaken belief about Jake's whereabouts and that I was acting on it. We pass through the world on the basis of our best information. Our knowledge is partial, and it sometimes leads us astray.

In many psychologists' opinion, this newly acquired understanding of others' ignorance would still not be quite enough to make Athena a true mind reader. Here's another, more formal game we played recently. I took two of her Tweenies dolls, Bella and Fizz, and sat them down on the floor in front of two lidded baskets, yellow and green. Athena then witnessed a routine in which Bella hid a chocolate in the yellow basket and went out to play. While Bella was off the scene, Fizz was seen to take the chocolate out of the yellow basket and move it to the green one, replacing both lids. Bella then arrived back from her outing, wanting her chocolate. After checking that Athena remembered where the chocolate was in the first place, and where it was in reality now, I asked her where Bella would look. Responding as most two- and three-year-olds would do, she pointed to the green basket (the one the chocolate had been secretly moved to). She seemed unable to represent Bella's false belief about the chocolate's location and use it to predict the doll's understandably wrong-headed behavior. Older children correctly judge that Bella will think—because she has seen no evidence to make her revise her belief—that the chocolate is where she left it (in the yellow basket). More than just being sensitive to ignorance, they can represent the *content* of that ignorance: the false beliefs, which, on the basis of incomplete information, actors in our human drama often entertain.

False-belief tasks, as they have become known, deliver robust findings. Universally, across cultural contexts and experimental settings, three-year-olds mostly fail them; four-year-olds mostly pass. So compelling is the evidence for this watershed in children's mind reading that many cognitive scientists have looked for biological or genetic causes. Perhaps something in the brain, charged with a fairly narrow set of mind-related responsibilities, lies dormant for the first few years of life and then switches on late in the preschool years. A module, in other words, underpinning our ability to predict and explain people's behavior on the basis of their internal states. More plausible, for a variety of reasons, is the idea of some innate structure allowing the brain to process social information and build up knowledge about the rules that underlie it. Nurture interacts with nature in allowing children to develop a body of core knowledge, which they can then use in unpicking the complexities of human social interaction. Children must surely come to understand other minds by interacting with them. By talking to them, listening to them, and seeing how they differ and converge, children can learn about what kinds of things minds are.

Acquiring a theory of mind, then, has much in common with acquiring other kinds of understanding. You start out with some basic foundation stones of knowledge and build on them, using the evidence you have drawn from your own researches to adapt and elaborate your existing knowledge structures. Piaget famously characterized children as little scientists, constantly constructing new theories about how the world works and testing them out through action. With all this talk of theory construction, Piaget has been accused of remaking children in his own image. Actually, some have argued that it should be the other way around: rather than children being like scientists, professional scientists are like big children who are simply applying childlike curiosity to the frontiers of knowledge. Whichever way the analogy works, it is certain that children do not learn about other minds from a process of solipsistic scientific endeavor. To construct a theory of mind, you need to build up a database of practical understanding about how people work, and use it to develop organized bodies of knowledge about the beliefs, desires, and intentions that make folk do what they do.

What sort of data do these little scientists need? One approach to this question is to focus on the natural differences that occur between children. If you can work out how such individual differences relate to other important features of children's lives, such as their social experience or genetic makeup, then you have a chance of understanding why some children acquire a theory of mind more quickly than others. As with any psychological variable, children of the same age will differ in their performance on theory of mind tasks. An important measure of any such variability, known as "variance," can be analyzed statistically to see how it is affected by factors such as genetics or life experiences. A recent study of twins found the genetic contribution to five-year-olds' theory of mind ability to be tiny in comparison with social and environmental influences. When it comes to mind reading, how your genes are configured is of much less importance than how your environment is. One obvious environmental influence is family size: the more people you have around you in the family, the richer your opportunities for learning how other minds differ. Brothers and sisters are also potent sources of conflict, which parents might try to resolve by making reference to the mental states of the combatants ("He took your Transformer because he thought you'd finished with it"). Sure enough, some studies report that children from bigger families, particularly those with older siblings, show a slight advantage in mind reading. In gathering the data they need, these little scientists don't even need to leave home.

And yet singletons like Athena learn about mind as well, so there must be more to it than the mind puzzles posed by all those inscrutable brothers and sisters. The list of influences proposed to affect theory of mind development is impressive, ranging from the quality of the emotional interactions that babies have with their mothers to children's mastery of particular kinds of sentence structure. What all of these important activities have in common is that they impart information about other people's private thoughts and beliefs. Humans hide their mental states in all sorts of ways, but they also have many channels for revealing them, the most eloquent of which is the language they use. For a patient listener, gathering information about other people's mental states is a simple business. If you want to know what's on a person's mind, just listen to her talk.

. . .

I wish we could go for a swim."

She looks out at the pool blanket, where two mynahs are having a bath in a puddle of rainwater. For most of the autumn we've been dragging its insulated mass across at night, trying to preserve what remains of the summer warmth. My last swim in there was an exhilarating lesson in whole-body coldness that seemed to loosen something in my head. But since the cold snap arrived earlier this month, the blanket has been drawn across permanently. The worst thing is the way it has obliterated an entire landscape of procrastination. Back in the summer, there was always a filter that needed cleaning or a suction pipe to be nudged back into motion. When I had run out of ideas for wasting time inside the house, there was usually something small and fluttery to rescue from the swimming pool using the long-handled tadpole-net accessory.

"Do you remember when we used to sit on the step in the water and drink pink champagne?"

She nods thoughtfully. "I wish we could go on that holiday again."

The air has the distinctive scent of winter in Australia: wood smoke mingling with suburban eucalyptus. Athena is wearing the blue fleece we bought her in Port Douglas, with the word "Australia" spelled out in letters formed from indigenous animals. Last night she sat and picked out the letters, which, because she was still wearing it, were all upside-down: *A* for Athena, *S* for snake, *R* for bunny rabbit. Her breath still smells faintly stale.

"Do you remember that time you told me you'd washed your hands after you'd been for a wee, when you hadn't?"

Her thoughtful look has turned to guilt. To me, that's the surest sign that she can represent what I might be thinking about her. Mind-blind creatures don't do guilty looks.

"I don't know. *N* for *don't know*."

I somehow doubt that she's answering the question.

"Do you remember how it made you feel that time, when you didn't tell the truth?"

"A bit sad . . ."

She thinks the lesson through. The reason you don't tell lies to people, or say nasty things to them, is not primarily for any painful consequences it might have for you. You restrain yourself because the recipient of your unpleasantries will feel hurt. The trouble is, you need a theory of mind, or something very like it, to work out that equation. In our hurry to grab the frailest thread of mind reading skill and pull it for all it is worth, we overdo it. Clonking me over the head with a storybook in the middle of the night is wrong because sleep deprivation "makes Daddy feel poorly and sad." Running around the house shouting "Kill! Kill!" makes Mummy "feel unhappy inside." Hitting, or being messy, or ignoring reasonable requests: they all press the button of parental sadness. We've sworn off smacking, but we are past masters at emotional blackmail.

She goes over to the trampoline and kicks off in a flail of blond curls. She wants to keep talking as she bounces: easy enough for her, with her hours of practice on her borrowed trampoline, but disconcerting for the person left on solid ground. Our conversations used to be awkward joint commentaries on the flow of her attention, all the desired things and mini-crises that crashed through her mind from minute to minute, about which I could only offer a spectator's opinion. Now, though, we have a meeting of minds. I feel open with her, not crabby and pressured like I do with adults. She's two and three-quarters, and I feel as close to her as I do to anyone.

"Lenore, Alyssa, and Faye think I'm coming to nursery, but I'm not."

I note another quiet breakthrough. If you judge her on what she says rather than her performance on a laboratory test, then she has just demonstrated a mastery of false belief. She has shown that she can represent what her nursery nurses will believe on the basis of false expectations. Lenore, Alyssa, and Faye think Athena is coming to nursery because they don't know (haven't been notified, or had any other inkling of the fact) that she isn't. Psychologists Karen Bartsch and Henry Wellman have made an intensive study of the "contrastives" that occur in young children's speech: utterances that, for example, incorporate both what a person believes about a state of affairs and how the situation is in reality. They found that children typically start producing such utterances some time before they would pass a false-belief test. Just as performance on search tasks doesn't tell the whole story about infants' understanding of objects, so laboratory tests of theory of mind probably make additional demands that obscure children's true abilities. As with her precocious real-world reasoning about the missing Jake, Athena's everyday abilities have just outstripped her formal performance.

But then again, language is particularly good at representing different points of view. Language's special ability to capture the to-and-fro of perspectives is one reason it has been attributed such a critical role in the development of social understanding. Researchers have found that simply exposing children to conversations in which different perspectives are presented, even when there is no explicit mention of mind-stuff like beliefs and desires, can boost children's false-belief performance. Maybe those environmental influences on theory of mind all boil down to the ways in which families—mothers, fathers, siblings, and beyond—express points of view in language. Perhaps some mums and dads are good at it, and others not so good.

"No. You're not going today."

"Why?"

"Because we're having a Daddy-day."

"Why?"

I notice that she has stopped bouncing. Just as I did when I spied on her as a fetus, I take a slowdown in her movements to betray an increase in mental effort.

"Well, you know what it is that I do. I don't go out to work like other daddies."

"Why?"

"Because I do my work at home. I'm writing a book."

I try to think what that means to her. To do that, I have to project myself imaginatively into her shoes; I have to perform a quick mental audit of what she understands (the long walks, the hours spent hunched over a notebook) and what she doesn't. For the brief moment that I am trying to get into her head, I have to enter her perspective as I would try to enter that of a character in a work of fiction. I have to novelize her. Perhaps that is what she is trying to do as well. In order to read my mind, she has to novelize me as I am novelizing her: work out where I am coming from, and then run a sort of mental simulation of my point of view, asking herself what *she* would do if she were standing where I'm standing. Some have argued that this is precisely what mind reading requires: the simulation of another person's thought processes on your own mental apparatus. In which case, theory of mind is a misnomer. It has more to do with fiction-writing than it does with science.

"Well, I work at home, too," she says.

"Really? What do you do?"

"I write a book. I write a book like Daddy."

She nods enthusiastically. It's not a lie this time, so much as a leap of imagination. If understanding others is all about running mental simulations, then it should be no surprise if little mind readers spend as much time in the world of make-believe as they do in the world of solid objects. The imagination, wrote William Hazlitt, must carry me out of myself into the feelings of others by one and the same process by which I am thrown forward into my future being. Following that shining thread of the self means being able to imagine things as they might be, rather than how they really are. Sometimes, along the way, the thread gets entangled. By imagining who I am, she becomes it. In mirroring me, Athena finds a reflection of herself.

Twelve

IT'S ABOUT A LITTLE MOUSE

The Story of Story

She wasn't really writing a book, but she was reading plenty. The owners of the house we were renting had left a lifetime's supply, and Athena was working through them methodically and, for much of the time, in solitude. The days when she would let us read to her were apparently over. *Listening* to stories was for wimps; she wanted to be doing it for herself. Although she could now pick out some letters of the alphabet, she couldn't yet put them together into words, and so her "reading" to herself was a mix of free-form improvisation and parroting of those bits of the story she could remember from our own renditions. "Trevor's Birthday," she would announce, as though she were trailing Radio 4's afternoon play. This was all about presentation. She sat cross-legged on the carpet and held the book before her in a hymn-book V, as she had seen her nursery nurses doing. "One-ee pon-ee time," she would begin, turning the pages quickly with only the briefest glances at their contents. "The little girl, and the rabbit . . ." and then there would be a lot of *buts*. A story was a sequence of descriptions, with a formulaic beginning and end and a telescopic chain of propositions for a middle. She could read them backward, and their message would be the same: an affirmation of temporal continuity, of the relentless flow of one-thing-after-anotherness.

Books went further than that, of course. They were memory albums, snapshots of moments in our past. She drew from them the same musty weight of nostalgia as we, her parents, did from the pop songs of our youth. When she pulled one of those slim, mushy-cornered volumes from the shelf, she pulled down a context of associated memories, often centered around the banal physicality of these heavy lumps of cardboard and bound paper. Months or even years after the event, she could recall how she had caught her finger in one, accidentally stabbed her cheek with the corner of another. They were postcards from her past, the heirlooms of her toddlerhood. They were also full of ritual and predictability. Everyone ended up asleep. The bigger the adventure, the more certain the author could be about pulling the plug on a bunch of exhausted characters in the end. The sleep message had all the inevitable power of a sermon, about a judgment no one can gainsay. Sleep, little reader: this is what *you* should be doing. No one escaped from its drowsy clutches. Just to break the monotony, I sometimes longed to read of a group of cuddly animal hell-raisers staying up and partying till dawn.

Not that the content of the books seemed to matter much. The pages were a canvas on which she could impose whatever structure she wanted. If she had chosen to, she could have made a story out of the metropolitan telephone directory. She would pull a baby's ABC board book from the shelf in a bookshop and start riffing around its bold, bright concepts. At home, she did requests. She would pick up our *Rough Guide to Australia*, stand on a chair, and flick hurriedly through its pages, as though she were the teacher directing a class toward a lesson in a textbook. She *was* the teacher, of course. "Allbody sit down!" she would intone. "Can you sing . . . the Galumph Puzzle?" "No," Lizzie and I would chorus, "we don't know that one." That set her flicking some more. If the camcorder was on her, she would slip glances at it with a prim, self-pleased, pursed-lipped smile. Her hair was still long and curly at the back, but had had a severe fringe-trim that suddenly gave her a look of authority. I didn't think I would mess with this teacher.

"Do you know a song about a Christmas tree?"

"No."

"Well, I'll sing it and you clap at the end."

"Okay."

She sang: "It's *about* a *Christ*mas *tree* . . ."

The world's literatures begin in song. Storytelling begins around a campfire, with warm sounds to ward off the darkness. Athena was reinventing that primeval genre for herself. Story presented her with structure, pegs upon which to hang ideas. Music provided a beat that drove it forward into the unknown. She didn't get her ideas for stories from books so much as impose story on the raw material that books presented her with. The prosaics of beginnings, middles, and endings gave her imagination wings.

It is partly the evidence for children's narrative drives that has made psychologists appreciate the importance of story for thinking in general. As much as it is an information-processing device, the human mind is now seen as a storytelling machine. This "narrative turn" in psychology is a recent development, but it probably had its roots in some simple experiments on how people process unfamiliar tales. Sir Frederick Bartlett, first professor of experimental psychology at the University of Cambridge, conducted a series of studies in the 1920s designed to shed light on the brain's capacity to organize incoming information. He presented his subjects with a North American Indian folktale called "The War of the Ghosts," which involved a battle between ghostly warriors that would have sounded quite alien to his Cambridge participants. By looking at the errors they made in their retellings of the story, Bartlett found convincing evidence that people fit an unusual story to existing knowledge structures. For example, they would expunge the supernatural element of the story and make it fit with their own characteristically Western understanding of how the soul survives the body after death. Bartlett concluded that our recollections of our own lives, like our recollections of an unfamiliar story, are constructed according to our knowledge of the prototypical narratives in our culture. When we try to make sense of our own past, we make it fit with the stories we already know, even if that means recalling the information inaccurately.

Psychologists now use the term "scripts" to describe the prototypical story structures that help us organize incoming information. When we go into a restaurant, for example, the context automatically activates a script for the events—being shown to a seat, handed a menu and wine list—that can be expected to unfold. What's more, we know about these story structures from an early age. Using carefully constructed interviews, developmental psychologists have found that children as young as three can give ordered and generalized accounts of what happens in prototypical events such as restaurant-going. At nearly three, Athena had the dining-out script down to a fine art. In the guise of a waitress, she would come up to us with a piece of paper and a pen, "write down" our orders, disappear off to the kitchen, and return moments later with a plate of "pasta and sugar" or "banana and sandwich mixed together." She knew that things happened in a certain order—that you didn't bring the customers' food, for example, before they'd even been shown to their seats—suggesting that she had abstracted a general story structure from all her different, unique experiences of restaurants. As an apprentice in the culture's way of doing things, she was already skilled. Going to a restaurant was not a baffling experience for her, because she knew the routine; she knew what to expect.

In a sense, you can think of scripts as our modern-day myths. They are the stories we carry around with us, the truths that our culture hands down to us, authorless and universal. Children pick them up from books, TV, and their own experience of ordered cultural scenarios, and project them back, in their enthusiastic narrativizing. But where story really makes a difference is in the way it gives toddlers a handle on time. In a story, stuff happens in a temporal order. For a child trying to understand herself as an entity with a past, a present, and a future, keeping track of what happened, and when, must be a formidable challenge. Athena's experience of how minds differ had given her the basis for splitting ideas away from their underlying reality, and thus escaping from the chains of the here and now. Story gave her a structure in which she could order these ideas in sequence.

We saw the proof in the way she narrativized herself. When I asked her about her past, I sensed a conspicuous effort to impose a story. It was around this time that we started our bedtime routine of "What We Did Today." Lizzie and I would lie down on the bed on either side of her and together we would go through the day's events. Beyond its value as a moment of shared intimacy, this was a way of putting some good research into practice. Psychologists Katherine Nelson and Robyn Fivush have shown that children get involved in conversations about past events soon after their second birthdays, and gradually take on ever-greater responsibility for joint storytelling about the past. Furthermore, parents' willingness or skill in supporting these dialogues has been shown to have a big effect on children's developing storytelling abilities. Longitudinal studies, following the same samples of families over periods of time, show that parents who have an "elaborative" style in their interactions have children who produce more-sophisticated memory narratives. Adopting an elaborative style means producing orienting information (details on where the event occurred, and who the actors in the drama were) and evaluative information (all the emotional details of how things looked, seemed, and felt that gave the event personal significance). More than simply reiterating the crucial information, our efforts were about allowing Athena to step back into the event and reexperience it. This was her drama, and we were helping her take center stage.

In our early attempts to reflect Athena's life to her, we tended to draw on an explicit narrative structure. One surefire way of settling her, if she was upset or overtired at bedtime, was to put her in a fairy tale. She found her appearance in a story as reassuring as she had once found her reflection in a mirror. *Once upon a time, there was a little girl named Athena who lived with her mummy and daddy in a house with a yellow door . . .* Nothing much happened in this story, except for the affirmation of our family values of togetherness, mutual love and respect, and the irrelevance of worldly fortunes. But it worked magic. In telling them stories, we ask children to identify with a character, to enter their perspective and see the world through their eyes. This was the easiest perspective of all for Athena to enter: her own. It was comforting, homely, and self-affirming, like going over old photographs. In their detailed study of the "crib speech" produced by one toddler named Emily, Katherine Nelson and colleagues showed that many of the improvised stories Emily told herself before sleep were simple recollections of the day's events. Like an old lady in a nursing home, she warded off the darkness with her memories. At both ends of life, the past can be a powerful comforter.

"What We Did Today" didn't begin *Once upon a time . . .* We didn't frame it as a bedtime story, but it nevertheless had a narrative structure. It looked like a story, even if it didn't start off like one. As well as the orienting information that established details of temporal and geographical location ("It was this morning. We were at the shops"), we put in the same background information that novelists would use to set a scene. Evaluative statements give characters the motives that fiction writers are always concerned to supply: if we know that someone is scared, or happy, it makes their actions easier to understand. We also glued our narratives together with what linguists call "cohesion devices": temporal markers such as *next, then,* and *after,* as well as more-complex causal connectives such as *because, if,* and *so.* Gradually these characteristics of an elaborative style began to feed through into her own stories. The *buts* and *thens* that threaded together her own improvised narratives were proof that she, too, could do cohesion. As story became more tractable, so life became more tractable. She could talk about it at one remove while remaining centered in it. Like those Hollywood stars who can hop from behind the camera to in front of it, she was directing this movie as well as starring in it.

But stories didn't only work with past events. Mental time travel had a forward gear as well as a reverse. By talking together with adults about the past, children are probably doing important work on their abilities to project themselves into the future. Thinking about the future requires that you have that sense of the temporal order of events, which allows you to organize your experiences before they even happen. In Nelson's study, Emily's crib speech often focused on her attempts to understand events that were forthcoming, such as a trip to the doctor or the seaside, as well as times that were gone. Stories were about what was going to happen, as well as what had.

We are sitting downstairs in our living room. It is a cold night in late June and the big wood-burning stove is glowing. Athena is in her white pajamas decorated with twirling pink ballerinas, and is flicking through the pages of the *UBD Complete Motoring Atlas of Australia*, making up a song about Lightning Ridge. At least, it starts off being about the mythical opal-mining town, and then metamorphoses into a song about the adventures of a little boy named Sammy:

> *Then he went in the car*
> *Then he got home*
> *Then the traffic lights*
> *Then the green traffic lights . . .*

She has already sung me some "songs" from the *Rough Guide*, on the topics of Australia, kangaroos, koalas, and a little mouse who says nothing but "Ding dong." These musical stories have involved a lot of running around, clapping, and diving on to the sofa. Earlier, in the bath, she was telling the future story of her forthcoming trip across the outback, ending it, reassuringly, with our safe return to the "green house" in Turramurra. We have been in the country for five months. Time is running out for our antipodean sabbatical. Winter, we're told, is a good time to see the country, unhindered by flies, sweaty tourists, and baking summer temperatures. Rug up at night, though: it gets cold out there.

For me, the outback means Lightning Ridge. I have heard talk of it on trains, in pubs, and in the enthusiastic chat of well-traveled back-packers. People who come back from Lightning Ridge come back with their eyes ever so slightly wider open. Haunting backpacker trails as a nostalgic family man is one thing I have tried to avoid: it is like refusing to accept that the party is over. But this is no ordinary backpacker trail. I don't understand it, but I feel that some past version of me is out there, in this outback town I have never visited; that, in some imagined continuation of my gap-year travels, my twenty-one-year-old self found its future lying there like an opal in the dirt. I have a story to fit together, too. Back then I felt incorporeal, adrift in time; I felt as though I could vanish from the face of the earth at any moment and no one would ever know. It can't be impossible for that life to bleed into this one. I want to understand those connections and rewire them in imagination: to see how the person I was became the person I am now, and how he might have become someone else. Narrative psychologists tell us that we are happier people when we can make sense of our lives in these terms, by sifting through these dreamy continuations until we find a story that makes sense.

That's the point about story. It gives us a handle on how things might have been, as well as how they are. Stories can be about what is not true. There are different ways in which things can be not true: because they haven't happened yet, or because they cannot possibly happen. Our trip across the outback is simply something that hasn't yet happened; making that trip in a blue car, as Athena has been describing in her stories, is more in the realm of the not-possible, since our Toyota Camry is bottle green. She needs a place in which the not-true can flourish, free from the pedantic demands of objective reality. She finds it in imaginative contexts, often created in collaboration with others, in which there is an agreement that a thing can become true just because someone says it is. Children's imaginative narratives take different forms—stories, pretending scenarios, role-playing, engaging with imaginary friends—but they all share certain key features. They are all a form of fictionalizing: the creation, as in a novel, of an invented world in which different rules may apply.

Like most children, Athena made her first forays into these imaginary worlds when she was about a year old. Just before her first birthday, she responded appropriately to a suggestion to "brush her hair" with a wooden spoon she was holding. Although the idea came from us, she showed that she could, in imagination, substitute one object for something else. She was demonstrating an early ability to use symbols, to make one thing (a wooden spoon) stand for another (a hairbrush). If toddlers' early symbolic play requires the presence of a concrete object to work upon, their pretending abilities soon break free of the shackles of materiality and create fantasy objects, actions, and locations wherever they please. In a pretend tea party at eighteen months, Athena would happily follow my suggestion to pick up and "eat" nonexistent pieces of cake. Our tea parties were civilized affairs, where real-world conventions (about passing the sugar and serving people in order) applied. Far from representing the outpouring of an unfettered, wish-fulfilling imagination that has no contact with reality, pretend play involves social codes that make somber demands on the people involved. One prominent social convention is that, if someone makes a stipulation about how the pretense should proceed, you go along with it. As soon as I had made the suggestion about the nonexistent cake, it would have been rude not to acquiesce. Athena soon understood that she possessed the same power to impose meaning on pretend events. When she lined up five cosmetics bottles on the floor and said, "This is a train," I complied obediently. When the storyteller clears her throat, we listen.

Part of that compliance with others' pretense stipulations means following the causal logic of the imagined events. If we're having a pretend tea party with sandbox toys, we follow the rules of the tea party, not the rules of the sandbox. If I spill imaginary tea on to an imaginary teddy bear, the imaginary teddy bear gets wet. As well as having a causal logic—effects follow causes just as they do in the real world—these imagined scenarios have an emotional logic. The characters who inhabit them feel the impact of events just as they would if they were real people. Furthermore, when we participate in these scenarios, we are invited to align ourselves with a particular character's perspective, and we remain true to that perspective: we respond emotionally in the same way that the protagonist would. If Athena insists that she is my mummy and I am her little baby, I do as babies do: I cry, I wet myself, I respond to her comfort-giving with joy. One of the rules of the game is that you stay in character. As in a work of fiction, characters are motivated. They respond to circumstances in appropriate ways, setting off events that are themselves plausible and meaningful responses by other characters. Because our imaginary worlds mostly follow the rules of the real one, these causal chains are secure. One thing leads to another, even if the things themselves have no basis in reality.

It seems, then, that complex pretense and role-playing draw on the same novelizing skills that mind reading appears to. Although they may take some of their structure from ready-made scripts—the routines of preparing a meal, for example, or changing a baby's diaper—Athena's play scenarios are flexible, creative, and rule-bound. Because they obey the dual logic of physical causation and emotional response, they cannot help but take the form of a story. These days she even creates characters of her own, with a skill that would make any creative writing tutor proud. One sunny day in June, we get a visit from "Elizabeth." Elizabeth rolls into our lives in a little toy car and says, "It's nice to meet you." She turns out to be a chatty little imaginary person. She tells us that she is two, that she has a brother called Declan (aged five) and sisters called Sammy (nine) and Rachel (fifteen). She has a fast blue car (also called Sammy), in which her mummy (a lecturer) drives to work while her daddy (a writer) stays at home. "That's interesting," I tell her; "you should meet my little girl, Athena; I'm sure you'd get on well." Athena/Elizabeth grins excitedly, as she always does when she can hardly dare believe that she is fooling a grown-up. This is not a masterpiece of creative effort—it draws heavily on facts, such as names, ages, and birthdays, that apply to her or to those around her—but the leap into imagination is complete. So too is the pleasure of the pretense. At one point Athena/Elizabeth even calls out for herself (the daughter we have been telling her about) to come downstairs and play. We can pretend to be ourselves as willingly as we slip into the shoes of others. Victorian psychologist James Sully described the case of two sisters, aged five and seven, who spent the afternoon pretending to be sisters. Sully noted that the game had a strangely civilizing influence: the pretend sisters were much nicer to each other than the real sisters had been. Be yourself for a change, the lesson seems to be. You might like what you find.

Although Athena will not take this next step for a while, older children progress from impersonating imaginary characters to engaging with them in elaborate dialogues and collaborations. Recent surveys have shown that a large proportion of children in Western cultures report having imaginary friends, and that these reports are usually validated independently by parents. Children's made-up companions can be demanding charges. Family mealtimes frequently have a ghost at the feast: the empty place laid for a little girl named Lolly, for example, who carries balloons around but does not like Korean food, or Jelly Monster, a monster made in a jelly mold who is "as big as a school." Long-suffering parents have been known to have to turn back halfway through a car journey, just because someone's imaginary friend has been left behind. Far from being a sign of introversion or strangeness, imaginary companions seem a natural extension of children's close engagement with the not-real.

What is the draw of these imaginary worlds? Research on children's imagination has long been haunted by a paradox. Given that there is so much at stake, for the survival of the species as much as for any individual child, in being able to accurately process life-or-death information about food sources, predators, and so on, why are children such suckers for potentially dangerous flights of fancy? For a long time, the Freudian orthodoxy (exemplified, for example, in Bruno Bettelheim's account of the enduring appeal of fairy tales) was that children's imagination gives free rein to the unconscious desires and wishes that are typically stymied by the strictures of real life. Frustrated by her own impotence, for example, Athena could overturn the balance of power in the family by becoming Mummy and putting me in diapers. Children's unconscious minds act out their fantasies in pretense, in the way that adults' wishes come true in their dreams.

Developmental psychologist Paul Harris has argued that the Freudian account simply doesn't add up. For one thing, Freud's explanation of children's fantasy-making sees it as a primitive mode of thinking that holds sway before infants have any understanding of objective reality. In fact, children's sophisticated responses to the social conventions of pretense prove that they are far from the little id-crazed solipsists envisaged by Freud. Furthermore, the idea that imagination is driven by primordial emotions fails to stand up to scrutiny. Children do not create imaginary companions, for example, just because they lack real ones. Rather, children who are skilled at role-playing and who spend time inventing friends for themselves turn out to show better social understanding than their less-dreamy peers.

Harris argues that the solution to the puzzle might lie in some experimental work on adults' responses to imaginary situations. Children's biologically risky fondness for unreality maps neatly on to another paradox: the question of how adult readers can become emotionally absorbed in a narrative while at the same time being fully aware of its fictional status. Psychologists have argued that this happens because readers, under the expert guidance of the author, create a mental model of the events described in the narrative and plunge into it wholeheartedly. The creation of these "storyworlds," as they are known, has been the subject of some vigorous research. Experimental studies have shown that readers often make inferences that go beyond the words on the page, and use their own background knowledge to fill in gaps in the author's literal description. This is because, in responding imaginatively to a narrative, readers create and constantly update a mental model of the situation, the characters involved, and their motivations and actions. Readers' minds don't represent the author's words: they represent the author's imagined world. When reading, they behave as though they were within that world, rather than looking in on it from the outside.

The technical term for these storyworlds is "situation models." When confronted with a new narrative, readers quickly assimilate instructions for building up a model of the world it describes. In a way, their responses are programmed, just as software programs a computer, by the author's instructions. It is not the author's actual turns of phrase that the reader is interested in (not at this stage, anyway) so much as the instructions they contain for building a storyworld. These instructions contain information in several different dimensions. First, the author provides spatial information that allows the reader to build up a picture of a physical setting. If that information is presented in an inconsistent manner (for example, by providing facts about the spatial layout of a room that don't fit consistently with any one particular perspective), the reader gets lost. Other dimensions include time (what happens when), causation (what causes what), character (who the actors in the story are), and motivation (what drives them to act as they do). A skilled author presents information—the right information, and in the right order—that allows a new reader to quickly and efficiently fill in the details of the model along these five dimensions. As fictional events intrude, readers can update their situation models and make appropriate emotional responses to the ebbs and flows of the plot. Importantly, the reader is also invited to take up a particular position within the model: to side with, or at least identify most strongly with, a particular protagonist, and to interpret events from that position.

The evidence from psycholinguistic experiments shows that readers accept these invitations willingly. For example, we interpret the verbs *come* and *go* from a particular reference point. Something moving toward that reference point *comes*; something moving away from it *goes*. In one study, adults read stories in which the use of these verbs was either consistent or inconsistent with the protagonist's perspective. When an inconsistent verb was used, the subjects read the sentence more slowly, and also made more errors in recall, tending to replace inconsistent verbs with consistent ones. It is because readers are participants in fiction, not spectators, that they can respond emotionally to a heroine's imaginary trials and tribulations as they do.

It is perhaps no surprise that children do something similar when processing narrative. In one study, the *come/go* distinction was presented to three- and four-year-olds in the context of a retelling of the "Little Red Riding Hood" fairy tale. The story first established Little Red Riding Hood, sitting in her bedroom, as the protagonist whose perspective was to be adopted. Characters were then described entering the bedroom, with verbs that were either consistent with Little Red Riding Hood's perspective (her mother *came* in) or inconsistent with it (her mother *went* in). Children made the same errors in recalling the story (replacing inconsistent verbs with consistent ones) as the adult participants had done in the earlier study. The conclusion is that children enter the perspective of a story protagonist as readily as adult readers do, because they are busy building up similar situation models. When Athena empathized with the little rabbit Max, who (in the story we were reading) wore the wrong sort of shirt on his first day at school, it was because she had taken up that position within the model she had constructed. Once in Max's shoes, she responded emotionally just as she would have done if she had really been in that situation.

The mental models that provide the mechanism for a child's reaction to a storybook seem the same, then, as those that underpin their other imaginary worlds. Returning to his question of why such a potentially dangerous capacity should ever have evolved, Harris proposes that our ability to construct situation models of nonpresent events might have been driven, evolutionarily speaking, by our need to process language in all its forms. When our early ancestors began to talk, they used their words to refer to events and situations that were not immediately visible to the eye: a future hunting trip, the presence of a food source some miles away. Making sense of that discourse would have required the construction of revisable situation models. For the modern child, entering into a community of language makes the same demands. The storyworlds that children create in making sense of the discourse of others are the same as they use in talking about the past and future, and in creating the imaginary worlds of pretense, role-playing, and narrative. The little scientist is usurped by the little novelist. Or perhaps, in the end, fiction-making has more than a little of science about it. To get on in the world, the child, like the novelist and the engineer, has to build her models and see how they run.

⌒

THE YOUNG
DOCTOR WHO

Adventures in Time and Space

I spy with my little eye, something beginning with . . . *T.*"

The car rattles and squeaks along a straight road fringed with salt-bush. The blacktop ahead of us is a ladder of heat-mirage, rungs of light and shadow mapping on to undulations in the dead-straight tarmac. Athena is sitting in the back in her booster seat, protected from the brilliant winter sun by a sheet of old muslin hooked in place at the top of her window. Outside the car, an unfixed strip of its fabric flaps in the wind.

"I'll give you a clue. What did Mummy say that we've passed lots of in the last three days? There's one there, and there's one there, and there's a few more over there . . ."

She looks out at the spindly eucalyptus that line the road. They are the most beautiful trees, skinny ladies in flowing dresses.

"Um . . ."

"Athena, where does the kookaburra sit?"

"On the sofa."

"No, the kookaburra in the song. The song you sing at nursery."

"Look, I can clap with my feet! Look, Mummy!"

"Mummy can't look at the moment, sweetheart. She's driving."

There's silence. At nearly three, Athena understands that looking is a straight arrow: if you're paying attention to one thing, you can't also be paying attention to another. But the unknowability of another person's mental content—the idea that she can be holding something in her head that you can't see—is a puzzle that this apprentice mind reader is still struggling with.

"Why?"

"Because we won't get to Lightning Ridge unless someone drives the car."

"Can you remember the song?" Lizzie offers. "*Kookaburra sits in the old gum . . .*"

"Oh."

She muses on this for a few moments. She has taken so enthusiastically to I Spy, we have to wonder whether she has played it before. She likes the to-and-fro of turns, the reassuring safety net its simple rules weave. The only thing she can't grasp is its name: it is variously Ice-Hock, Icing, and Ice Cream. We have been trying to drum into her the fact that initial letters have wide applicability: *T* is for teddy, but it is also, just as appropriately, for telephone, tortoise, and teapot. Having grasped this principle, she can't help applying it promiscuously. Unfamiliar words are strange beasts whose heads you grasp firmly, but whose tails metamorphose into fantastical shapes before your eyes.

"Trees," she says at last.

"You got it! Now it's your turn."

She chooses *T*. I'm sensing a pattern.

"Tractor?" I venture.

She shakes her head.

"Telegraph pole?"

"No! Try again!"

"Could it be . . . trees?" Lizzie suggests.

Athena grins, as though she had just done something extremely clever.

"But that's what *I* just chose. Wouldn't it be better if you chose something different?"

Now Daddy is splitting hairs. There's nothing in the rules of I Spy to say you have to pick something different each time. Mixing up the topics might be in the spirit of the game, but it's not there in the letter.

Victorious in the last bout, Mummy has chosen *stones*. "Something beginning with S."

"Um . . . You give me a clue."

"What do you like picking up?"

"Beetles!"

"That doesn't begin with S."

I mouth the answer to her.

"Stones!" she declaims. "My turn!"

It goes quiet in the back. I can hear the roar of the road, the general rattle-and-hum of the cabin. That familiar cicada-like chirp from somewhere near the back and middle of the roof, which has followed us all the way from Sydney.

"Have you thought of something?"

"Uh-huh!"

"What does it begin with?"

"*A* for *Athena*."

So: something beginning with *A* . . . I look out the passenger window, seeing objects flash up, in my mind's eye, with convenient ghostly name tags, as though I had woken up in an episode of *Sesame Street*. I would like to say ancient ruins, or abbeys, or art galleries, but there aren't any. There is just a tree-scattered plain, flooded with shiny billabongs of heat-haze. In the middle distance, the acacias adjust their configurations in expected ways, flashing past us in close-up, twisting slowly ahead of us farther away. But there is another, changeless world beyond this familiar parallax, impossibly distant, where, as far and as fast as we drive, nothing moves at all.

"Aerials," I venture.

"What? What did you say?"

"Aerials. TV aerials." There are none, not even any houses, but it's all I can think of.

"No-oo. . . ." she says sneakily.

I hear myself sighing. "Are you sure you've thought of something? Something that you can actually see with your eyes right now?"

"Um . . ."

This is drawn-out, thoughtful; self-consciously so. Suddenly she is looking for answers, rather than withholding them.

"Say something else," she says.

"Athena?"

"Is it inside or outside?"

"No, sweetheart. Remember, *you* have to think of something and *we* have to guess it. Are you sure you're thinking of something?"

She nods.

"Okay," I say. "*A* for . . ."

"Is it . . . sky?" she guesses.

Perhaps this is a tall order. *Do you know your own mind?* we're asking her. If you hold a word in your head, and keep quiet about it, do you appreciate that it is a secret only you can know? To get these judgments right, children have to understand quite a lot about how thinking works: not so much *what* other people are thinking (the key to success on standard false-belief tasks), as what kind of thing thinking is. Part of becoming conscious involves understanding something of the workings of your own consciousness. At what age do children realize that thought is a flow of words and images, imperceptible to anyone but the thinker? In one experimental task, we ask children about what is going on inside an experimenter's head while she is silently looking out the window, engaged in no specific activity. Children of Athena's age are reluctant to attribute an ongoing stream of consciousness to an individual who isn't actually doing anything. Four-year-olds, in contrast, are much more likely to acknowledge that the tap of thought doesn't just get turned off in quiet moments. They will judge that ideas and impressions keep flowing through the experimenter's mind, even when there are no external clues to this mental hubbub.

In another respect, Athena knows her own mind too well. As in those phone conversations when she assumes that the person on the other end of the line automatically shares her point of view, her way of looking at the world tends to squeeze out all others. She struggles with I Spy because she struggles with the idea of mental privacy; the world is as she sees it, and can't yet be carved up into different points of view. Piaget called this "egocentrism," and saw it as the main hurdle that children have to overcome before they can do the kinds of rational thinking—geometrical, mathematical, social, moral—that involve considering other perspectives. In his famous phrase, young children are rooted in their own viewpoints. To make further progress in their scientific endeavors, they first have to escape from themselves.

"It's takin' a long *toime.*"

"Do you want to play another game? What about the Counting Game?"

The Counting Game is the one where we each pick an object likely to be seen from the car window—trucks, wind pumps, houses—and score points each time we pass one of our adopted landmarks. It's good for counting practice, of course, and it's also good for ticking off the hours. Like I Spy, it comes with a network of rules that liberate at the same time as they constrain. One of the reasons toddlers appear so bossy is that they have fallen in love with this new way of organizing people's behavior. Armed with a rule, a little person can exert awesome control over a bigger one. "You have to run holding hands," she barks at me, as we while away some moments in a playground. "You have to stand at the top of the steps and when I reach the tree you can come down." A rule is not just Mummy or Daddy telling you to do something; it comes from somewhere transcendental, like God. Under the democracy of a rule, everyone is an equal.

You can apply your rules to the wider world, but you can also turn them back on yourself. When a child can hold a rule in mind and use it to guide her own behavior, she gets a handhold out of her own egocentrism. Rules are about *if* and *then*. They give you a way of structuring time, of orienting yourself within it. Rules give your Tardis self a little nudge into the future. "If the little hand has gone past six, then it's all right to get up." "If I finish my fromage frais, then I can have some chocolate." Rules are stories; they allow events to unfold over time, with plausible contingencies. Pretense has rules (if you are playing at being sisters, you have to follow the rules of sisterhood), although the rules can change at a moment's notice. The games we are using to while away the miles to Lightning Ridge have rules that are on public display, fixed elements of assumed knowledge. When you play a game with rules, you have to leave your egocentrism at the door. As Piaget noted, games with rules are deeply social. It takes two to have a rule; otherwise you should call it something else.

"No, I don't want to play the Counting Game. I want to read."

She flicks through one of the books that lie scattered on the seat beside her. I see her picking out a few *the*s, the one word she can now confidently recognize. The back of the car is littered with books, jigsaw puzzles, sun hats, muslins, towels, water bottles, tissues, baby wipes, coats, pink notebooks, scraps of paper covered with felt-tipped tadpole-people. It is extraordinary that someone so portable should trail so much that is not portable.

"I want to go to Lightning Bridge."

"We *are* going to Lightning Ridge."

"Just now?"

I think about what this journey means to her. We set off this morning from Coonabarabran, deep in rural New South Wales. Some time went by, and we didn't arrive anywhere. Does that mean that we aren't going there anymore? This isn't that classic of childhood impatience, *Are we nearly there yet?* This is something more fundamentally anxious: *Are we still going to that place?* She is asking, *Does that place still exist?* Am I the same person I was when I last asked the question? Have I ever even asked this question before?

If a vehicle sets off from point A with a velocity v, how much time t will elapse before it has covered distance d . . .? As any GCSE student knows, distance, time, and speed are locked together by their mathematical interdependence. At a constant speed, distance unfurls as neatly as time. Within a fixed time period, the distance traveled is proportional to the available speed. Piaget claimed that children must learn to coordinate their schemas of time and distance, much as they use their experience of the world to adapt and coordinate their schemas for acting on objects. In becoming rational beings, children have to learn to do with the objects of thought what they have already achieved in interactions with their objects of play. All those hours of investigating how things fit into containers pay dividends when children are learning how abstract ideas fit together.

Piaget thought that a watershed in this process was reached around the age of six or seven. Before this age, children's imprisonment within their own viewpoint means that they cannot think flexibly enough to tackle some apparently simple reasoning problems. Consider, for example, how they come to understand that the properties of an object can change in two dimensions at the same time. In Piaget's classic "conservation" task, children are asked to judge whether a quantity of material that has been distorted in some way (for example, a beaker of orange juice poured into a tall thin container) remains the same quantity after the transformation. Even though nothing has been added or taken away, preschoolers usually say that the quantities are different after the change. In the orange juice example, they appear not to comprehend that, although the height of the liquid has increased (once it has gone into the taller, thinner container), the width has decreased. They cannot understand that the liquid has changed in two dimensions (height and width) simultaneously. Piaget termed these children "preoperational," because they have not yet acquired the flexible, reversible knowledge structures, or "operations," that are the building blocks of logical thought.

Piaget saw further evidence for his theory in his little participants' judgments about speed, time, and distance. Piaget notes how he was put up to the challenge by a certain Albert Einstein, with whom he shared an academic symposium in 1928. Having already turned the world upside down with his ideas about how speed and time are defined relative to the point from which they are observed, Einstein now wanted to know whether a child's intuitive grasp of time was the basis on which she made judgments of speed and distance, or whether ideas about motion were more fundamental. Picking up on Einstein's challenge, Piaget's Genevan researchers presented children with various scenarios involving moving objects, such as clockwork snails crawling across a table, or two small dolls that were made to pass through tunnels of unequal length. Preoperational children would get hopelessly confused by questions about how long and how far. Failing to take differences in speed, or starting and stopping points, into account, they might judge that something that had traveled farther had also been traveling for more time. Slightly older children could use information about relative speed, such as the fact that one doll had overtaken another, but still tended to answer questions about temporal order in terms of spatial order: that is, interpreting questions about before and after in terms of distance rather than time.

From a modern perspective, Piaget's studies seem a little too wrapped up in the complexities of relativity theory. What if you take speed and distance out of the equation, and simply ask your little Einsteins to judge temporal durations? In one such paradigm, researchers show children a picture of an animal, such as an owl called Barney, who, it is explained, makes a certain kind of sound (a tone lasting half a second). Children are then shown pictures of some other owls who make sounds of differing lengths, some longer, some shorter than Barney's. On each of the test trials, participants have to say whether the sound played is Barney's (the half-second sound) or not. Five-year-olds (the youngest children tested so far) tend to claim that sounds shorter than half a second are Barney's sound: that is, children remember the tone as being shorter than it was in reality. It is as though their own internal clocks are running too fast, causing them to judge that time is passing more quickly than it really is. Those children who pester their parents with pleas of "Are we nearly there yet?" may simply have speeded-up body clocks. Appealing to concrete intervals measured in conventional units of time ("We'll be there in half an hour") is no solution, since a five-year-old's half an hour is quite a bit shorter than that of the person behind the wheel.

Athena's problem was not so much that of a fast-running clock as a difficulty in situating herself within a time frame at all. Philosophers distinguish between two ways of thinking about time: time as relative to a perspective, and time as an absolute ordering of events. Most of our talk about time is perspectival. Past, present, and future only make sense relative to a specific standpoint (the year 2020 is currently part of my future, but one day it will be in my past). Sure enough, many of children's first tryouts in the language of time are perspectival. Athena would use words for relative time before she could deal with days of the week, months, and years, the standard vocabulary of our discourse about absolute time. Something in the past happened "yesterday," no matter how long ago it was. Shortly after our arrival in Australia, she saw a picture of the Eiffel Tower in Ludwig Bemelmans's book *Madeline* and remembered that it was something to do with our marriage. "There, yesterday, I marry Mummy," she announced, retelling an event that had happened almost nine years earlier. In the other direction along time's arrow, she struggled with the word *tomorrow*, and instead everything in the future was scheduled to happen "the next day." "The next day," she would proclaim, "I go to my nursery." When it suited her, she could do *later*, as in, "I'll brush my teeth later." I suspected, though, that *later* was less about perspectival time than about fobbing us off, punting a troublesome event into the long grass.

As Piaget noted, living your life by perspectival time is more than a little egocentric. Histories and autobiographies would not get written if the author's past, present, and future were the only concepts available. Preoperational children need to learn to decenter from their own perspective in all sorts of ways, not least in their judgments about how their own selves extend through the fourth dimension. Just as the Doctor can plug an absolute, numerical A.D. or B.C. date into his onboard computer, so Athena's Tardis self needed a sense of objective time that was distanced from her own perspective on it. Our little Time Lord was certainly interested in absolute time, as evidenced by her obsessive questioning, as a birthday went past, about exactly (to the day) how old she was. Other people's ages mattered enormously as well. "How old is your birthday?" she might ask a newish acquaintance for whom that key information had not yet been supplied. Once she knew the days of the week, she knew that, if yesterday was Monday, today must be Tuesday. Those building blocks of story known as scripts may also have helped her get a grasp of the objective ordering of events, since scripts are all about generalizable sequences, successions of occurrences that lie outside any particular historical context. If you know the restaurant script, you have a handle on the past, present, and future of restaurant-going. In time, recognizing these pervasive, repeating patterns of human activity may help toddlers toward a more profound understanding of their own temporal continuity.

That still doesn't explain how children come to locate their own selves within a temporal framework. In order to understand their own past *as* past, they need to understand that the time frame they inhabited at the time of the remembered event (the now of the past) is different from the time frame they inhabit currently (the now of now). They need to step up a level of consciousness and reflect on their own passage through time. Without that ability, they must feel like strangers to their historical selves, just as they were once strangers to themselves in the mirror. In fact, learning how to shift flexibly between these time frames may be one of the most enduring benefits of family memory-sharing routines like What We Did Today. Talking about the past, and shaping it into a story, is about learning to connect all those different nows. When I asked her to recall an event from her infancy, it wasn't just going there that was important; it was coming back again. In becoming time travelers, children aren't just resigning themselves to a life lived in memory, or in some fantasy of the future: they are acquiring a passport for traveling there, and making a safe return.

For the Doctor, as for Einstein, the journey across the universe is measured in miles traveled as well as hours passed. Our Toyota Camry is bearing us toward a point in the future, but also toward a place that is different from the one we set off from. We have heard people speak about it, this town where ordinary people dig fortunes out of the dust. We have built up a picture of it, a perfectly proportioned situation model, a Lightning Ridge of the mind. The trouble is, Lightning Ridge is taking its time in appearing. If distance is time, Athena has waited a long way. Long enough to strain a young lady's trust, you might think. How does she know for sure that this legendary opal-mining town really exists? Since the end of babyhood, she has had no problem in continuing to believe in things she has seen with her own eyes. But when distances are measured in days' traveling, that certainty breaks down. None of us has ever set eyes on Lightning Ridge. We can look it up on our road atlas, and see how it is depicted relative to places we do have firsthand knowledge of, like Sydney and Broken Hill. Personally, I have enough trust in the cartographers of Universal Publishers Pty Ltd to know that, when we arrive at that yellow dot near the Queensland border, it will be a real, buzzing, bricks-and-mortar town. Athena has less reason to be convinced. For a start, a map is a representation of a thing rather than the thing itself. Learning about representations is part of what's difficult about learning about other minds: who is representing what, and how they might be getting it wrong. My false belief about a thing is like an inaccurate map, liable to lead me, like the map reader, astray. Asking her to read a map might be like asking her to read a mind: difficult enough for small children, even if one can trust in its validity.

Empirical research shows that young children certainly do struggle with schematic representations of space. Give a group of children a scale model of a thing, such as a room in which an object is hidden, and even two-year-olds will understand how the model relates to the reality. A scale model differs from a true map, though, because it is simply a smaller version of the real thing. It has been argued that, to use a map correctly, you have to understand at least two important aspects of it. First, you have to know that it is a representation, or symbol, of a thing rather than the thing itself. Second, you have to be able to work out how the spatial layout of the map corresponds to the physical space being represented. Young children have difficulties meeting both of these challenges. In one study, psychologists showed children a collection of maps and recorded their responses to tentative interpretations of their contents. For example, the researcher pointed to a line on the map and said, "Hmm . . . I think maybe this is a road . . ." Children's reactions were frequently withering. While they seemed willing to accept that the map represented a place of some kind, they got things very wrong in their judgments of scale and orientation. One four-year-old, asked to comment on the possibility that a thin line on the map was a road, responded, "It's too skinny for two cars to fit on."

Shown a plastic relief map with mountains depicted as little rubbery bumps, a child commented that they could not be hills because they weren't high enough. Children also made errors when asked to identify objects and locations in aerial photographs. A triangular parking area in a photo of Chicago was described as a "hill," a baseball field as an "egg," and, when asked whether a prominent building might be the place where his father worked, a four-year-old boy replied, "Oh, no, his building is *huge*! It's as big as this whole map!"

We won't be passing the road atlas to Athena, then. I know that her problems with understanding representation go beyond visualizing splotches of cartographer's yellow as built-up areas. Pictures, like words, have powers that far exceed their status as representations (have you scrubbed out that sentence about the imagined death of a loved one yet?). There is a further similarity between linguistic representations and pictorial ones, like road atlases. Just as you have to find your way into the protagonist's perspective in a story, so you have to understand your own perspective within a map. Even quite old children fail to use a map correctly when it is supplied in the wrong orientation. I personally am incapable of following one without twisting it amateurishly in my hands until it is aligned with the lay of the land, so it is perhaps not surprising that children are similarly challenged. In one classic study of children's perspective-taking, Piaget and his colleague Bärbel Inhelder presented children with a three-dimensional model of a mountain scene and asked them to select pictures that depicted what a doll would see from different positions around the model. Young children were fairly inept at putting themselves in the doll's shoes, tending instead to choose the picture that represented their own perspective on the model. Piaget interpreted these findings as more evidence for preoperational children's egocentrism, or inability to shift out of their own viewpoint in order to consider another person's point of view.

Halfway between nowhere and nowhere, she pipes up: "I want to go on a playground."

"We're coming into a little town. There must be a playground here somewhere."

There isn't, but there is a coffee shop with a dusty little play area out back. A sign proudly announces that they have just taken delivery of a new cappuccino machine, which can make cappuccino with a choice of three kinds of instant coffee: Nescafé, Maxwell House, and the famous International Roast, a brownish dust that looks much like the stuff that has been filtering through our air-conditioning vents. We're a long way from soy latte country. Some Aboriginal children in striped tracksuit tops are hanging around outside a video store. Bruce Chatwin's controversial bestseller *The Songlines* tells of his search for the network of lines crisscrossing Australia, along which the creator ancestors roamed in the time of the Dreaming, singing the features of the landscape—trees, mountains, lakes—into being. In theory, Chatwin wrote, the whole of Australia could be seen as a musical score. The concept of territory that emerged was not one of areas of space bounded by frontiers, but rather of lines of ancestry along which a man could travel and know that he was with people who shared his Dreaming. "Sometimes," Chatwin's songline-tracing companion, Arkady, declares, "I'll be driving my 'old men' through the desert, and we'll come to a ridge of sandhills, and suddenly they'll all start singing. 'What are you mob singing?' I'll ask, and they'll all say, 'Singing up the country, boss. Makes the country come up quicker.'"

Chatwin was too fond of a good story for his account to be taken as scholarly gospel. Still, it seems plausible that doing the semi-nomadic thing in a country as empty as this would give you a different perspective on space. Sure enough, studies with Aboriginal children have found them to perform better than white Australian children in certain spatial memory tasks, such as remembering the configuration of a set of objects laid out in a rectangular array. Whether this has anything to do with a cultural history in which people were required to navigate huge tracts of land with little to aid them but their own memories we cannot tell. But cross-cultural research of this kind does highlight the importance of keeping an eye on children's background knowledge when studying their reasoning about space and time. As their critics have pointed out on many occasions, Piaget and Inhelder measured their Genevan participants' perspective-taking ability using fairly formal tasks that made little sense to the child. Modify the Three Mountains task so that it involves, say, a guilty boy trying to hide from a policeman, and children show a much better understanding of perspective: what the policeman can see, and where the boy would have to hide in order to avoid being caught.

Athena's thinking is likely to be just as powerfully shaped by the culture she is growing up in. She has little understanding of historical time, for example, so she would be at a complete loss to know how old those mountains are, or when white people first settled in Australia. In traditional Aboriginal cultures, the Dreaming represents a past time that is nevertheless eternally in the present, out of which people emerge at birth and return at death, and in which the spirits of the creator ancestors are endlessly renewed. In which case you might also expect Aboriginal children to show subtle differences in their understanding of time. In some studies, Aboriginal participants have shown a tendency to recall items in a spatial order rather than a temporal one, as though they organized their memory by geometry rather than temporal succession. If time is seen as a circle rather than an arrow, it is plausible that it might be of less use in organizing one's knowledge. Assuming that Chatwin was right in arguing that space, not time, is the linear principle in Aboriginal thinking, perhaps thinking in spatial terms is going to be the most straightforward way of doing things.

In other respects, a typical Western child is much like a typical Aboriginal one. Ask a child, as Piaget did, who made the sun and moon, and you are likely to get a creationist answer. For children growing up on the shores of Lake Geneva, the stars of the constellation

Pleiades might have been scattered there by God. For the Aboriginal people of the Melville and Bathurst islands, they are a group of kangaroos being endlessly chased by a pack of dingoes (the stars of Orion). Piaget's interpretation was that young children suffered from an "artificialist" bias, mistakenly inclined to see a creative agency in inanimate objects. As their thinking becomes flexible enough to give them a basic grasp of the laws of physics, they become better able to see how the landmarks of nature could have arisen without human or divine intervention. Piaget saw artificialism, of the kind demonstrated by some Aboriginal peoples, as a wrinkle of cognitive immaturity that is ironed out by further development. As you grow into more-sophisticated reasoning about the physical world, he argued, you rely less on God for your cosmology.

Although Piaget explicitly denied it, it was easy to take his arguments as suggesting that traditional cultures are, like children, entrenched in immature ways of thinking. A better explanation is that human beings' thinking about different areas of knowledge is affected by the particular culture in which they are growing up. In one recent study, white Australian and British children were tested on their knowledge of cosmology, such as their understanding that the earth is a sphere on which people can live without falling off. Even controlling for general intelligence, the Australian kids showed a significantly richer and more scientific understanding of cosmology than their British peers. One might say that they could not help but do so. Australian children grow up well aware of their distinctive location (relative to other English-speaking nations) below the equator. Their allegiance to the Southern Cross, as depicted on their national flag, is emphasized in their elementary school curriculum, which introduces cosmology at an earlier age than in the UK. For all their sophistication, however, Australian children are no less likely to give an artificialist answer to the question of who made the sphere to which they cling. They simply have bodies of knowledge that develop at different rates depending on the specific cultural influences they are exposed to. These little scientists' topics of study are split into distinct disciplines—cosmology, biology, physics, and so on—and their understanding progresses at different speeds for each particular scholarly specialty.

To get over artificialism, then, you need to make progress in that realm of reasoning that is specifically about physical causes. Children's minds are not like computers that, armed with a software upgrade or new memory chip, deliver enhanced performance across the board. They are assemblies of disparate skills and quasitheoretical knowledge systems that rattle along, helping each other out when the need arises. Sometimes children use a theory developed in one domain, such as social reasoning, to solve problems in another, such as physical causation. Psychologist Paul Bloom has asked whether some of children's errors in this respect might arise because children are thinking in mentalistic terms about entities that are really only physical. In Bloom's view, seeing the hand of a Creator where there is none, or attributing intention to objects that have no mind at the wheel, arises because children are simply overdoing the mind reading. When Athena told us that a car wasn't moving because it needed to wake up first, she was attributing intentionality a little too generously. Far from being a sign of cognitive immaturity, artificialism is a natural result of the human tendency toward mind reading, toward seeing intention where there is only blind physics. And it's not just children who show that tendency. Those who complain about the teaching of intelligent design in American schools, for example, might just be coming up against a deeply human bias toward making sense of the world in terms of mind. Western children do not have a monopoly on artificialism. Western adults are using it too.

We finish our coffee, extract Athena from the climbing frame, and start walking back to the car. The stripped white trunks of a stand of river gums connect red earth to a jasper-blue sky. Everything has a shadow. On the other side of the road, away from the creek, I can discern the curvature of the earth. It's easy to see why people believe in a Creator. So much is mysterious: why the sun rises, how gases fuse to make water, how blind natural selection could have launched birds into the air. Through the centuries, children have wanted answers to these questions, and adults have had to try to find ways of explaining them. If Bloom is right, those adults needn't have bothered. The explanations were already at hand. Until children's thinking is sufficiently developed to cope with the hard science, the belief that God or some other supernatural being is responsible for all these miracles comes to youngsters as naturally as language does. I like to think that one day Athena will be able to see the thing in all its wonder, that she will be able to step into her Tardis and take herself off to the birth of the universe, in her scientifically schooled imagination at least. But, until then, God will have to do. You might even argue that He was invented for children. If we were born grown-up, knowing what we know, He might find himself out of a job. But then there would be no children to explain things to.

Fourteen

LIGHTNING RIDGE IS FALLING DOWN

A Portrait of the Artist

I was right about Lightning Ridge. It does exist, and Athena is making a movie about it. She holds the camcorder with her hand hooked into the grip belt and points the lens at anything that comes to mind. With Athena in the director's chair, we will get footage of things that interest her, rather than things I think she should be interested in. This is a location shoot from her point of view. She turns the camcorder to the sky quite often, as though it were a kaleidoscope, or one of those toy cameras that come free with her comics, which click through different character cartoons when you hold them up to the light. She also turns it to the ground, where the textures of grass, carpet, or wooden flooring, or perhaps the prospects of finding minibeasts, are satisfying. She usually has the zoom on full, and she doesn't pause the recording when she is opening doors or going up stairs, which makes watching her first movies a slightly dizzying experience. There is much footage of shoes, and people's knees, and close-ups of clothing, and a fair amount of replacing the lens cap when the camera is still running. "T'is it on?" is a frequent question on the voice-over. Eventually she learns to switch the camera on by herself, and months later we come across bizarre secret footage, strange rituals involving dancing teddy bears and carefully configured totems: artfully arranged canvas backpacks, rudimentary cities built from colored stationery. It is as though the door that conceals her imagination from us has suddenly blown open, and we can see how she would arrange the world if she had the chance. But the opportunity is short-lived. Grown-ups are coming up the stairs, their voices and footsteps caught on the audio, and she is snatching up the camera and trying to fiddle the lens cap back on, then dropping its switched-on bulk as though it had electrocuted her, so that the last moments of the reverie are a close-up of a chalk-scrawled desk, the abstract textures of a carpet's shag pile, or the grain of a wooden table.

Today, though, in a neat inversion of the usual order, she is turning the camcorder on us. We have hours of videotape in which she is the subject under interrogation, as though our home movies' authenticity depended on them coming with an enforced commentary from her. Now she is getting us back.

"Where are we today?" she asks.

Lizzie's face appears, in sunglasses, in bright afternoon sunlight. "We're in Lightning Ridge."

"And what have we been doing in Lightning Ridge?"

"We've been looking around at the shops and all the places that are selling opals."

Athena swings the camera around at a row of cars, parked with their noses facing obediently outward from the curb. For a supposedly lawless town, they sure are sticklers for the regulations.

"And what . . . did I go on Daddy's shoulders?"

"You did, didn't you?"

"And what else did we do?"

She zooms in on a noticeboard smothered with advertisements for odd-job services and freeholds on residential mining claims. The idea is that you set up home above a claim—a small mine—and rummage until you find your fortune. On the drive in, the sign says LIGHTNING RIDGE / POPULATION: ? The attraction of these easy riches draws such crowds to the town that no one is really sure how many people are here.

"Well," Lizzie says, "this morning we stayed in our hotel room and did some drawing, didn't we?"

"With my new pens?"

"That's right."

As a reward for being such a patient traveler, we bought Athena a new set of Winnie-the-Pooh felt-tip pens as soon as we arrived in Lightning Ridge. Her first task was to test out all the colors with little scribbles in her sketchbook, as though to confirm that the rainbow was as she remembered it. Then she drew a ladybug and a jellyfish. Apart from the fact that the ladybug had more legs, they were indistinguishable. In fact, if she hadn't named her creations for us before she began, we would still be guessing. Where previously she would have gone ahead with the drawing and then opportunistically slapped a label on afterward, now she sets out her intentions in advance. That's part of the game of making art: you have foreknowledge of what it is that you are making. Michelangelo didn't just throw some paint on the ceiling and then remark: "Oh, it looks like the Creation of the Universe." He set off up his ladder with certain intentions in mind. The point at which children start making art, as opposed to seeing artistic shapes in the tea leaves, is the point when their creative intentions assume control. Athena had set out to draw a ladybug, and so a ladybug was what resulted. It was drawn with ladybug-intent, not jellyfish-intent. As with pretend play, the stipulations of the imaginer are binding.

At this age, the intention behind a drawing would seem to be as important a guide to its meaning as its actual appearance. Psychologists have confirmed this with more-formal tests of children's sensitivity to artistic intentions. In one study, three-year-olds were asked to draw a series of similar-looking objects, such as balloons and lolli-pops. In the hands of these unskilled artists, such drawings would be expected to be indistinguishable. And yet, when asked later what their own sketches depicted, children named them according to the intentions they had had in creating them. If a circle attached to a stick was meant to be a lollipop, then that was how the child described it later, even if it looked more like a balloon. Kids respond similarly to pictures made by other people. In one study, children were shown simple drawings, such as one that looked like a teddy bear. Half of the participants were told that the picture had been painted intentionally by a child in an art lesson, and the rest that the image had resulted from the accidental spilling of some paint. In the "intentional" group, even two-year-olds showed a greater tendency to name the picture according to the object it represented, compared with their age-mates in the "accidental" group (who were more likely to say that it looked like a random splotch of paint). Just as they understand that the inten-tion to hand over a toy is valid even if the action itself is unsuccessful, so toddlers understand the intention to represent as separable from the actual success of the representation. The implication is clear: for very small children as well as adults, it is only a picture of something if it is meant to be a picture of that thing. There is no representation without intention to represent. A picture is what you mean it to be, not what it accidentally or contingently is.

Making and understanding art, then, would seem to draw on the same mind-reading skills that children use to make sense of the social world. That is hardly surprising, since making art is inherently social. If a painting goes up in an art gallery and there is no one around to see it, then it may as well not have happened at all. Many of Athena's early artworks had compelling social functions. If one of us was ill and needed cheering up, then her picture-producing factory went into overdrive. That's one reason I find it so difficult to throw any of these creations away. With children's artworks, the usual laws of supply and demand don't apply. Abundance does not diminish them. The more tadpole-people and rainbows she produces, the more valuable they become.

As she continues with her variations on the ladybug theme, I look back at some of the video footage she took yesterday. I'm not sure that describing these shaky handheld clips as artworks is as appropriate as it is for her drawings and narrative songs. The first thing she does with a picture is come and show it to us. There is an element of performance involved. These home movies, in contrast, are only indirectly for public consumption. As well as being intentional in its symbolic or representational sense, art has a second, more subtle way of being intended: as an entity that should be taken as art by other people. A crack in the floor can be an artwork if it is made in the floor of an art gallery (where the context is saying, *Please consider this art*), but not anywhere else. It must set out, in other words, to announce its own aesthetic credentials. It can't just be made with representation in mind; it must have an artistic reception in mind too.

Did Athena intend her drawings, songs, and movies to be appreciated in this second, aesthetic sense? Could we really call them artworks, if she did not fully understand the reflexive complexities of how art works? We faced similar questions with other products of her imagination. Jokes, for example, rely on the same reciprocal broadcasting of intentions as art does. Something is only a joke if it is intended that it should be taken as a joke, and if the person who is listening also recognizes that intention. This complexity meant that Athena's understanding of humor had a rocky development. We used to play a game in the car on the way home from nursery where we would say the name of an animal and she would have to supply the sound it made, or we would make the sound and she would name its source. When that became too easy for her, we would give it a twist, like this:

Mummy: So what does a doggy say?
Daddy: Quack!
Athena: No! A doggy doesn't say quack!

It wouldn't have them rolling in the aisles at the Comedy Club, but toddlers find this kind of twisting of representations hilarious. Athena did something similar herself, perhaps picking up the pattern from the jokers around her. When, as a baby, she pointed to her mother's face and said "Bear," she knew she was being funny. Although she could not have understood its full social ramifications, she had nevertheless grasped one of the key principles of humor: Say what isn't so. Like art, much of comedy involves playing on the audience's expectations. We know that the world is a certain way, and we expect things to turn out a certain way. As long as the consequences are not too troubling, we laugh when our expectations are confounded.

Understanding an act of imagination, like a joke, would seem to require some sophisticated sensitivity to the audience's expectations. Like stories, jokes require us to represent the world as it is not. We hear someone playing fast and loose with the facts, and our model-building mechanisms spring automatically into action. You can't hear that rudimentary joke of mine without conjuring up an image, however fleeting, of a quacking dog. I had to be careful, though. I knew that Athena was using me as a source of knowledge for building up representations of how the world was: for everything she couldn't see with her own eyes, she had to trust the testimony of others, primarily her parents. Perhaps it was the not-quite-knowing that was part of the thrill. As she gained confidence in her judgment of what was funny and what was not, she came to grips with the social conventions about when you can reasonably expect someone to see a joke rather than a lie or an impertinence. As she got older, I would cut it finer. Sometimes it would backfire, resulting in the blossoming of that chuckle even when I was being deadly serious. My announcement, one night over dinner, that I am going to give up drinking wine is met with rills of songbird-ish laughter. Why should I be dismayed? She has learned that laughter is appropriate when people say things that cannot possibly be true. Even if I didn't intend it to be humorous, she took it to be so.

I ask her to tell me a joke. She thinks hard for a moment.

"A mouse crept up me."

"And then?"

"A tree fell on me."

It's funny, in an absurdist kind of way. But is it a joke? She doesn't tell a proper, formal joke until after her third birthday, and even then she rushes the punch line, leaving no time for any stagy protestations of my ignorance. Perhaps she has simply come to associate these formulaic exchanges with other people's laughter: they might do nothing for her, but they are clearly the sorts of things that the rest of the world finds funny. Perhaps she knows full well what a joke is, but simply isn't very good at executing them. Or perhaps there is a deeper confusion here. A mouse was the topic of a dream she reported this morning. When I ask her to tell me a joke, she actually tells me a dream. Both are stories. Both are about what is not true. Both interested Freud, who argued that both were manifestations of primordial desires that the conscious mind could not countenance. I'm not sure what a quacking dog tells me about my unconscious mind, but in other respects the equation makes sense. My giving up drinking is a good joke because it is also a good dream. When Athena was two, Lizzie asked her what dreams are. "Colored things," she replied. She proceeded to act out strange puppeted routines with her hands, asking her mother to copy them. "This dream," she instructed. "Now this dream." When Piaget interviewed children about where dreams came from, he obtained answers that were works of art in themselves. One four-year-old replied that dreams were made of little lights that came "from the moon. It breaks up. The lights come in the night." Other youngsters proposed that dreams were sent by pigeons, or from "the smoke that comes from the bedclothes." Slightly older children claimed that dreams were sent by God, or by those who were being dreamed about, eventually endorsing the commonsense view that dreams are pure products of thought with no external agency involved. When Athena was three, I tried my own version of Piaget's interview, and the answer was more prosaic. "Athena, where do dreams come from?" She thought for a moment and replied, "Apples."

Perhaps dreams are interesting because they are one aspect of their consciousness that children know is secret to everyone but themselves. Athena's desire to express herself in imaginative endeavors may reflect her growing acknowledgment of this fact. Does she understand that words and video images can represent her view of the world, just as scribbles on the page can? Is she *intending* to represent her point of view, perhaps to help me in my own footsore quest to understand it? Her desire to express herself is certainly strong. We sometimes feel as though we are drowning in tadpole people. But, for her, we *are* tadpole people, so perhaps the feeling is appropriate. If human beings are mirrors to each other, then my reflection is taking some getting used to. Being constantly depicted as a potato with cotton-bud limbs is bound, eventually, to affect your self-esteem. In one picture, she draws Lizzie as a haunted, saucer-eyed refugee running from some unspecified peril. I, on the other hand, can look strangely disconnected, my features a Picasso-esque jumble of eyes, nose, and hair. I have dreams in which she makes little pieces of me fall off just by looking at me. At least the sun is always shining in these renditions she makes of us. Whatever psychological torments she visits on us, she never fails to consider the weather.

We shouldn't take it personally, of course. If one motive behind Athena's self-expression is her recognition that there are aspects of her consciousness that are private, then it is wrong to assume that her artworks must always be directed toward others. At least some of the attempts to represent her point of view may be exclusively for her own consumption. Commenting on the strange beauty of one toddler's crib speech, famous linguist Roman Jakobson considered it an outstanding example of infant art. But a child like Emily, lying in her cot in the twilight, could not have known that her bedtime soliloquies were being overheard, let alone recorded for posterity. Far more likely was that she was representing the events of her life for herself, and therein lay the beauty of her words. Perhaps, like language, art can be for self as much as for others. You can talk yourself through an intellectual problem, but you can also do wonders for the continuity of your own experience by making beautiful things out of it.

We drive out to the claims the next day. On the rough red-dirt track that leads to the Three Mile open cut, ripped-out car doors, fashioned into house nameplates, point out tin-roofed shacks with huge air-conditioning units clamped on like parasites. A sign reads MAD DOGS, STAY IN CAR. All the houses have suspiciously tall aerials, as though trying to outgrow nonexistent mountains. A white sport-ute speeds past us, trailing red dust. Athena is filming the courtesy light in the middle of our car's soft-lined roof. "T'is it on?" she says. "I'm doin' my video in'." We stop at a scrap yard in the middle of nowhere, where we've been told to wait for a bloke named Brian. A lone dog sniffs around us, but otherwise there is no sign of life. Athena films the scattered machinery and broken-down vehicles, the drooping leaves of gum trees against the horizon. She keeps the view screen folded away and instead composes the scene through the tiny viewfinder. She seems to enjoy the correspondence between what she can see with her own eyes and what she observes through this little rectangular optic. It is another way of looking out at the world and yet seeing the same thing. The blue sky, the red-earthed scree, the dusty ground beneath our feet: yes, everything in its place. Looking out at reality like this might simply be an interesting confirmation of the way the unfilmed world looks to her. *Thirty Seconds in Lightning Ridge*, she might entitle it, or *Ennui with Light Machinery*. She understands that the video record will persist, and that we will be able to look at it again, in a context very different from the heat of rural New South Wales. *It's like this,* she is saying to herself, *and here is the documentary evidence.*

We walk on to the quarry. There is an open cut, hundreds of meters across, and only a chicken-wire fence to stop us from falling into it. Athena thinks the quarry looks like a big empty swimming pool. I point out the strata of sandstone that lock in layers of opal-bearing clay, and try to explain to her that we are looking at the graves of prehistoric marine animals who lived in the sea that covered this land a hundred twenty million years ago. Perhaps she wasn't so wrong to liken it to a swimming pool. At the Walk-In Mine this morning, they told us that they find fossils here made of black opal, the skeletons of platypuses, pleiosaurs, and ammonites reconstructed, through a miracle of silica deposition, into a gem as valuable as diamond. I think of the nineteenth-century explorers who were tempted to their deaths by the promise of an inland sea. They were right about the sea, but not about the timing. What they were looking for had vanished eons ago. Athena thinks she can see some little dinosaurs in among the orange-red clay, but I suspect she is just trying to make me feel better about coming all this way just to look at a hole in the ground. She tries to film the dinosaurs, unaware that whatever she can see will never reproduce at this distance. Perhaps that doesn't matter. She can see them, and I can't. There are certain truths that not even hard video evidence can fully reveal to me.

She falls asleep on the drive home. I sit in the car with her outside the motel, listening to her breathing. In one of the rooms in the strip below us, the occupants have put up a sign announcing that they are buying opal. A steady trickle of lads turns up, clutching precious nobbies—chunks of opal ore—in handkerchiefs and bags. A busload of American tourists looks on. In her booster seat in the back, Athena sleeps with her face upturned to the roof, as though bathing in warm rain. Now and then she makes a suckling motion in her dream. In her resting mind, that secret footage is still playing. I flick through my notebook, reading lines of her conversation, observations scribbled down before I had a chance to forget them. The pages are crammed with her own drawings. They are observations she has made while I have been observing her, snippets of testimony about the impressions that flow through her mind, all the wonders I will never be able to witness. They represent all the ways in which she is strange to me. They are precious for all sorts of reasons, but not least because they tell it how she sees it. As long as I have these notebooks, I will still have something of her.

On our last Daddy-day in Sydney, we take the fast catamaran to Watson's Bay. It is a bright breezy day in July, and the wave tops are foaming to white as we scoot close by the Opera House. In January, when the two of us first took the fast cat to the southern side of the harbor, it was baking hot. Athena remembers how she spent most of the afternoon jumping off the wall on to the sand with no clothes on. If I had asked her then, at two and a half, about something we had done six months earlier, she would not have known what to say. There's a tape in the camera now. Which means I can expect her to remember *this*, six months from now.

"You know, when I was on the roundabout I was the only little child there."

She's remembering her ride on the carousel at the Italian Forum in Leichhardt, a few days ago.

"Yes, you were all alone, weren't you? Why did you just remember that?"

She stands on her seat and looks out at the opulence of Vaucluse. She sees brushed water, white boats frozen in speed, tall houses tilted toward us like offerings on a velvet cushion. And, behind these immediate attractions, there are the prospects that today holds. Fish-and-chips from Doyle's, consumed with the gulls on the wall above the beach. One of those spectacularly messy chocolate ice creams.

"Happy," she says.

"Were you happy when you were on the carousel?"

"Yes."

"And did you remember it because you're happy now?"

She nods.

"So another time, when we're back in England and you're feeling happy, you might remember today?"

Her smile is dimply and self-conscious, constructed according to some internal plan of how it will appear to others. As with her art-works, she is professing an intention that this image should be taken in a certain way. There is no camera on her; I haven't brought it today. But she still seems to have one eye on posterity, or at least a new aware-ness that she figures in a social drama. She can see herself in the mir-ror without the mirror actually being there. When you learn to look out through other people's eyes, you catch sight of a different kind of self: one that is for others, as well as for you.

"When I get back to England, will I be little again?"

"No, sweetheart. You're just going to get bigger from now on."

"I want to go back to England."

"We *are* going back to England."

"No, but at England, I want to play with my colored pens at England."

"You can take your colored pens to England. We're taking enough other stuff."

I think of the sense of ordered dismantlement that reigns at home. We have already packed some of Athena's most precious belongings into two big cardboard boxes and posted them off by surface mail. The next time she sees her orange scooter, it will be at home. I tell her that the big ship will take about six weeks to sail from Australia to England. She listens in awe. If car time is slow, sea-mail time is slower still.

"Will it still be almost my birthday when we get back to England?"

"Of course it will. Nothing's going to change. We're still going to be together."

"Are I going to go to big school?"

"I think so. We'll see if we can find a school that you like."

"And are I going to sleep in my bedroom?"

"That depends on whether we have another little baby."

I see her searching her memory, testing the idea for seriousness. We've discussed it in the abstract, as a family, for as long as Lizzie and I have been discussing it. I've asked her questions like, "If Mummy has another baby, where will it grow?" and she has given answers like, "In the garden!" I'm not sure that her understanding of biology has progressed much, but her attachment to the idea has. She has taken to saying it spontaneously, catching us off guard, as though something were already decided.

"I want to have a baby."

"Do you?" I try not to sound too relieved. "Do you want to be a big sister?"

"Is it going to be a little boy or a little girl?"

"We don't know yet. What would you like it to be?"

"Um . . . boy!"

I can tell that either alternative would please her. Like us, the prospective parents, she is more concerned that the baby actually gets made than with how its sex chromosomes might be configured. She has a sense now of the permanence of these categories—if she is a girl now, then she will always be a girl—and so the self that she projects into the future has at least one of its characteristics inked in. Most of the practical implications of that identity, though, will have to wait for those days ahead. At nearly three, she has little understanding of the expectations that come with being a member of one or the other sex. She is part of the club of girlhood, but not yet aware of the responsibilities that go with it. Dressing up in beads and a fairy costume is just another way of presenting her social face; she has no reason to believe that her imagined little brother would behave any differently.

"Well, we'll see what we can do."

She accepts this with a shrug. She wants things to stay the same, but she also wants them to change, in the most fundamental way imaginable. She approaches our impending departure with the same disarming equanimity. This is another way in which things will never be the same again, and yet she has shown little anxiety about getting ready to go. She has been tolerant of the upheaval, responsible beyond her years. It suggests that, deep down, this is something she wants to happen. You need memory in order to be able to feel homesickness, of course, but you also need a sense of how you will fit in to that imagined future. You've got to be able to weigh the past, but you also need to be able to anticipate a return.

We avoid the queue for the main restaurant and head for the take-away kiosk. I order a box of fish-and-chips while Athena runs around the wharf waving a sandwich bag, scaring the pigeons. We sit on the wall and look back along the level of the water at the city skyline, which glows with a pale light, as though lit from elsewhere. When we've finished eating, it's warm enough to take our shoes and socks off and paddle. Athena throws sand up in the air and watches it falling. "It's like rain," she says. She is not pretending, although the mental challenges of understanding this connection are similar. In symbolic play, her focus would be on making the sand look like rain. Here, she is trying to say something about the sand. It is the first time I have been conscious of her using a metaphor. She has attained that fundamental capacity of humankind: to see one thing as something else.

By the time the ferry arrives for the post-lunch return to the city, the afternoon has already taken on sunset colors. We sit at the back, near the engines. Athena is yawning but won't admit to tiredness. I suggest that she put her head on my lap and have a sleep, but she seems afraid of missing something. "At nursery I don't have a sleep," she lies.

She wants a cake, even though we have only just had lunch. As we pull into Circular Quay and the ferry turns around to dock, the skyline is pink and yellow in the wintry afternoon light. It's cold, and she has finally allowed me to put her green cardigan back on her. She stands on her seat with her hands on the rail on either side, and together we marvel at the amazing common sense that has structured Circular Quay: the ferry wharves with the trains running above them, and then the road going over the top, like in a masterpiece by Richard Scarry. She is wearing her green dress, a purple T-shirt, and green sneakers. Her blond hair curls loosely around her ears. The woman in the next seat wants to engage her, but the most beautiful girl in Sydney is playing hard to get. She tells me that she likes coming out with me, and I say that I hope we will always be able to have Daddy-days together. It's a vain hope. If she likes the nursery school we are planning for her, she will be going five days a week. The Daddy-days are coming to an end; I could probably count them on my fingers if I dared to try. My work, for this project, is nearly over. The notebooks are almost full. Already she resists these efforts to make sense of her. Where once I had to attribute thoughts and feelings to a mentality I had constructed for her, impose my own pattern on the compelling mysteries of her behavior, now the task of making meaning is hers. She is no longer a set of facts that need to be interpreted; she interprets herself, supplies the hypotheses and empirical tests, proves her coherence with every word and action. She's a miracle: a mind that can understand itself, a center of experience where once there was nothing. I like to think that happiness will be her emotional key to this memory. For me, it will be a particular kind of wistfulness: that warm, anxious desolation that comes from leaving something you love.

IF YOU GO TO THE SEA OF LIFE, BE SURE TO WEAR YOUR ARMBANDS

Love and Loss

No matter what state of repair you find it in, a return home always calls for a certain amount of rebuilding. When the absence has been a long one—seven months, in our case—you are reminded of what has altered in your life as much as what has stayed the same. The yellow house in County Durham was as we had left it, but much had changed for its smallest occupant. She investigated the rooms, audited her toys, teddies, and books like an amnesiac trying to reassemble a forgotten life. "I haven't played with this for a long time," she would remark, picking up an obscure piece of injection-molded plastic and trying to remember what she used to do with it. The secrets of her transformation were to be found here, in the tat of babyhood. Six months earlier, there would have been no threads to reweave. She would have recognized the house, and the view from the window, but not herself. Now, she could celebrate her own continuity. She was remembering what used to matter to her, what she cared about, how these dustily familiar objects made her feel. "When I was a little baby," she would ask, "did I play with this?" Back then, before Australia, she had been a "little baby." Now she had come back as a little girl, whose experience could be organized around the structure of a self. She was reassembling herself after a hiatus. We all do it, probably, every time we wake from a night's sleep. We grasp at the threads of memory that make us what we are. Sometimes eagerly, sometimes thankfully, we pick up the story where we left off.

The best thing about that rediscovered life was that much of it unfolded on TV. Starved of cathode rays in Turramurra, she applied herself to compensating for her missed viewing hours with professional dedication. Each videotape or children's TV program was both a new discovery and a reunion with an old friend. She had a lot of catching up to do. For a few days in that cool July, she was probably the only child in England who didn't know the names of the four Teletubbies. I would find her lying on the sofa, staring in a trance at our small color portable, her mouth open, her face seeming to form an apex of concentration, all her features sharpened by the effort of assimilating every last detail of televisual reality. She could hold the pose with preternatural stillness. As though trying to position herself for optimal absorption, she would roll over on to her back and watch it upside down. I had never seen her so transported. Those who doubt that TV is a drug should witness the effect it has on children. I could have led a baby elephant into the room and she would not have noticed, until the point at which it began to obscure her view. Perhaps it was my own fault for depriving her for so long. Forbid a child sweets and you're bound to have a chocoholic later in life. Athena's seven-month abstinence might just have been the start of an addiction.

The trance was reassuringly short-lived. Her orgy of watching only served to make the exotic familiar again. Another aspect of the dynamic of homecoming is the way the knowledge of what has changed eventually succumbs to the realization of what has stayed the same. You've traveled so far; how come life hasn't kept up with you? We all shared that feeling of faint disappointment. For all the immediate demands of reorganizing our lives, we were waiting. We were waiting for the big ship to arrive, with the boxes that contained our Australian possessions. We were waiting for the new school year, and for Athena to start at her new nursery. But these predictable excitements were all, more or less, about reinstalling what we'd had before. We had become hungry for something else. It would be the biggest transformation of all, and it would start quietly.

The teddies are acting up. Athena has gone to all that effort to put them in clean diapers and they repay her by filling them straightaway. The rate at which her teddies soil themselves suggests either an alimentary complaint or a deliberate conspiracy. Motherhood is demanding, but surely not quite as demanding as Athena makes it out to be. A certain amount of exaggeration is doubtless valuable for a mind bent on pretending. When you've got to create the reality for yourself, there is no harm in cranking it up a little. But I can't help thinking that there is a warning, too, in the frenetic activity of these imaginary babies' bowels. You have chosen this path, Athena is telling us. Look what is in store for you.

There was no dramatic, soap-operatic announcement. The first inkling Athena could have had would have been on the level of pure emotion, the thrilling recognition of a change in the family mood. Even before we confirmed the news with a DIY testing kit, an inexplicable happiness seemed to have settled on the house. She could not have known what to make of the white plastic stick with its inscrutable blue line, which sat on the piano like the calling card of some mysterious visitor, who had dropped by in our absence to tell us about the world we would soon inhabit. Even more bemusing would have been our constant visits to the piano to check on it, as though we wanted proof of something that was otherwise hard to believe. But believe it we should. Even the faintest blue line, the information leaflet told us, is evidence that your life is about to change.

How can you love someone you have never seen? We had made the decision to start trying for a second child, and that had started with the feeling that we had more love to give, more than we could expend on Athena alone. But love is not a limited resource, like dishwasher detergent, which can be topped up when it runs dry. Nor is it something that is produced continually on the off-chance that it might be needed one day. This wasn't a case of physiological excess, some freak of hormonal overactivity. The heart has its reasons, and love has its targets. Like any mental state, love has aboutness. It has to take an object, or it is not what it says it is.

But this was an emotion that had no object to take. Athena's baby brother was still all in our minds. When we saw Athena for the first time, on the day of her twelve-week scan, she became powerfully, unquestionably real. We gave her fetal form a name, and graced her movements on the ultrasound with all sorts of intentional nuances, alternating bouts of exuberance and thoughtfulness. As soon as she was born, we set about interpreting her grimaces as smiles, her vocalizations as rudimentary attempts to communicate. Even before that, we had loved the idea of her, and the potentiality of her. We start constructing our children when they are still little more than a faint blue line. We don't know for sure that these imaginative exploits had really made a difference to Athena's development, but they had made a difference to us. They gave her humanity a head start, and made her a target for our emotions. The fact that we were filling in many of the details for ourselves was no obstacle to our loving her.

Now that scrutinized infant was herself a mind reader. Athena, too, witnessed intention where there was only blind physics, saw mind forming before its time. Calling it love, when her understanding of the emotion was so limited and its object still only an idea, might seem far-fetched. But that would be to underestimate the groundwork she had been laying. Our early dawn-tinged love-ins had shown us how a human child is wired up for adoration from her very first days. Those smooch-fests witnessed by visitors to a maternity ward are there for a solemn purpose: getting love off the ground. Just by being there, adorably, she called the appropriate responses out from us. From an evolutionary perspective, it makes sense that vulnerable infants develop behaviors that will trigger instinctual caregiving from those with the greatest interest in those infants' survival. We would not have gotten very far as a species if we hadn't answered our babies' cries.

It was the recognition of this fact that inspired British psychiatrist John Bowlby to devote his career to some profoundly important studies of the growth of love. In his trilogy *Attachment, Separation,* and *Loss,* Bowlby described how babies' initially untargeted efforts to attract emotional attention give way to concerted strategies for forming attachments to specific individuals, predominantly the mother. As infants' behavior becomes more sophisticated—as they begin to get around under their own steam, for example—they become better able to regulate their own interactions with the loved one. In a series of groundbreaking studies conducted in Africa and the United States, Bowlby's colleague Mary Ainsworth showed that infants' attachment behaviors fall into distinct patterns that seem to reflect qualitatively different types of relationships. In the standard procedure, known as the Strange Situation, babies of about twelve months are observed in a series of carefully arranged separations from and reunions with their caregiver (usually the mother). Securely attached children may get quite distressed by the separations from their mother, but they are readily comforted on her return. Infants who are insecurely attached, in contrast, seem to gain less, emotionally, from their mother's reappearance. One group of babies, known as "resistant," can seem overly clingy in the episodes when the mother is present and become extremely upset when she leaves the room. On her return they are inconsolable, unable to use her renewed presence in reestablishing their previous mood. Children in another category, termed "avoidant," seem to make proximity to the mother a lower priority, and might hold back from interacting with her altogether. A fourth category of children, whose attachment is classified as "disorganized," demonstrates bizarre and contradictory behavior toward their caregivers. For example, they might cleave to the mother with all their might, at the same time screaming and averting their gaze from her. Disorganized babies have also been observed to lash out at their mothers while appearing to be in a cheerful mood, or to get to their feet when the caregiver returns, only to fall in an inanimate huddle when she approaches. These forms of insecure attachment are not necessarily a cause for concern, in terms of pointing to strange emotional behavior later in life, but they do make up a minority. In Western samples, around one-third of infants tested in the Strange Situation show an insecure attachment pattern.

It may not be the sort of fact that people need psychologists to tell them, but the consequences of these primordial emotional connections are profound. Bowlby argued that the first relationship forms the template for all subsequent emotional attachments. If a child forms no attachment at all, as is sometimes the case for children who have been orphaned, neglected, or abused, then mental and physical ill health are often the results. For the majority who do form some kind of attachment, experiences in these relationships become crystallized into relatively stable structures, which lend their qualities to new relationships as they are formed. A child who is secure with her mum will be secure across the board: with new friends, a new stepfather, a new Tamagotchi. Crucially, the lessons children learn about their caregivers' behavior become set into generalized representations of how social interaction works. A toddler who has gotten used to unpredictable caregiving behavior will represent other people as unreliable targets of her affection, and relationships as stressful and emotionally risky. These schemas, or internal working models, represent children's expectations about how people will behave in social contexts. A securely attached child expects affection, sees others as emotionally reliable, and feels confident that her relationships will survive temporary separations. Just as scripts for everyday events structure children's homegrown narratives, so internal working models influence the kinds of social information that children pay attention to. In one study, securely attached children were better than their insecure peers at remembering stories depicting sensitive behavior by a caregiver. It was as though the insecure children didn't process the information as well, simply because it didn't fit with their experience. When you are securely attached, you see the world through security-tinged spectacles. An insecure child, on the other hand, sees unpredictability and ambivalence everywhere.

In the years since the publication of Bowlby's trilogy, the idea that our early relationships write the script for all our later ones has transformed the study of social and emotional development. Today's attachment psychologists study adults' representations of their relationships with their own parents, their attachment to their romantic partners, to their pets, and even to God. Bowlby's theory has been used to explain how attachment patterns are handed down from generation to generation, such that recalling your childhood attachment to your own parents in a secure manner makes it more likely that you will have a secure child yourself. What all these diverse studies have in common is the idea that we possess models of how the social world works, built up through our own sometimes painful lessons in love. Our internal working models give us a schema, if you like, to which we can assimilate new attachment objects. That object may only be a faint blue line, but it can be loved.

If the theory is right, it explains how we can come to love a representation almost as powerfully as a body of flesh and blood. When parents-to-be talk to their fetus, or give it a pet name, they are demonstrating attachment behaviors toward the invisible object of their affection. When the image of that new baby slots into a healthy internal working model, the result can be hard to suppress. It was probably one reason we broke the news to Athena when we did. She had proved herself tolerant of upheaval, even eager for it, and she seemed ready to join with us in contemplating this new transformation. There seemed no reason to exclude her. When she drew us as a family of four tadpole-people, instead of three, she was showing that her own internal working models had already found space for the new addition. While our own excitement was tempered by a faint concern not to tempt fate (we certainly weren't telling *everyone*), Athena's excitement was uncontaminated. Emotions flow through toddlers like water through a sieve. Anyone who has tried to calm an overexcited child knows that a young heart has no truck with reason. Feelings come from a place that thoughts don't get to. For a toddler, there is no such thing as qualified joy. And clouds do not have silver linings.

Things were changing, though, behind that rawness of feeling. Her understanding of the basic emotions, like fear, disgust, and surprise, had been in evidence from the days of our earliest emotional dialogues. Language had given her a way of talking about these invisible affairs of the heart, and so of learning more about her own and others' emotional states. Her developing skill in mind reading soon meant that she could predict what others would feel on the basis of her knowledge about what they wanted and didn't want. At three, she had mastered the rules of the basic emotions. She understood how they drive human behavior: how people will do things that make them happy, and avoid doing things that hurt them. Emotions are the currency of social exchanges, but they are also the fundamental facts that make people do anything at all. Without emotion, the whole game grinds to a halt.

The emotions we live and die for, however, are rarely so black-and-white. Basic emotions like surprise and joy have long evolutionary histories. They are the province of subcortical regions of the brain, like the amygdala, which are out of bounds to higher forms of thought. Other emotions, like love and shame, are a little less animal. These are feelings with cognition built in. Love at first sight may make for a good story, but it is the exception rather than the rule. Compared with the basic, innate emotions, these higher cognitive emotions take more time to build up, and persist longer before dying away. They draw on cortical regions associated with advanced levels of cognitive processing. You can't feel shame without some representation of the social audience who might be watching you. To do pride, you have to have a certain mental ideal for yourself. To feel these emotions in all their poignancy, you have to put thought and feeling together. Athena certainly shared our joy at Lizzie's pregnancy—her unflinching attention to her teddies' diapers was proof of that—but did she share, say, that bittersweet acknowledgment that a precious time was coming to an end, even if it was going to be succeeded by something new and wondrous? Her internal working models gave her the cognitive basis for love, certainly: how to represent the loved thing in its absence, and how to connect it with her other experiences of that emotion. If the object was insubstantial, she could love the idea of it. If, one day in the future, she fell in love with a pop star or a pen pal, it would be a relationship molded by this basic pattern. The trouble is, loving ephemeral things leaves you open. Trust in love too much, as the secure child is bound to do, and love trips you up. Love comes at a cost, and insubstantial objects push the price up. If you can feel an idea, you can also feel its loss.

There is a certain predictability about the video footage we have taken up until now. The record is selective, and the criterion seems to be a relentless cheerfulness. It is as though our home movies had been edited by a censor who didn't want to see our footage wasted on anything but happy times. But stuff happens, even when the tape is rolling. Our little performer will be doing something preposterous, gleeful, rattling around in self-conscious joy, when all of a sudden an obstacle will frustrate her plans. Or perhaps she is dancing, showing off for the camera, unaware of what accident is about to befall her, how quickly a stubbed toe or bumped head will ruin her game. In the last few frames before the recording is stopped, the world is knocked out of whack. The camera might catch on her face, contorted by misery, before furniture looms jerkily into unfocus. The sound track is a disembodied wail. I have never tried to edit them out, and so these moments of grief remain, like bookmarks, between one scene and the next. This is where it all went wrong, they tell us. This is where we stopped laughing.

I take the call one gray afternoon in October. I am in the car, on my way to pick Athena up from nursery. I hear Lizzie's voice, almost unrecognizable with grief. I can hardly understand what she is saying, but I know that we have lost the baby. She sounds like I have never heard her. This is the sort of prodigious, exotic agony you hear on TV, in the screams of women who have had their families wiped out by missiles, and it has come to our home. I feel the old sick turmoil, the chatter and glow of low-level hallucinations, the shivery phantasmagoria of grief. This time I can't stop the tape. This time there is nothing to do but cry.

How can you mourn a child you have never seen? We tried to love an idea into existence, and now that love had lost its target. The idea became real too soon. Its only chance for survival was to stay invisible, nourished in our minds. Death is supposed to be where we lose our footholds in the physical world, say good-bye to corporeality. This was the opposite. Dying made our baby substantial. It ejected it from its dream into the world of cold flesh. I felt compelled to look at it, to know it in its final form. The sight of it—him? her?—was a comfort, because it proved we had not been wrong. This little sac of skin would have been a baby, a child, a person. Just as we had always loved Athena, in part, for what she had the potential to become, so we had loved this child for what he or she might have been. Love is not just about what you are giving to a person now. Love is a promise for the future. It is about saying "I will" as much as "I do."

That promise could not now be kept. When my father died, my grief was qualified by a feeling of redemption: his suffering was over, his waiting had come to an end. This loss held nothing back. We were the toddlers now, with the emotions pouring right through us, unable to temper our feelings with any glimmer of consolation. There was no cognition in it; this grief was like a black hole, swallowing thought. What little thinking we could do was distorted by this tearing at our souls: it was over, we would never have another child, our last chance was gone. We hadn't just lost a baby; we had lost a family, or the hope of one.

We buried that hope in the garden, wrapped in a little square of green craft paper. In the tiny grave, among the stones and crocus bulbs, we placed brief messages, saying how we would never forget him, we would love him forever. That night we told Athena that the baby in Mummy's tummy had gone away. There was a seed, we said, and it hadn't grown properly. We hoped that there would be another seed, and another little baby, soon. Although we weren't quite sure that we believed it ourselves, we told her that we still hoped she would be a big sister one day. We were trying to protect her, but we didn't realize that we were giving her a complicated emotional burden of her own. She had to respond to the fact of what we were grieving about, but she also had to respond to the immediacy of our grieving. She had seen us distraught before, but only ever as individuals. If one of us was crying, the other adult would be there as an ally in her attempts to stem the tears, a colleague in comforting the one who was upset. Now sadness was a family affair: bewildering, inclusive, filling the room.

We tried to draw her into it, but it was too strange. We could laugh together as a family, but it would be some time before we could cry.

I tried out some words that I thought might match her feelings. She was slouching on the sofa with her feet up on either side. She looked guilty, as though this was somehow her fault. I realized that, for the first time in her life, she was experiencing an emotion that had nothing to do with her own immediate needs. This was a pain that was bigger than her existing scope for feeling pain, that had to be understood in ways that went beyond what it meant for her. She looked miserable, but her reaction could not have been any further removed from the rawness of our own grief. She was grappling with what must be one of the most mentally challenging of all the higher cognitive emotions: the purity of selfless, useless sadness. Her reaction to the miscarriage was not to cry. It was to think.

There is a famous myth that elephants, when a member of their social group dies, enter a phase of mourning. They stay with the dead body, "bury" it with foliage, and are sometimes observed to pause thoughtfully at the spot where a group member has died. Elephants live in complex social groups. A recent study has shown that they recognize their own selves in a mirror, putting them on the same level of self-understanding as chimps, bottlenose dolphins, and human children. Can human children mourn? Bowlby thought so. Rejecting the Freudian view that young children's egos were too weak to bear the pain of adultlike mourning, he proved that even toddlers' reactions to the loss of a parent can show similar patterns of yearning, persisting memories and images of the loved one, anxiety, anger, and guilt. When it came to grief, there was no such thing as sparing the children. Two tasks face the mourner, Bowlby argued: to accept the new reality of the loved one's now-permanent absence, and to adjust one's internal working models to accommodate the loss. Mourning is the successful completion of these readjustments, and the prospect of continuing one's life without any serious unresolved trauma surrounding the bereavement.

There is a purpose to love. Love gets you a mate, and it helps you keep it. Love looks after your children and feeds you in your old age. Grief is pointless. From an evolutionary point of view, it is unattractive, a waste of precious resources. Those tears and cries could be turned to better use. We should be wired to forget and move on, not to dwell and brood. And yet grief is a by-product of our evolution as a species, as surely as elephant graveyards are a roundabout proof of that species' success. Mourning shows that you have a complex social life, that you show empathy for other members of your species, and that you can create internal models of the social relationships that matter to you. It shows that you have a concept of self, that you know your own feelings, that you can travel in time and imagine what might be, as well as what is. Just as we had loved an idea, we mourned an idea. For Athena, it was the image of a future playmate, a little brother she could dress up as a dolly and terrorize with her bossy games. In some ways, her mourning of our lost baby was an understated affair. The facts didn't square with the little she knew about death. Granddad Philip had died, and he was in heaven. She had no memories of him—he died a couple of years before she was born—but there were photographs of him, paintings he had owned, bits of furniture that he had left behind. The baby in Mummy's tummy had never been here in the first place. When people mourn a parent, they are grieving for a past. When it comes to mourning a child who was never born, bereaved parents report particular difficulties, when interviewed by researchers, in resolving their grief about a future that can now not come to be. You can reach closure about what has gone, but not about what never happened.

In the weeks that followed, Athena talked more about her grandfather than she did about the baby. One morning we were in the car,

on the way to her nursery. We have always had some of our best conversations in the car. The family power dynamic shifts dramatically
when Dad has to concentrate on the road. Booster seats put toddlers
up with the adults, in terms of vantage point, but the playing field is
leveled in other important ways too. In the back, freed from the comforting constraints of eye contact, children open up. If you want to
know a toddler's mind, put her in her car seat and drive.

"Why did Granddad Philip die?" she asks, out of the blue.

"Because he was poorly."

"Why was he poorly?"

"Well, you know we all get poorly sometimes and we have to go
to the doctor's. Granddad Philip had a bad disease and the doctors
couldn't make him better."

"Is Granddad Philip in heaven?"

"I think so, yes."

I hear her thinking this through. I'm starting to wish that I hadn't
said anything about heaven. Bowlby tells the story of a four-year-old
girl whose mother died suddenly after a chronic illness. Her father
broke the news in a car journey. He told Wendy and her little sister
that their mother had stopped breathing. She could not feel anything;
she was gone forever and would never come back. On hearing that
her mother was to be buried in the ground, protected by a coffin from
rain and snow, Wendy asked, "How will she breathe and who will
feed her?" Her father explained that, when you are dead, you don't
breathe anymore and you don't need food. Wendy seemed to accept
her father's kindly materialism quite readily. Other members of her
family, on the other hand, thought young children needed spiritual
guidance through their grief. On a visit to relatives shortly afterward,
someone mentioned that Wendy's mother was now an angel in heaven.
Wendy protested that it was not true, that her mother was in a coffin
in the ground, and she cried hysterically.

Asking a child to understand that a person can have two fates, a bodily one and a spiritual one, seems a tall order. Children of this age cannot even grasp the principles of the conservation of matter; how, Bowlby complained, can they be expected to resolve such metaphysical complexities in the fraught aftermath of a bereavement? Do away with all this confusing talk of souls, and we might just be doing kids a favor. That would leave us with another problem, though. Ask an average sample of Western adults and a large proportion will say that they believe in heaven, hell, and angels. The materialism espoused by most psychologists and neuroscientists—that there is nothing more to our consciousness than patterns of neural activity—is sharply at odds with popular belief. To some extent, that is because it is at odds with everyday experience. We didn't invent God to explain the physicality of death, but the continuity of the self. It is not the biological facts of death that children struggle with so much as the idea that a person they know, with whom they may have been talking and playing only recently, has gone and is not coming back. Children invest so much in understanding themselves as continuous entities, with a past, present, and future, that it is little wonder that they find it hard to imagine how that continuity can be broken.

Anyway, it is not just death that convinces us that flesh and spirit go different ways. Rather than saying that souls, heaven, and angels are cultural inventions created to ease the task of explaining death to children, Paul Bloom has argued that children's belief in the afterlife is a natural consequence of their dualism: that is, their adherence to the doctrine that mind and body are made of very different stuff. Children start off knowing nothing about death, but instead assume that both body and soul go on forever. When they learn the hard truth, they need to make sense of the idea that the soul can continue when the body drops out of the race. A belief in the afterlife is just a logical result of being a dualist. We are mentally programmed to see bodies as inhabited by souls. Heaven just comes with the territory.

"The doctors couldn't do anything, couldn't they not?"

"No. Sometimes these things just happen and there's nothing anyone can do about it."

"Why?"

Another reason for believing in a spiritual world is as a cause of things happening. If Athena had had a sound grasp of biological causation, she might have been able to understand the blameless physicality of her grandfather's death. She needed agency, though. She was like a headteacher trying to get to the bottom of a misdemeanor: *someone* in this room must be responsible. Piaget saw this relentless search for culprits at the root of children's animism. Death was certainly one of those aspects of reality over which, try as she might, she herself could exert no influence. Like the solidity of objects or the suck of gravity, our own efforts bounce right off it. She had to get this one thing straight about death: it can't be helped.

"Because that's just the way things are."

It was a feeble answer, but I had no other.

"And God couldn't do anything, couldn't he not?"

Thus do children reason their way to a metaphysics. If we didn't do it, and the doctors didn't do it, then who did? When human agency reaches its limits, other kinds of agencies can take over. In their search for causes, children see the work of supernatural hands where there is no evidence of human ones. Rather than simply seeing God as mopping up all the causes that can't be explained through human or physical means, young children have very clear ideas about who God is and what His powers consist of. In many ways, He appears frighteningly human. In the observations gathered by nineteenth-century philosopher and psychologist James Sully, God was a simple old man who lived in an apple tree, or who hung out with Santa Claus in a park full of birds. Athena's God is not the all-powerful being of the Old Testament. He is a human God, who comes up against the limits of his agency as often as we do.

"No, God couldn't do anything. Maybe God wanted Granddad Philip back in heaven with him."

Note the caginess. I'm doing my best not to sound like I know what I'm talking about.

"Was God angry? Is that why he wanted Granddad Philip back?"

I think of her expression of guilt as we told her about the miscarriage. If you don't understand causes, you can't really understand guilt and innocence. Which is why, in their innocence, children often end up shouldering blame. In one naturalistic study of empathy in toddlers, two-year-olds would sometimes take responsibility for their mothers' distress, even when they had no part in it. They would see her crying and say, "Did I make you sad?" or apologize and promise to behave better in the future. It seems a harsh lesson, but thinking through what she can and can't be held responsible for is already helping Athena plot the limits of her own agency. She is learning that life is a story that pays only scant attention to human wishes. That's a tough one, in terms of what it means for your ego, but it can also save you a lot of pain.

"No, God wasn't angry. There's nothing anyone could have done differently."

"I wish Granddad Philip wasn't in heaven. I wish he didn't die."

"So do I."

She is silent again. In the rearview mirror I can see her trying to put aside what did happen, in favor of what might have happened. Among the higher cognitive emotions, regret is probably the one that puts the greatest strain on your cortex. You can't feel regret until you have some ability to think about how things might have happened differently, and that means building situation models, traveling imaginatively into the future, constructing that alternative world in which you didn't make the fateful error. What really marks us as a species, though, is our ability to regret things that couldn't possibly have turned out differently. Wistful humanity, beating itself up over the passing of time. If we had any sense we would, as in the Alcoholics Anonymous desideratum, accept what we cannot change and have the wisdom to know the difference. But that would be to misunderstand the emotion. It might be sensible to restrain our regret in that way, but it wouldn't be human.

"If the baby is in heaven, will I see him when I get there?"

"Sweetheart, you won't be going to heaven for a very long time."

For once, I'm not regretting the inevitable. I'm regretting hurting her with these lessons, when I could have left her innocent for a little longer. We had no right to tell her about a pregnancy that wasn't properly established. We should have known better than to build up her expectations and then let life dash them. Freud argued that childhood amnesia draws its veil, most conveniently, over a period of maximum sensitivity to trauma. All the stuff that messes us up happens in the first five years. The young ego is not strong enough to bear the weight of these lessons, and the seeds of neurosis are sown. Have we traumatized her? Will she remember this as the moment that her trust in life failed? Perhaps we'll know one day, if she ever understands it herself. All I know is that, if we hadn't hurt her with this truth, someone else would have. She would have picked it up in the playground, in the queue for the school canteen: Haven't you heard? Didn't you know that we all die? We were simply learning the hardest lesson of parenthood: you can't protect them forever.

We arrive at the school parking lot, which is full of coffee-morning mums and four-wheel-drives too wide for the parking spaces. The school spreads around us like a blueprint for Athena's childhood. If she stays here, she will follow its benign strictures to the letter. We could stand here and pinpoint the classroom where she will study for her GCSEs, the playing field where she will feel the first wet smart of a hockey ball. Her social self will be polished in interactions in these color-coded playgrounds. The school has it all worked out for her. It will spit her out at eighteen, confident, knowledgeable, with a healthy sense of her own immortality. She and her imposing friends won't even notice the three-year-olds trooping into nursery. She will know what she values, what she fears, what makes her laugh and cry. At three, she knows her own mind; when she emerges, she will know her own heart.

I don't dread this predictability. It gives a structure to my own life, a sense of where I'll be when those milestones are happening to her. For me, now, the prospect of being fifty means having a daughter at university. If I make it to eighty, she'll be contemplating middle age. Children time our dying. They give us a guide-rail, a measuring tape. Without them, we would be flailing into the unknown. They show us the road ahead, and how much of it is left.

"There's Katie!" she says.

We unload her green-and-gold liveried baggage and wait for her friend to be unstrapped. Athena wants to walk into school with Katie and her mum. Turning up at nursery without a parent in tow appeals to her ruthless drive for autonomy. There's not much she'll let me do, these days, if she can do it for herself.

"I love you," she says, as I kiss her good-bye.

The afterthought is unexpected. Usually she is in a hurry to shake me off as quickly as possible and get on to the social whirl of the playground. She knows who her parents are; through the smooth operation of her internal working models, she can track them in her heart every minute of the day. She doesn't need to make a performance about good-byes.

"I love you too," I reply.

And then, because I can't help trying it on: "What do you think love is?"

She looks thoughtful. Her eyes are big and reflective. Her lips are tense with a smile.

"You like somebody very much and you give them a hug and somebody says, 'Can I play with you?' and you say yes and they don't know how to do it and they say it's nice."

"You're right," I say. "There's not much more to it than that."

At last Katie is ready. Athena has a different smile for her, the face you put on when you enter society, the mask that hides all manner of emotions. She has learned that you smile even when you don't feel happy, just as you would hold your tongue to spare somebody's feelings. As you gain more understanding of your emotions, and of how other people might be hurt by them, you learn to put them on a leash. Perhaps it was easier when feelings ran through her like water. The emotions were less complex, and there was less for them to be complex about. She has seen more of life now; she has felt the sting of things happening. For the first time, her heart has something to hide.

I stand at the top of the steps and watch them dawdle down toward the playground. Athena keeps looking across and checking that her little friend is still with her, as though she can't quite believe this gift she has been given. I feel an urge to call out after her, to make her turn back and acknowledge me. But I don't know what I would say. Time is pressing on. I have work to get on with, empty pages to fill up with ghosts. The living has already become the remembering. As life sweeps her away, I'll follow along with my notebook, trying to scribble it all down. I'm hitched to her star, tugged out of myself by her relentless velocity, trying to remember things before they have even finished happening.

Sixteen

⌒

WHERE IT TAKES YOU

Casting into the Future

I can still find my way around Sydney on autopilot. The Grace Brothers department store has been rebranded, the Little Girls' Toilet has migrated from the second to the fifth floor, but you can still get a five-dollar rice special at the Korean stall downstairs in the food court and, across the way in the QVB, the Old Vienna Coffee House is still serving weary shoppers. After four years, this city of golden light is still trying to baffle me with a version of my past. The crowds that mill through the underground walkway from Town Hall station could be the same people who brushed past me two decades ago, each individually convinced that they are on a one-way trip through time, but actually recycling like water in a swimming pool, recurrently familiar. They are amnesia personified, the flow of time made flesh. Once, I even see someone I am convinced I remember from a previous visit, and I run after her, tap her on the shoulder, and pose my embarrassed question. I am wrong, of course. The person I remember would be twice her age by now. I apologize and let her go on her way, still bizarrely convinced by the coincidence, half certain that this hurrying stranger is mistaken about her own identity. Nostalgia is rich with these fleeting delusions, the feeling that everything you believe in has shifted without you quite becoming aware of it. Memory plays tricks, but so does time. Gaining a sense of your own continuity as a person is no guarantee that you won't sometimes be fooled.

I watch a blond child scamper up the escalator toward Pitt Street Mall. He has the same wavy golden hair as the child in my memory, grown long because we can't bring ourselves to cut it. That earlier avatar, now grown preternaturally tall, runs up behind him, grabs his shoulders too roughly, and makes him protest with a brief whine. She is big sister, deputy parent, tormentor-in-chief. Her brother's growing up is happening unflinchingly under her gaze. The baby we lost still tugs at our hearts, dragging down little tides of grief like the moon tugs at the sea. But there is also an acceptance that, if that child had survived, we wouldn't have this one. We mention the baby occasionally, but it is as much for our sakes as it is for Athena's. If she does one day forget about the brother or sister who never was, we don't want it to be through any negligence on our part. So much of what we do as parents is about warding off our own imagined guilt. It is not just Athena who is building a sense of how this will look from the perspective of history. I'm casting a line into the future as well.

Outside it is a showery day in July. We are in Australia for an academic conference, and have headed to Sydney for a couple of weeks' holiday before flying home. Isaac is going shopping for stickers with his mum, and I have persuaded Athena to take the bus up George Street to Circular Quay with me. I want to see what she remembers. Not much has stirred so far, but then she hasn't seen the big sights yet. Surely the Harbour Bridge and the Opera House will dislodge something? She remembers the time when, on a visit to the Blue Mountains, the door joining the hotel rooms wouldn't open because a radiator was in the way. She remembers a visit to Dee Why beach and a particularly messy chocolate ice cream. But the big memories, the unique experiences that were supposed to enrich her life and widen

her horizons, have almost uniformly fallen away. What are they telling me, these weird bits of flotsam that do survive to wash up on the
shore of her consciousness? Was I wasting my time with my life-
enhancing schemes? It is like realizing that the person with whom you
have apparently been conducting a conversation has been plugged in
to headphones the entire time. Perhaps she is simply proving that the
things that matter to you when you are small are not the same things
that matter when you're bigger. Or perhaps I am learning that not
everything that is valuable in life takes the shape of a memory. Ninety
percent of what I've recalled in this book will be news to her. That
doesn't mean that it wasn't worth doing.

Which, if I'm honest, is the real reason I want to talk to her now.
She knows about this thing I've been writing: I have been floating the
idea of it for as long as I can remember. Ever since she saw me jotting
down our interview in the Old Vienna Coffee House, she has been
well used to the frequent reemergence of my black notebooks. They
have paintings in them, ballpoint-pen scribblings; she has decorated
the pages with stickers, thumbprints, and handprints, spiky attempts
at the initial A of her name. I have dated the entries, like some assiduous bird-watcher, and, when the record has spilled over into other
notebooks, I have numbered the pages for ease of cross-referencing.
Some pages have been torn out, by her hand or mine, to assuage some
long-vanished need to scribble. I sometimes wonder how much I have
encouraged these intrusions, wanting this to be a collaboration even
in the writing of it. It is as though I have needed her comments on
what I am doing, like a schoolboy wants to see his teacher's marks in
the margin, approving, correcting, justifying the exercise. Or perhaps
it's simply obvious to me that this is her story and she's the one who
ought to be telling it. The words are mine, but the guiding spirit is all
hers. When the time comes, and if she feels the inclination, she can
tell it in her own way.

Perhaps that time is coming closer now. In the years since we have been away, Daddy's book about Athena has grown in front of her eyes. The scribblings with which she adorned my notebooks have now colonized its manuscript pages, in lines of loopy handwriting and coy tryouts of a young lady's signature. She has got practice in her new literacy skills from reading over my shoulder what I have been typing in to the computer. She reads it back to me in a slightly sarcastic voice: now that she can decode text, she can own it, boss it about. Keeping her involved with the project has always been a big part of ensuring that she is happy with its outcome. And yet I know that her approval as a seven-year-old is not the far-reaching, informed approval I really need. As with her memories, perhaps things that don't matter to her now will start mattering to her in the future. It's that future I'm thinking about today.

We get off the bus at the back of Circular Quay station, where the old Chinese couple is still selling doughnuts. Hunger is a condition of being, even now.

"You know Daddy's writing a book, don't you?"

She nods, biting deep into a crust of chocolate icing.

"And you know it's about children in general, but mostly it's about you?"

"Yeah," she says.

"Well . . . how do you feel about that?"

She shrugs. "Okay."

"You don't mind that it's going to be about things you did when you were little? You don't think it will be embarrassing?"

"Not really."

I consider what I am asking her to do. I'm asking that she imagine other people reading a book that isn't even finished yet, and predict her own emotions about being at the center of their attention. I'm asking her to guess how it might feel to meet a stranger, some sunny day in the future, and find that they already know the story of your toddler-hood. Whatever she has learned about the continuity of her own self, and all the subtle ways in which thought feeds into emotion, she will need it now. That's one reason consent is such an issue in our dealings with children. Immature minds cannot be expected to fully understand the consequences of their actions now, let alone consequences that might unfold at some unspecified point in the future.

We wander through into the bustle of Circular Quay. The rain has stopped and the Harbour Bridge is resplendent in winter sunlight. It is Athena's first sight of it since we said good-bye to the harbor at the end of our last visit. When I ask if she remembers it, I get that bluff reassurance that tends to greet a dumb question, as though I were quizzing her about the fact of the bridge's existence rather than her own personal experience of it. I suspect that she remembers something about it, but it may just be a memory of its picture in our well-thumbed *Rough Guide*. It reminds her of the Tyne Bridge, often wrongly assumed to have been the model for Sydney's marvel, or perhaps it's the Tyne Bridge that reminds her of the Sydney version. All I know is that her impressions of four years ago will have been thoroughly overwritten by all the intervening reminders of those impressions. Four years from now, will she remember this moment on the wharf at Circular Quay, or only some mediated version of it? Will her grip on the thread of time be any surer? I imagine asking her about the book in four years' time, or eight, or twelve. If I can't trust her in her approval now, would it help if I put the book on ice and asked her as a teenager? She is bound to be embarrassed as a teenager; she will be embarrassed by my very existence on the planet when she is a teenager. In Western societies, the late teenage years are when individuals are judged capable of assuming most forms of legal responsibility. Under British law, lawyers can make a case for children acquiring decision-making competence before they reach these formal ages of consent, if they show the cognitive and emotional maturity necessary for weighing the consequences of their actions. There is a legal age of consent, but there is also a mental age of consent. However judges and lawyers choose to assess it in practice, it must have something to do with memory, mental time travel, the construction of situation models and imaginary worlds. Even at age three, Athena was gaining some mastery of these skills. When you put it this way, it seems as though she doesn't have so much left to learn.

Should I worry, then, if I have her approval for this project on the basis of the best understanding I can give her now? If I have the additional proof that she can reason about beliefs and emotions, and construct a representation of the future that she can use in shaping her judgments, then perhaps I can sleep more soundly. What I'm doing here will be part of Athena's past, whatever happens. There have been times when I have thought about making her anonymous, expunging her name from the record, but that seems dishonest. Although some famous child participants in psychological studies have regretted the experience, efforts to prove that this kind of attention is harmful have largely failed. The daughter of famous behaviorist B. F. Skinner may have had reason to complain about the way she was portrayed in a recent book about her experiences, but that had more to do with her being misrepresented than with anything her father did or did not do to her. Being raised in a blanketless air-conditioned cot had *not* messed her up, she insisted. My intervention in Athena's upbringing has been less dramatic. Apart from the fact that I have spent time writing about her when I could have been playing with her, we have not done anything as observing parents that we wouldn't have done as nonobservers.

Here's another reason her antics as a toddler may not cause her mortal embarrassment later in life. You weren't the same person as an infant that you are now. That baby in those funny stories from your childhood: that wasn't *you*. If it is true that toddlers don't have personalities, then there is nothing for their future selves to be embarrassed about. Witness, again, my fruitless quest to find small children appearing as characters in adult novels. There are babies in fiction, without any agency of their own but with plenty of scope to cause trouble for the women, and sometimes men, who are left holding them. There are a few brilliantly observed three-, four-, and five-year-olds. But toddlers, as owners of the sorts of belief systems and emotions that drive fiction, are largely invisible. When choosing who to put into their narratives, writers seem not to believe that a toddler's personality is up to the job. This is a striking irony in itself, given how much the little scientist moonlights as a little novelist.

It also makes scant sense in the light of parents' oft-voiced convictions that they are watching a little personality unfold. For all that I have said about adults' preconceptions and interpretations giving infants a leg up into social interaction, one's overwhelming impression as a parent—particularly a parent of two or more—is that one is watching the emergence of a character that is in many ways already partly formed. When Number One arrives, you try to mold her to your own image; when Number Two pops out, you see how determined Homo sapiens is to do its own thing. I have said little about the biological basis of Athena's personality: the patterns of traits, preferences, habits, and cognitive biases that carry the ghosts of her genetic inheritance. The science of behavioral genetics is all about explaining the differences between people in terms of their unique genetic endowment and their specific experiences. It is hard to focus on differences when your lens is trained on one particular child. If I asked the question again now, and thought about all the ways in which Athena differs from her brother, it might give me more of a handle on those aspects of her personality that had the force of biology behind them. I don't know if I was right about her personality at age two. I don't know if she is the same person now as she was then, any more than I know if I'm the same person I was when I was her current age. It is probably too soon to tell. But I know that she was a person. If this book makes any sense as a story, then that personality will have proved itself.

"So would that be all right, then, if I finish it and send it off to David?"

"Who's David?" she winces.

"David's the person Daddy sees when he goes to London. You know, who gave you the Kit Kat."

"Oh. Okay."

That was easy persuasion. Perhaps she anticipates another Kit Kat.

"Will my name be in it?"

"Of course your name will be in it. It's about you."

She sounds impressed.

"Can I read it?"

"Whenever you want."

I imagine the day that will happen. She is nine, or nineteen, and she holds a finished copy of this book in her hands. I try to look away, to give her space and privacy for this encounter with her past, but I can't help studying her expression. She still has the quizzical eyebrow that I observed in her as a toddler, although that mischievous under-bite grin has faded. I wait for her reaction. Then, when she closes the book and puts it down, I ask her what she thinks. She takes issue with something. "I don't remember that bit," she says. "It didn't happen like that." I smile, relieved that my only error in this is in a matter of fact. What do I know? She remembers all sorts of things that I don't remember. She remembers the owl that sat on the fence post outside our front door and scared her when she was not even two. She remembers what shorts she was wearing that day in Dee Why when she plastered herself with ice cream. She remembers how she caught her finger in the peephole of *Peepo!,* and that happened eons ago, when she was still a little tiny baby. If she quibbles with the narrative, with my own partial, skew-eyed telling, then it means she has a narrative of her own to compare it with. It's her word against mine, her story against my story. The point is, there's a story. In a way, that's all I've been trying to say.

Acknowledgments

Many people have contributed to the making of this book. My sincere thanks are due to my agent, David Grossman, and to my editor at Granta, Sara Holloway, whose good sense and wisdom have been invaluable for my telling of Athena's story. Sara's colleagues at Granta have been supportive at every stage of the book's production, and I have benefited in particular from the skills of Amber Dowell, Julio Ferrandis, Christine Lo, Brigid Macleod, Aidan O'Neill, Lindsay Paterson, Angela Rose, Pru Rowlandson, Bella Shand, and Sarah Wasley. Miranda van Asch and her colleagues at Allen and Unwin gave me a warm Australian welcome. Jeff Galas and his colleagues at Avery made the preparation of the U.S. edition a great pleasure.

Several books on children's development have inspired me. Brian Hall's *Madeleine's World* (Houghton Mifflin, 1997) uncovered parts of a toddler's world that science is only beginning to reach. Daphne and Charles Maurer's *The World of the Newborn* (Basic Books, 1988) remains the most careful attempt to understand neonatal consciousness from a scientific perspective. Daniel N. Stern's *Diary of a Baby* (Basic Books, 1992) is a poetic and well-informed reconstruction of a baby's emotional world. Paul Bloom's *Descartes' Baby* (Basic Books, 2004) is a model for popular writing about developmental psychology. Margaret Donaldson's venerable *Children's Minds* (Norton, 1979) remains the best introduction to Piaget's theory and its immediate critical reception. Among the many fine textbooks on this topic, my own choice is Helen Bee and Denise Boyd's *The Developing Child*, now in its eleventh edition (Allyn and Bacon, 2006). Other recommendations for further reading are marked in the Notes.

Several people read and commented on earlier drafts: Richard Bentall, Clare Connor, Christine Dyer, Rhett Griffiths, Sue Leekam, Chris Moore, Edward Platt, Vincent Reid, James Russell, and Valerie Webb. Leo Hollis and Philip Gwyn Jones provided helpful input. Daphne Tagg and Charles Boyle were exemplary copy editors and proofreaders. Kathleen and Alan Meins gave invaluable day-to-day support with child care while the book was being written. Kirsty Gordon and Emma Wilson helped spread the word. I have received financial assistance from the Arts Council of England, the Northern Writers' Awards, and the Authors' Foundation. Thanks for endless, unquantifiable support to Claire Malcolm and her colleagues at New Writing North, the literary development agency for the north of England.

Many colleagues answered queries while I was researching the book, and I am grateful to members of the dev-europe mailing list for their tolerance of, and responsiveness to, my e-mailed questions. I hope that my scientific colleagues will also tolerate some necessary simplifications of what are often still-lively debates. For settling matters of fact, thanks are due to Peter Barnes, Peter Bryant, Robin Campbell, Julia Carroll, John Clibbens, Marc de Rosnay, Stephan Desrochers, John Findlay, Mike Forrester, Juliet Goldbart, Paul Harris, Peter Hobson, Britta Jensen, Mark Johnson, Elena Lieven, Anthony McGregor, Morag MacLean, Paul Magrs, Sara Maitland,

Alan Slater, Les Smith, Jon Sutton, and Suzanne Zeedyk. Needless to say, all errors and omissions are my responsibility.

I cannot even begin to properly thank the people who have really made this book possible: Lizzie, Isaac, and of course my dear little scientist, Athena.

Notes

Suggestions for further reading are marked in bold type.

CHAPTER 1:
IT'S LIKE THIS

3 *There has not . . . this fact* Sigmund Freud, *The Standard Edition of the Complete Psychological Works of Sigmund Freud*, vol. 15 (translated and edited by James Strachey), p. 200, London: Hogarth Press, 1963.

3 *Childhood amnesia* Carole Peterson, Valerie V. Grant, and Lesley D. Boland, "Childhood amnesia in children and adolescents: Their earliest memories," *Memory*, 13, pp. 622–37, 2005.

4 *Explanations of childhood amnesia* Josef Perner and Ted Ruffman, "Episodic memory and autonoetic consciousness: Developmental evidence and a theory of childhood amnesia," *Journal of Experimental Child Psychology*, 59, pp. 516–48, 1995.

4 *The two-and-a-half-year watershed* M. J. Eacott and R. A. Crawley, "The offset of childhood amnesia: Memory for events that occurred before age 3," *Journal of Experimental Psychology: General*, 127, pp. 22–33, 1998.

5 *The blooming, buzzing confusion* William James, *Principles of Psychology*, vol. 1, p. 488, New York: Holt, 1890.

7 *Something that it is like* When they want to know about the consciousness of another being, philosophers sometimes ask, "Is there something that it is like to be that being?" This subjective, "something-that-it-is-like" quality is the aspect of consciousness that has proved most resistant to scientific explanation. See Thomas Nagel, "What is it like to be a bat?" *Philosophical Review*, 83, pp. 435–50, 1974; Adam Zeman, *Consciousness: A User's Guide*, London: Yale University Press, 2003.

CHAPTER 2:
PRECONCEPTIONS

11 *Cycles of love* Peter Fonagy, Howard
Steele, and Miriam Steele, "Maternal representations of attachment
during pregnancy predict the organization of infant–mother attachment at one year of age," *Child
Development*, 62, pp. 891–905, 1991.

11 *Projecting infant personality* Bro-
nia Arnott and Elizabeth Meins,
"Continuity in mind-mindedness
across the transition to parenthood," *Infant Behavior and Development*, 31, pp. 647–54, 2008.

12 *Noise in the womb* D. Walker, J.
Grimwade, and C. Wood, "Intra-
uterine noise: A component of the
fetal environment," *American Journal of Obstetrics and Gynecology*,
109, pp. 91–5, 1971.

13 *Learning mother's voice* Barbara S.
Kisilevsky et al., "Effects of experience on fetal voice recognition,"
Psychological Science, 14, pp. 220–
24, 2003.

13 *Fetal memory* P. G. Hepper, "Fetal
memory: Does it exist? What does
it do?" *Acta Paediatrica Supple-
ment*, 416, pp. 16–20, 1996.

13 *Memory for the* Neighbours *theme
tune* P. G. Hepper, "Foetal 'soap'
addiction," *Lancet*, 11 June 1988,
pp. 1347–8.

13 *The basics of remembering* Carolyn
Rovee-Collier and Peter Gerhard-
stein, "The development of infant
memory," in *The Development of
Memory in Childhood* (edited by
Nelson Cowan), Hove, England:
Psychology Press, 1997.

13 *Neural proliferation . . .* Paul Casaer,
"Old and new facts about perina-
tal brain development," *Journal of
Child Psychology and Psychiatry*, 34,

pp. 101–9, 1993; **Lise Eliot, *What's
Going On in There? How the
Brain and Mind Develop in the
First Five Years of Life,* New**
York: Bantam Books, 1999.

14 *. . . and neural pruning* P. R. Hut-
tenlocher, "Synaptogenesis, synapse
elimination, and neural plasticity in
human cerebral cortex," in *Minne-
sota Symposium on Child Psychology*,
vol. 27, Hillsdale, N.J.: Lawrence
Erlbaum Associates, 1994; Denis
Mareschal et al., *Neuroconstructivism: How the Brain Constructs
Cognition*, vol. 1, Oxford: Oxford
University Press, 2007.

15 *Forming connections* Eliot, *What's
Going On in There?*

15 *Activity dependence* Mareschal
et al., *Neuroconstructivism*.

15 *Cortical differentiation* Mark H.
Johnson, "Functional brain devel-
opment in humans," *Nature Reviews
Neuroscience*, 2, pp. 475–83, 2001.

16 *New ultrasound technologies* Stuart Campbell, *Watch Me Grow! A
Unique, 3-dimensional Week-by-
week Look at Your Baby's Behavior and Development in the Womb*,
London: Carroll and Brown, 2004.

16 *Movement patterns in the womb*
J. I. P. de Vries, G. H. A. Visser,
and H. F. R. Prechtl, "Fetal motil-
ity in the first half of pregnancy," in
*Continuity of Neural Function from
Prenatal to Postnatal Life* (edited
by H. F. R. Prechtl), London: Spas-
tics International Medical Publica-
tions, 1984.

17 *Something that it is like* See note for
p. 7.

17 *Consciousness before birth* Roland
Brusseau and Laura Myers,
"Developing consciousness: Fetal
anesthesia and analgesia," *Seminars
in Anesthesia, Perioperative Medicine and Pain*, 25, pp. 189–95, 2006;

Stuart W. G. Derbyshire, "Can fetuses feel pain?" *British Medical Journal*, 15 April 2006, pp. 909–12; Susan J. Lee et al., "Fetal pain: A systematic multidisciplinary review of the evidence," *Journal of the American Medical Association*, 294, pp. 947–54, 2005; K. J. S. Anand, "Consciousness, cortical function, and pain perception in nonverbal humans," *Behavioral and Brain Sciences*, 30, pp. 82–3, 2007.

19 *Fetal dreaming* . . . H. P. Roffwarg, J. N. Muzio, and W. C. Dement, "Ontogenetic development of the human sleep-dream cycle," *Science*, 152, pp. 604–19, 1966.

20 . . . *and fatal dreaming* G. A. Christos, "Infant dreaming and fetal memory: A possible explanation of sudden infant death syndrome," *Medical Hypotheses*, 44, pp. 243–50, 1995.

CHAPTER 3: BLOOMING, BUZZING

22 *Remembering birth* Otto Rank, *The Trauma of Birth*, New York: Harper & Row, 1973 (original work published 1929).

23 *Tactile sensitivity in fetuses* Davenport Hooker, *The Prenatal Origin of Behavior*, New York: Hafner, 1969.

24 *Birth pains* **Daphne Maurer and Charles Maurer, *The World of the Newborn*,** New York: Basic Books, 1988.

25 *Knowing redness* Frank Jackson, "Epiphenomenal qualia," *Philosophical Quarterly*, 32, pp. 127–36, 1982.

25 *Neonatal hypoxia* Maurer and Maurer, *The World of the Newborn*.

26 *Imitation at forty-two minutes* Andrew N. Meltzoff and M. Keith Moore, "Newborn infants imitate adult facial gestures," *Child Development*, 54, pp. 702–9, 1983.

26 *Breath rehearsals* A. H. Jansen and V. Chernick, "Fetal breathing and development of control of breathing," *Journal of Applied Physiology*, 70, pp. 1431–46, 1991.

27 *Thalamic switching* Maurer and Maurer, *The World of the Newborn*.

28 *Sleep cycles* A. W. de Weerd and Renilde A. S. van den Bossche, "The development of sleep during the first months of life," *Sleep Medicine Reviews*, 7, pp. 179–91, 2003.

28 *Newborns and the visually evoked response* R. Ellingson, "Variability of visually evoked responses in the human newborn," *Electroencephalography and Clinical Neurophysiology*, 29, pp. 10–19, 1970.

28 *Bat consciousness* Nagel, "What is it like to be a bat?"

30 *Lens changes* J. S. Werner, "Development of scotopic sensitivity and the absorption spectrum of the human ocular media," *Journal of the Optical Society of America*, 72, pp. 247–58, 1982.

30 *Contrast insensitivity* **Philip J. Kellman and Martha E. Arterberry, *The Cradle of Knowledge: Development of Perception in Infancy*,** Cambridge, Mass.: MIT Press, 1998.

31 *Learning and forgetting in sleep* J. J. Campos and Y. Brackbill, "Infant state: Relationship to heartrate, behavioral response, and response decrement," *Developmental Psychobiology*, 6, pp. 9–19, 1973; Maurer and Maurer, *The World of the Newborn*.

31 *Jerky objects* Maurer and Maurer, *The World of the Newborn*.

31 *S.'s synesthesia* A. R. Luria, *The Mind of a Mnemonist: A Little Book About a Vast Memory* (translated by Lynn Solotaroff), p. 23, New York: Basic Books, 1968.

32 *Synesthesia in newborns* Robert Hoffmann, "Developmental changes in human infant visual-evoked potentials to patterned stimuli recorded at different scalp locations," *Child Development*, 49, pp. 110–18, 1978; Daphne Maurer, "Neonatal synesthesia: Implications for the processing of speech and faces," in *Developmental Neurocognition: Speech and Face Processing in the First Year of Life* (edited by B. de Boysson-Bardies et al.), Dordrecht: Kluwer Academic Publishers, 1993; Simon Baron-Cohen, "Is there a normal phase of synesthesia in development?" *Psyche*, 27, 1996.

33 *Neonatal echoes* R. K. Clifton, B. A. Morrongiello, and J. M. Dowd, "A developmental look at an auditory illusion: The precedence effect," *Developmental Psychobiology*, 17, pp. 519–36, 1984.

CHAPTER 4: THOSE DRIVEN THINGS

36 *Taste memory* P. G. Hepper, "Adaptive fetal learning: Prenatal exposure to garlic affects postnatal preferences," *Animal Behavior*, 36, pp. 935–36, 1988.

36 *Benefits of poor eyesight* Gerald Turkewitz and Patricia A. Kenny, "Limitations on input as a basis for neural organization and perceptual development: A preliminary theoretical statement," *Developmental Psychobiology*, 15, pp. 357–68, 1982.

37 *"What" and "where" streams* Andreas Burkhalter, Kerry L. Bernardo, and Vinod Charles, "Development of local circuits in human visual cortex," *Journal of Neuroscience*, 13, pp. 1916–31, 1993.

37 *Sticky fixation* Mark H. Johnson, "Cortical maturation and the development of visual attention in early infancy," *Journal of Cognitive Neuroscience*, 2, pp. 81–95, 1990.

38 *The busy subcortex* H. T. Chugani and M. E. Phelps, "Maturational changes in cerebral function in infants determined by 18FDG positron emission tomography," *Science*, 231, pp. 840–43, 1986.

38 *Synapse growth and loss* Eliot, *What's Going On in There?*

39 *Myelination* Casaer, "Old and new facts about perinatal brain development."

40 *Sound localization* D. W. Muir, R. K. Clifton, and M. G. Clarkson, "The development of a human auditory localization response: A U-shaped function," *Canadian Journal of Psychology*, 43, pp. 199–216, 1989.

41 *Tracking faces* Mark H. Johnson et al., "Newborns' preferential tracking of face-like stimuli and its subsequent decline," *Cognition*, 40, pp. 1–19, 1991; Catherine J. Mondloch et al., "Face perception during early infancy," *Psychological Science*, 10, pp. 419–22, 1999.

41 *Eye contact* Teresa Farroni et al., "Eye contact detection in humans from birth," *Proceedings of the National Academy of Sciences*, 9 July 2002, pp. 9602–5; Tricia Striano, Anne Henning, and Daniel Stahl, "Sensitivity to social contingencies between 1 and 3 months of age," *Developmental Science*, 8, pp. 509–18, 2005.

42 *Perceiving bodies* Virginia Slaughter, Michelle Heron, and Susan Sim, "Development of preferences for the human body shape in infancy," *Cognition*, 85, B71–B81, 2002; **Tricia Striano and Vincent M. Reid, "Social cognition in the first year,"** *Trends in Cognitive Sciences*, 10, pp. 471–6, 2006.

42 *Expectations about objects* Elizabeth S. Spelke and Katherine D. Kinzler, "Core knowledge," *Developmental Science*, 10, pp. 89–96, 2007; **Paul Bloom, *Descartes' Baby: How Child Development Explains What Makes Us Human,*** London: William Heinemann, 2004.

43 *Learning from eye contact* Striano and Reid, "Social cognition in the first year."

43 *Proto-conversations* Colwyn Trevarthen and Kenneth J. Aitken, "Infant intersubjectivity: Research, theory, and clinical applications," *Journal of Child Psychology and Psychiatry*, 42, pp. 3–48, 2001; Manuela Lavelli and Alan Fogel, "Developmental changes in mother–infant face-to-face communication: Birth to 3 months," *Developmental Psychology*, 38, pp. 288–305, 2002.

44 *Iris color* Robert A. Moses, "The iris and the pupil," in *Adler's Physiology of the Eye: Clinical Application*, 6th edition (edited by Robert A. Moses), St. Louis: C. V. Mosby Company, 1975.

44 *Still faces* Lauren B. Adamson and Janet E. Frick, "The Still Face: A history of a shared experimental paradigm," *Infancy*, 4, pp. 451–73, 2003; Kellman and Arterberry, *The Cradle of Knowledge.*

45 *Altered states of consciousness* Dieter Vaitl et al., "Psychobiology of altered states of consciousness," *Psychological Bulletin*, 131, pp. 98–127, 2005.

45 *Unblinking eyes* John G. Lawrenson, Rosalind Birhah, and Paul J. Murphy, "Tear-film lipid layer morphology and corneal sensation in the development of blinking in neonates and infants," *Journal of Anatomy*, 206, pp. 265–70, 2005.

CHAPTER 5: WHO'S PLAYING THAT PIANO?

49 *Organized action* Claes von Hofsten, "Action in development," *Developmental Science*, 10, pp. 54–60, 2007.

49 *Motor cortex as a piano keyboard* W. Penfield and E. Boldrey, "Somatic motor and sensory representation in the cerebral cortex of man as studied by electrical stimulation," *Brain*, 60, pp. 389–443, 1937.

50 *Blueprints for walking* Esther Thelen and Donna M. Fisher, "The organization of spontaneous leg movements in newborn infants," *Journal of Motor Behavior*, 15, pp. 353–77, 1983; Esther Thelen, "Treadmill-elicited stepping in seven-month-old infants," *Child Development*, 57, pp. 1498–506, 1986.

51 *The illusion of conscious will* Daniel M. Wegner, "The mind's best trick: How we experience conscious will," *Trends in Cognitive Sciences*, 7, pp. 65–9, 2003.

54 *Widening circles of influence* Emily W. Bushnell and J. Paul Boudreau, "Motor development and the mind: The potential role of motor abilities as a determinant of aspects of perceptual development," *Child Development*, 64, pp. 1005–21, 1993; von Hofsten, "Action in development"; Kellman and Arterberry, *The Cradle of Knowledge.*

CHAPTER 6: CLOSING THE CIRCLE

60 *Piaget's theory* Jean Piaget, *The Origin of Intelligence in the Child* (translated by Margaret Cook), Harmondsworth, England: Penguin, 1977 (original work published 1936).

60 *He immediately sucks it . . . for a long time and thoroughly* Ibid., p. 39.

61 *The A not B error* P. L. Harris, "Object permanence in infancy," in *Infant Development* (edited by A. Slater and J. G. Bremner), Hillsdale, N.J.: Lawrence Erlbaum Associates, 1989.

63 *Choosing what to see* Immanuel Kant, *Critique of Pure Reason* (translated and edited by Paul Guyer and Allen W. Wood), Cambridge: Cambridge University Press, 1997.

63 *Self and world* James Russell, *Agency: Its Role in Mental Development*, Hove, England: Lawrence Erlbaum Associates, 1996.

CHAPTER 7: WHERE'S THE BEAR?

69 *FOXP2* Wolfgang Enard et al., "Molecular evolution of *FOXP2*, a gene involved in speech and language," *Nature*, 418, pp. 869–72, 2002.

69 *Experts in phonology* P. D. Eimas et al., "Speech perception in infants," *Science*, 171, pp. 303–6, 1971.

70 *Sensitivity to foreign phonemic distinctions* J. F. Werker and R. C. Tees, "Cross-language speech perception: Evidence for perceptual reorganization during the first year of life," *Infant Behavior and Development*, 7, pp. 49–63, 1984.

70 *Brain responses to consonants* Maritza Rivera-Gaxiola, Juan Silva-Pereyra, and Patricia K. Kuhl, "Brain potentials to native and non-native speech contrasts in 7- and 11-month-old American infants," *Developmental Science*, 8, pp. 162–72, 2005.

70 *Critical periods for language* Elissa L. Newport, "Maturational constraints on language learning," *Cognitive Science*, 14, pp. 11–28, 1990.

71 *Statistical regularities* Patricia K. Kuhl, "Early language acquisition: Cracking the speech code," *Nature Reviews Neuroscience*, 5, pp. 831–43, 2004.

71 *Stress patterns* Peter W. Jusczyk, Derek M. Houston, and Mary Newsome, "The beginnings of word segmentation in English-learning infants," *Cognitive Psychology*, 39, pp. 159–207, 1999.

73 *Fanciful interpretations* Jerome S. Bruner, *Actual Minds, Possible Worlds*, Cambridge, Mass.: Harvard University Press, 1986; Elizabeth Meins, "The effects of security of attachment and maternal attribution of meaning on children's linguistic acquisitional style," *Infant Behavior and Development*, 21, pp. 237–52, 1998.

75 *For there is a kind of universal language . . . nothing to do with it* Saint Augustine, *The Confessions*, p. 29, Harmondsworth, England: Penguin, 1961.

77 *Gone* Alison Gopnik, "The acquisition of gone and the development of the object concept," *Journal of Child Language*, 11, pp. 273–92, 1984.

78 *Mommy sock* Lois Bloom, *One Word at a Time*, The Hague: Mouton, 1973.

80 *Radical nativism* **Steven Pinker, The Language Instinct: The New Science of Language and Mind,** London: Allen Lane, 1994; Steven Pinker, *The Blank Slate: The Modern Denial of Human Nature*, London: Allen Lane, 2002.

81 *Mutable genes* Matt Ridley, *Nature via Nurture: Genes, Experience and What Makes Us Human*, London: Fourth Estate, 2003.

82 *Fixation points* **Philip David Zelazo, Helena Hong Gao, and Rebecca Todd, "The development of consciousness in ontogeny,"** in *Cambridge Hand-*

book of Consciousness (edited by P. D. Zelazo, M. Moscovitch, and E. Thompson), Cambridge: Cambridge University Press, 2007.

82 *Overextension* Eve V. Clark, *"Meanings and concepts,"* in *Handbook of Child Psychology: Cognitive Development*, vol. 3 (edited by J. H. Flavell and E. M. Markman), New York: Wiley, 1983.

CHAPTER 8: UM . . .

89 *Thought before language* Jean M. Mandler, "Thought before language," *Trends in Cognitive Sciences*, 8, pp. 508–13, 2004.

90 *Linguistic relativity* Benjamin Lee Whorf, *Language, Thought and Reality*, Cambridge, Mass.: MIT Press, 1956.

90 *The Great Eskimo Vocabulary Hoax* Pinker, *The Language Instinct.*

90 *Tight shoes* Susan J. Hespos and Elizabeth S. Spelke, "Conceptual precursors to language," *Nature*, 430, pp. 453–6, 2004; Paul Bloom, "Children think before they speak," *Nature*, 430, pp. 410–11, 2004.

92 *Building blocks of thought* **Elizabeth S. Spelke, "Core knowledge,"** *American Psychologist*, 55, pp. 1233–43, 2000; Spelke and Kinzler, "Core knowledge."

93 *Mentalese* Jerry A. Fodor, *The Language of Thought*, New York: Crowell, 1975; Steven Pinker, *The Stuff of Thought: Language as a Window into Human Nature*, London: Allen Lane, 2007.

93 *Chess players* T. W. Robbins et al., "Working memory in chess," *Memory and Cognition*, 24, pp. 83–93, 1996.

93 *Thought sampling* Russell T. Hurlburt, *Sampling Normal and Schizophrenic Inner Experience*, New York: Plenum, 1990.

98 *Remembering Vygotsky* Gita Vygodskaia, "Remembering Father," *Educational Psychologist*, 30, pp. 57–9, 1995.

100 *Piaget and Vygotsky on private speech* Jean Piaget, *The Language and Thought of the Child* (translated by Marjorie and Ruth Gabain), London: Kegan Paul, Trench, Trubner & Co., 1959 (original work published 1926); **L. S. Vygotsky, "Thinking and Speech,"** in *The Collected Works of L. S. Vygotsky*, vol. 1 (edited by Robert W. Rieber and Aaron S. Carton, translated by Norris Minick), New York: Plenum, 1987 (original work published 1934).

100 *Colored balls* Charles Fernyhough and Emma Fradley, "Private speech on an executive task: Relations with task difficulty and task performance," *Cognitive Development*, 20, pp. 103–20, 2005.

100 *Teachers' attitudes to private speech* Carla Deniz, "Early childhood teachers' awareness, beliefs, and practices toward children's private speech," in *Private Speech, Executive Functioning, and the Development of Verbal Self-regulation* (edited by A. Winsler, C. Fernyhough, and I. Montero), New York: Cambridge University Press, 2009.

101 *Private speech in adults* Robert M. Duncan and J. Allan Cheyne, "Private speech in young adults: Task difficulty, self-regulation, and psychological predication," *Cognitive Development*, 16, pp. 889–906, 2002.

102 *The blue-walled room* Linda Hermer-Vazquez, Elizabeth S. Spelke, and Alla S. Katsnelson, "Sources of flexibility in human cognition: Dual-task studies of space and language," *Cognitive Psychology*, 39, pp. 3–36, 1999.

104 *Mind chapels* Steven Mithen, *The Prehistory of the Mind: A Search for the Origins of Art, Religion and Science*, London: Thames and Hudson, 1996.

104 *Language as a common language* Peter Carruthers, "The cognitive functions of language," *Behavioral and Brain Sciences*, 25, pp. 657–726, 2002.

CHAPTER 9: ALL BY MYSELF

107 *Hot thoughts* Antonio Damasio, *Descartes' Error: Emotion, Reason and the Human Brain*, London: Papermac, 1996.

108 *Identify the needs . . . in one direction or another* Vygotsky, *Thinking and Speech*, p. 50.

110 *Judging self-efficacy* Zelazo et al., "The development of consciousness in ontogeny"; Jerome Kagan, *The Second Year: The Emergence of Self-awareness*, Cambridge, Mass.: Harvard University Press, 1981.

115 *Doddy in the mirror* **Charles Darwin, "A biographical sketch of an infant,"** *Mind*, 2, pp. 285–94, 1877.

115 *The abomination of mirrors* Jorge Luis Borges, "Tlön, Uqbar, Orbis Tertius," in *Collected Fictions* (translated by Andrew Hurley), London: Allen Lane, 1999.

116 *Mirror self-recognition* **Philippe Rochat, "Five levels of self-awareness as they unfold early in life,"** *Consciousness and Cognition*, 12, pp. 717–31, 2003; Robert W. Mitchell, "Mental models of mirror-self-recognition: Two theories," *New Ideas in Psychology*, 11, pp. 295–325, 1993.

117 *The rouge test* B. Amsterdam, "Mirror self-image reactions before age two," *Developmental Psychobiology*,

5, pp. 297–305, 1972; G. G. Gallup Jr., "Chimpanzees: Self-recognition," *Science*, 167, pp. 86–7, 1970.

118 *The mirror and imagination* Henri Wallon, *Les origines du caractère chez l'enfant*, Paris: Presses Universitaires de France, 1949 (original work published 1934), cited in Michael Billig, "Lacan's misuse of psychology: Evidence, rhetoric and the mirror stage," *Theory, Culture & Society*, 23, pp. 1–26, 2006.

119 *Lacan's debt to Wallon* Ibid.

120 *The "flutter of jubilant activity"* Jacques Lacan, "The mirror stage as formative of the function of the I as revealed in psychoanalytic experience," in *Écrits: A Selection* (translated by Alan Sheridan), London: Routledge, 2001.

120 *Delayed self-recognition* Daniel J. Povinelli, "The self: Elevated in consciousness and extended in time," in *The Development of the Extended Self in Preschool Children: Theory and Research* (edited by K. Skene and C. Moore), Cambridge: Cambridge University Press, 2001.

120 *Capgras delusion* For a fictional exploration of this delusional state in which a familiar individual is believed to have been replaced by an impostor, see Richard Powers, *The Echo Maker*, London: William Heinemann, 2006.

CHAPTER 10: THE SHINING THREAD

122 *Mental time travel* Thomas Suddendorf and Michael C. Corballis, "The evolution of foresight: What is mental time travel and is it unique to humans?" *Behavioral and Brain Sciences*, 30, pp. 299–313, 2007.

125 *Mindful dots* Paul Bloom and Csaba Veres, "The perceived intention-

ality of groups," *Cognition*, 71, B1–B9, 1999; György Gergely et al., "Taking the intentional stance at 12 months of age," *Cognition*, 56, pp. 165–93, 1995.

125 *Dualist babies* Bloom, *Descartes' Baby*. Strictly speaking, it is possible to make this distinction between minded and non-minded beings without being an adherent to mind–body dualism; for further discussion, see Paul Bloom, "Religion is natural," *Developmental Science*, 10, pp. 147–51, 2007.

125 *Stages in intentional agent understanding* Michael Tomasello et al., "Understanding and sharing intentions: The origins of cultural cognition," *Behavioral and Brain Sciences*, 28, pp. 675–735, 2005; Amanda L. Woodward, "Infants selectively encode the goal object of an actor's reach," *Cognition*, 69, pp. 1–34, 1998; Tanya Behne et al., "Unwilling versus unable: Infants' understanding of intentional action," *Developmental Psychology*, 41, pp. 328–37, 2005.

127 *Primary and secondary intersubjectivity* Colwyn Trevarthen, "The foundations of intersubjectivity: Development of interpersonal and cooperative understanding in infants," in *The Social Foundations of Language and Thought: Essays in Honor of Jerome Bruner* (edited by D. Olson), New York: W. W. Norton, 1980.

128 *The primordial sharing situation* Heinz Werner and Bernard Kaplan, *Symbol Formation*, Hillsdale, N.J.: Lawrence Erlbaum Associates, 1984 (original work published 1963).

129 *Autism develops* **Peter Hobson, The Cradle of Thought: Exploring the Origins of Thinking**, London: Macmillan, 2002.

130 *Sharing intentionality* Tomasello et al., "Understanding and sharing intentions: The origins of cultural cognition."

131 *Childhood animism* **Jean Piaget, The Child's Conception of the World** (translated by Joan and Andrew Tomlinson), London: Routledge and Kegan Paul, 1929.

139 *Vegemite sandwich* Mem Fox and Julie Vivas, *Possum Magic*, San Diego: Harcourt Brace & Company, 1983.

141 *Opaque pretense* Alan M. Leslie, "Pretense and representation: The origins of theory of mind," *Psychological Review*, 94, pp. 412–26, 1987.

CHAPTER 11: BELIEVE ME

148 *The unexpected transfer task* Heinz Wimmer and Josef Perner, "Beliefs about beliefs: Representation and constraining function of wrong beliefs in children's understanding of deception," *Cognition*, 1, pp. 103–28, 1983.

148 *The fourth birthday watershed* Henry M. Wellman, David Cross, and Julanne Watson, "Meta-analysis of theory of mind development: The truth about false belief," *Child Development*, 72, pp. 655–84, 2001.

149 *Theory theories* Josef Perner, *Understanding the Representational Mind*, Cambridge, Mass.: MIT Press, 1991; Henry M. Wellman, *The Child's Theory of Mind*, Cambridge, Mass.: MIT Press, 1990.

149 *Children and scientists* Jean Piaget, *Psychology and Epistemology: Toward a Theory of Knowledge* (translated by P. A. Wells), London: Allen Lane, 1972; Alison Gopnik, "The scientist as child," *Philosophy of Science*, 63, pp. 485–514, 1996.

150 *Genetics of theory of mind* Claire Hughes et al., "Origins of individual differences in theory of mind: From nature to nurture?" *Child Development*, 76, pp. 356–70, 2005.

150 *Environmental influences* Judy Dunn et al., "Young children's understanding of other people's feelings and beliefs: Individual differences and their antecedents," *Child Development*, 62, pp. 1352–66, 1991; Ted Ruffman et al., "Older (but not younger) siblings facilitate false belief understanding," *Developmental Psychology*, 34, pp. 161–74, 1998; Elizabeth Meins et al., "Security of attachment as a predictor of symbolic and mentalising abilities: A longitudinal study," *Social Development*, 7, pp. 1–24, 1998; J. G. de Villiers and P. A. de Villiers, "Linguistic determinism and the understanding of false beliefs," in *Children's Reasoning and the Mind* (edited by P. Mitchell and K. J. Riggs), Psychology Press, 2000.

153 *Contrastives* Karen Bartsch and Henry M. Wellman, *Children Talk About the Mind*, New York: Oxford University Press, 1995.

153 *Exposure to differing perspectives* Charles Fernyhough, "Getting Vygotskian about theory of mind: Mediation, dialogue, and the development of social understanding," *Developmental Review*, 28, pp. 225–62, 2008.

154 *Mental simulation* R. M. Gordon, "The simulation theory: Objections and misconceptions," *Mind and Language*, 7, pp. 11–34, 1992; Paul L. Harris, "Desires, beliefs, and language," in *Theories of Theories of Mind* (edited by P. Carruthers and P. K. Smith), Cambridge: Cambridge University Press, 1996.

154 *The imagination . . . my future being* William Hazlitt, "An essay on the principles of human action," in *The Selected Writings of William Hazlitt*, vol. 1 (edited by Duncan Wu), p. 3, London: Pickering & Chatto, 1998.

CHAPTER 12: IT'S ABOUT A LITTLE MOUSE

158 *The War of the Ghosts* Frederick Bartlett, *Remembering: A Study in Experimental and Social Psychology*, Cambridge: Cambridge University Press, 1950 (original work published 1932).

159 *Restaurant scripts* R. C. Schank and R. P. Abelson, *Scripts, Plans, Goals and Understanding*, Hillsdale, N.J.: Lawrence Erlbaum Associates, 1977.

159 *Testing script theory* Gordon H. Bower, John B. Black, and Terrence J. Turner, "Scripts in memory for text," *Cognitive Psychology*, 11, pp. 177–220, 1979.

159 *Children's scripts* K. Nelson and J. Gruendel, "Generalized event representations: Basic building blocks of cognitive development," in *Advances in Developmental Psychology*, vol. 1 (edited by M. E. Lamb and A. L. Brown), Hillsdale, N.J.: Lawrence Erlbaum Associates, 1981.

160 *Talking about the past* Katherine Nelson and Robyn Fivush, "Socialization of memory," in *Oxford Handbook of Memory* (edited by E. Tulving and F. I. M. Craik), New York: Oxford University Press, 2000; Elaine Reese, Catherine A. Haden, and Robyn Fivush, "Mother–child conversations about the past: Relationships of style and memory over time," *Cognitive Development*, 8, pp. 403–30, 1993; Catherine A. Haden, Rachel A.

Haine, and Robyn Fivush, "Developing narrative structure in parent–child reminiscing across the preschool years," *Developmental Psychology*, 33, pp. 295–307, 1997.

161 *Emily's crib speech* Katherine Nelson, "Monologue as representation of real-life experience," in *Narratives from the Crib* (edited by K. Nelson), Cambridge, Mass.: Harvard University Press, 1989.

163 *Narrative psychology* Joshua M. Smyth, "Written emotional expression: Effect sizes, outcome types, and moderating variables," *Journal of Consulting and Clinical Psychology*, 66, pp. 174–84, 1998; Tilmann Habermas and Susan Bluck, "Getting a life: The emergence of the life story in adolescence," *Psychological Bulletin*, 126, pp. 748–69, 2000; Laura A. King, "The health benefits of writing about life goals," *Personality and Social Psychology Bulletin*, 27, pp. 798–807, 2001.

164 *Children's imaginative narratives* **Paul L. Harris, *The Work of the Imagination*,** Oxford: Blackwell, 2000.

166 *Sisters being sisters* James Sully, *Studies of Childhood*, London: Longmans, Green and Co., 1896.

166 *Imaginary friends* **Marjorie Taylor,** "Imaginary Companions and the Children Who Create Them," Oxford: Oxford University Press, 1999; Paige Davis, Imaginary companions and auditory hallucinations in a typical child population: A replication study, unpublished M.Sc. dissertation, Durham University, 2006.

167 *The enduring appeal of fairy tales* Bruno Bettelheim, *The Uses of Enchantment: The Meaning and Importance of Fairy Tales*, London: Penguin Books, 1991 (original work published 1975).

167 *The Freudian account* Harris, *The Work of the Imagination*.

168 *Situation models* Rolf A. Zwaan and Gabriel A. Radvansky, "Situation models in language comprehension and memory," *Psychological Bulletin*, 123, pp. 162–85, 1998.

169 *Perspectives in narrative* John B. Black, Terrence J. Turner, and Gordon H. Bower, "Point of view in narrative comprehension, memory, and production," *Journal of Verbal Learning and Verbal Behavior*, 18, pp. 187–98, 1979; Jaime Rall and Paul L. Harris, "In Cinderella's slippers? Story comprehension from the protagonist's point of view," *Developmental Psychology*, 36, pp. 202–8, 2000.

CHAPTER 13: THE YOUNG DOCTOR WHO

174 *Children's understanding of thinking* J. H. Flavell, F. L. Green, and E. R. Flavell, "Children's understanding of the stream of consciousness," *Child Development*, 64, pp. 387–98, 1993; J. H. Flavell, F. L. Green, and E. R. Flavell, "Young children's knowledge about thinking," *Monographs of the Society for Research in Child Development*, 60 (1, serial no. 243), 1995.

175 *Rooted in their own viewpoints* Jean Piaget and Bärbel Inhelder, *The Child's Conception of Space* (translated by F. J. Langdon and J. L. Lunzer), London: Routledge and Kegan Paul, 1956 (original work published 1948).

176 *Social rules* Jean Piaget, *Play, Dreams and Imitation in Childhood*, London: Routledge and Kegan Paul, 1962 (original work published 1951).

177 *Time and distance* Jean Piaget, *The Child's Conception of Time* (trans-

lated by A. J. Pomerans), London: Routledge and Kegan Paul, 1969 (original work published 1927); *The Child's Conception of Movement and Speed* (translated by G. E. T. Holloway and M. J. Mackenzie), London: Routledge and Kegan Paul, 1970 (original work published 1946).

177 *Conservation tasks* Jean Piaget and Bärbel Inhelder, *The Psychology of the Child* (translated by Helen Weaver), London: Routledge and Kegan Paul, 1969; **Margaret Donaldson, Children's Minds**, London: Fontana Press, 1987 (original work published 1978).

178 *Barney's tones* Teresa McCormack et al., "A timing-specific memory distortion effect in young children," *Journal of Experimental Child Psychology*, 87, pp. 33–56, 2004; Richard A. Block, Dan Zakay, and Peter A. Hancock, "Developmental changes in human duration judgments: A meta-analytic review," *Developmental Review*, 19, pp. 183–211, 1999.

180 *Perspectival time* Piaget, *The Child's Conception of Time.*

181 *Levels of consciousness* Zelazo et al., "The development of consciousness in ontogeny,"

182 *Understanding maps* Lynn S. Liben and Roger M. Downs, "Understanding person–space–map relations: Cartographic and developmental perspectives," *Developmental Psychology*, 29, pp. 739–52, 1993; Lynn S. Liben and Roger M. Downs, "Investigating and facilitating children's graphic, geographic, and spatial development: An illustration of Rodney R. Cocking's legacy," *Applied Developmental Psychology*, 24, pp. 663–79, 2003.

183 *The Three Mountains task* Piaget and Inhelder, *The Child's Conception of Space.*

185 *Boy and policeman* Donaldson, *Children's Minds.*

185 *Aboriginal children's cognition* Graham R. Davidson and Leon Z. Klich, "Cultural factors in the development of temporal and spatial ordering," *Child Development*, 51, pp. 569–71, 1980; Judith M. Kearins, "Visual spatial memory in Australian Aboriginal children of desert regions," *Cognitive Psychology*, 13, pp. 434–60, 1981.

186 *Kangaroos and dingoes* Ragbir Bhathal, "Astronomy in Aboriginal culture," *Astronomy & Geophysics*, 47, 5.27–5.30, 2006.

186 *Artificialism* Piaget, *The Child's Conception of the World.*

186 *Australian children's cosmology* Michael Siegal, George Butterworth, and Peter A. Newcombe, "Culture and children's cosmology," *Developmental Science*, 7, pp. 308–24, 2004.

187 *Overactive mind reading* Bloom, "Religion is natural."

CHAPTER 14: LIGHTNING RIDGE IS FALLING DOWN

191 *Artistic intentions* Paul Bloom and Lori Markson, "Intention and analogy in children's naming of pictorial representations," *Psychological Science*, 9, pp. 200–4, 1998; Susan A. Gelman and Karen S. Ebeling, "Shape and representational status in children's early naming," *Cognition*, 66, B35–B47, 1998.

193 *A crack in the floor* Doris Salcedo, *Shibboleth* (2007), Tate Modern, London, September 10, 2007–June 4, 2008.

193 *Aesthetic credentials* Bloom, *Descartes' Baby.*

194 *Trust in testimony* Paul L. Harris, "Trust," *Developmental Science*, 10, pp. 135–8, 2007.

195 *Children's understanding of dreams* Piaget, *The Child's Conception of the World.*

197 *Infant art* Roman Jakobson, "Anthony's contribution to linguistic theory," preface to Ruth Hirsch Weir, *Language in the Crib*, The Hague: Mouton, 1970 (original work published 1962).

197 *Art for self* Peter van Sommers, *Drawing and Cognition: Descriptive and Experimental Studies of Graphic Production Processes*, Cambridge: Cambridge University Press, 1984.

200 *The social self* Rochat, "Five levels of self-awareness as they unfold early in life."

CHAPTER 15: IF YOU GO TO THE SEA OF LIFE, BE SURE TO WEAR YOUR ARMBANDS

208 *The growth of love* **John Bowlby, Attachment, Separation, and Loss**, London: Penguin, 1969, 1973, 1980.

208 *Varieties of attachment* M. D. S. Ainsworth et al., *Patterns of Attachment: Assessed in the Strange Situation and at Home*, Hillsdale, N.J.: Lawrence Erlbaum Associates, 1978.

209 *Disorganized attachment* Eric Hesse, "The Adult Attachment Interview: Historical and current perspectives," in *Handbook of Attachment: Theory, Research and Clinical Applications* (edited by J. Cassidy and P. R. Shaver), New York: Guilford, 1999.

209 *Attachment legacies* John Bowlby, *Maternal Care and Mental Health*, Geneva: World Health Organization, 1951; Ross A. Thompson, "The legacy of early attachments," *Child Development*, 71, 145–52, 2000.

210 *Security-tinged spectacles* Steven J. Kirsh and Jude Cassidy, "Preschoolers' attention to and memory for attachment-relevant information," *Child Development*, 68, pp. 1143–53, 1997.

212 *Basic and higher cognitive emotions* Dylan Evans, *Emotion: The Science of Sentiment*, Oxford: Oxford University Press, 2001; Paul L. Harris, *Children and Emotion: The Development of Psychological Understanding*, Oxford: Basil Blackwell, 1989.

215 *Self-recognition in elephants* Joshua M. Plotnik, Frans B. M. de Waal, and Diana Reiss, "Self-recognition in an Asian elephant," *Proceedings of the National Academy of Sciences*, 103, pp. 17053–57, 2006.

215 *Childhood mourning* John Bowlby, *Loss: Sadness and Depression*, London: Penguin, 1980.

216 *Perinatal grief* Keith Brownlee and Jodie Oikonen, "Toward a theoretical framework for perinatal bereavement," *British Journal of Social Work*, 34, pp. 517–29, 2004; J. A. M. Hunfeld, J. W. Wladimiroff, and J. Passchier, "The grief of late pregnancy loss," *Patient Education and Counseling*, 31, pp. 57–64, 1997; Bernadette Susan McCreight, "A grief ignored: Narratives of pregnancy loss from a male perspective," *Sociology of Health & Illness*, 26, pp. 326–50, 2004.

218 *Children's belief in the afterlife* Bloom, *Descartes' Baby*. For more on childhood dualism, see Wellman, *The Child's Theory of Mind.*

219 *The search for culprits* Piaget, *The Child's Conception of the World.*

219 *The old man in the apple tree* Sully, *Studies of Childhood.*

220 *Responsibility on little shoulders* Carolyn Zahn-Waxler, Marian

Radke-Yarrow, and Robert A. King, "Child rearing and children's prosocial initiations toward victims of distress," *Child Development*, 50, pp. 319–30, 1979.

221 *Amnesia's veil* Sigmund Freud, *Moses and Monotheism: Three Essays*, London: Hogarth Press, 1974.

CHAPTER 16: WHERE IT TAKES YOU

228 *Consent and assent* D. S. Wendler, "Assent in paediatric research:

Theoretical and practical considerations," *Journal of Medical Ethics*, 32, pp. 229–34, 2006; Alison J. Cocks, "The ethical maze: Finding an inclusive path toward gaining children's agreement to research participation," *Childhood*, 13, pp. 247–66, 2006.

229 *Skinner's daughter* Deborah Skinner Buzan, "I was not a lab rat," *Guardian*, March 12, 2004.

Index

WITHDRAWN